The British Muslim Convert Lord Headley, 1855–1935

Islam of the Global West

Series editors: Kambiz GhaneaBassiri and Frank Peter

Islam of the Global West is a pioneering series that examines Islamic beliefs, practices, discourses, communities and institutions that have emerged from 'the Global West'. The geographical and intellectual framing of the Global West reflects the role played by both the interactions between people from diverse religions and cultures in the development of Western ideals and institutions in the modern era, and the globalization of these very ideals and institutions.

In creating an intellectual space where works of scholarship on European and North American Muslims enter into conversation with one another, the series promotes the publication of theoretically informed and empirically grounded research in these areas. By bringing the rapidly growing research on Muslims in European and North American societies, ranging from the United States and France to Portugal and Albania, into conversation with the conceptual framing of the Global West, this ambitious series aims to reimagine the modern world and develop new analytical categories and historical narratives that highlight the complex relationships and rivalries that have shaped the multicultural, poly-religious character of Europe and North America, as evidenced, by way of example, in such economically and culturally dynamic urban centres as Los Angeles, New York, Paris, Madrid, Toronto, Sarajevo, London, Berlin, and Amsterdam where there is a significant Muslim presence.

Also available from this series:

American and Muslim Worlds Before 1900, Edited by John Ghazvinian & Arthur Mitchell Fraas
Amplifying Islam in the European Soundscape: Religious Pluralism and Secularism in the Netherlands, Pooyan Tamimi Arab
Islam and Nationhood in Bosnia-Herzegovina: Surviving Empires, Xavier Bougarel
Islam as Critique: Sayyid Ahmad Khan and the Challenge of Modernity, Khurram Hussain
Sacred Spaces and Transnational Networks in American Sufism, Merin Shobhana Xavier

The British Muslim Convert Lord Headley, 1855–1935

Jamie Gilham

BLOOMSBURY ACADEMIC
LONDON • NEW YORK • OXFORD • NEW DELHI • SYDNEY

BLOOMSBURY ACADEMIC
Bloomsbury Publishing Plc
50 Bedford Square, London, WC1B 3DP, UK
1385 Broadway, New York, NY 10018, USA
29 Earlsfort Terrace, Dublin 2, Ireland

BLOOMSBURY, BLOOMSBURY ACADEMIC and the Diana logo are trademarks of Bloomsbury Publishing Plc

First published in Great Britain 2020
This paperback edition published in 2022

Copyright © Jamie Gilham, 2020

Jamie Gilham has asserted his right under the Copyright, Designs and Patents Act, 1988, to be identified as Author of this work.

For legal purposes the Acknowledgements on pp. ix–xi constitute an extension of this copyright page.

Series design by Dani Leigh
Cover image © Brian Stablyk / gettyimages.co.uk

All rights reserved. No part of this publication may be reproduced or transmitted in any form or by any means, electronic or mechanical, including photocopying, recording, or any information storage or retrieval system, without prior permission in writing from the publishers.

Bloomsbury Publishing Plc does not have any control over, or responsibility for, any third-party websites referred to or in this book. All internet addresses given in this book were correct at the time of going to press. The author and publisher regret any inconvenience caused if addresses have changed or sites have ceased to exist, but can accept no responsibility for any such changes.

A catalogue record for this book is available from the British Library.

A catalog record for this book is available from the Library of Congress.
Library of Congress Control Number: 2020945433

ISBN: HB: 978-1-3500-8442-1
PB: 978-1-3501-8817-4
ePDF: 978-1-3500-8443-8
eBook: 978-1-3500-8444-5

Series: Islam of the Global West

Typeset by Deanta Global Publishing Services, Chennai, India

To find out more about our authors and books visit www.bloomsbury.com and sign up for our newsletters

For Jyh-Jer Cho and Chiu-Chu Chen

Contents

List of figures	viii
Acknowledgements	ix
Glossary	xii
List of abbreviations	xiv
Note on quotations and spelling	xv
Introduction	1
1 A conventional start: Early years, 1855–92	7
2 Imperial engineer, 1892–1900	29
3 Troubles, 1900–13	43
4 Conversion to Islam, 1913	57
5 Muslim peer of the realm: The first decade, I: 1913–18	85
6 Muslim peer of the realm: The first decade, II: 1918–23	109
7 Pilgrimage to Mecca, 1923	123
8 Ambassador for British Islam, 1923–29	147
9 Twilight years, 1929–35	175
Epilogue	195
Notes	201
Select bibliography	242
Index	255

Figures

1	The Honourable Rowland George Allanson-Winn with his sisters and mother, Margaretta Stefana Allanson-Winn, Oxford, *c*.1869	11
2	The Honourable Rowland George Allanson-Winn, London, *c*.1874	14
3	The Honourable Rowland George Allanson-Winn with young servant, Kashmir, 1893	33
4	The Honourable Rowland George Allanson-Winn (left) demonstrating a boxing position, *c*.1890s	40
5	Teresa Allanson-Winn with Tommy Allanson-Winn, Dalkey, Ireland, 1903	47
6	The Honourable Rowland George Allanson-Winn with his sons at Margate, *c*.1912	51
7	Lord Headley with Khwaja Kamal-ud-Din, November 1913	88
8	The wedding of Lord Headley and Barbara Baynton, London, February 1921	112
9	Group photograph outside Woking mosque, November 1922	126
10	The 'Woking' pilgrims at Mecca, July 1923	135
11	Lord Headley at home in St Margarets after completing the Hajj, August 1923	144
12	Lord Headley at the Khyber Pass, India, January 1928	168
13	Lord Headley and Catharine, Lady Headley, in front of the Great Sphinx of Giza, Egypt, December 1929	177
14	Lord Headley with members of the Arab Palestine delegation at Woking mosque, March 1930	179
15	Lord Headley at *'Id al-Adha*, Woking, April 1932	187

Acknowledgements

I wanted to write this book for many years, having first encountered Rowland Allanson-Winn, the fifth Lord Headley, while researching my first book *Loyal Enemies: British Converts to Islam, 1850-1950* (2014). The research for that book took over a decade and, realizing then that Lord Headley was a significant and intriguing but little understood figure in the history of British Islam, I collated much more information about him than I could possibly use in *Loyal Enemies*. I continued to research his life with a view to eventually writing a full biography. Reading Headley's private papers in January 2018, however, transformed my understanding of the man and his life, and made the writing of a biography much more feasible. First and foremost, then, I thank the Honourable Janet Webb for granting me access to Lord Headley's private papers and permission to reproduce his published and unpublished writings, as well as most of the photographs in this book. I am extremely grateful to Janet and her husband David Webb, who welcomed me to their home, showed me family documents, and answered my questions about Headley. I am also indebted to Lord Headley's great-granddaughter, Pat Scott, who shared precious papers and photographs as well as personal memories of Headley in the early 1930s.

Dr Zahid Aziz has patiently answered my questions about the Woking Muslim Mission since I first met him almost twenty years ago, and he continues to generously share his own research about the history of the Mission and its personalities. The pages of the Woking Muslim Mission website edited by Dr Aziz and the online archive of *The Islamic Review* hosted by the Ahmadiyya Anjuman Isha'at Islam Lahore (UK) were invaluable during the research and writing of this book, and are an essential online resource for the historian of Islam and Muslims in Britain and the West.

I also thank the late David Cowan (Arabic scholar and imam of Woking mosque in the 1940s) and the late Patricia Gordon (granddaughter of Abdullah Quilliam), both of whom gave me first-hand accounts of Lord Headley and the Woking Muslim community between the wars. I am indebted to Dr and Mrs Roger Eltringham, who gifted me a collection of Catharine, Lady Headley's private papers, and Eunice Doswell of the Marden History Group who arranged the gift. Members of the Muslim UK History WhatsApp Group, coordinated by Yahya Birt, kindly translated material and shared their own research on the history of British Islam.

Thanks to staff at the following archives and libraries: British Library, London; General Register Office, Southport; The National Archives, London; The National Archives of Ireland, Dublin; School of Oriental and African Studies Library, University of London; and Thomas Wales, Churchill Archives Centre, Churchill College, University of Cambridge; Debbie Usher, Middle East Centre Archive, St. Antony's College, University of Oxford; and Patricia Moloney, Richmond upon Thames Local Studies Library and Archive.

At Bloomsbury Publishing, I thank Lucy Carroll and Lalle Pursglove for their support, and the Islam of the Global West series editors, Professor Kambiz GhaneaBassiri and Dr Frank Peter, for their encouragement and excellent advice on the manuscript. Thanks also to the anonymous reviewers of the original book proposal and the first draft for their helpful comments, and to Claire Smithson, who provided very useful feedback on the first draft.

Finally, I thank Yen-Ting and my family on two continents for their support and encouragement. This book would simply not have been completed without the support of Jyh-Jer Cho and Chiu-Chu Chen, and so it is to them that I dedicate it with gratitude and affection.

Jamie Gilham
March 2020

The author and publisher gratefully acknowledge the permission granted to reproduce the copyright material in this book.

Extracts from Lord Headley's published and unpublished works and correspondence are reproduced with permission of Janet Webb / The Estate of the Fifth Lord Headley. © The Estate of the Fifth Lord Headley.

The quote from Sir Winston Churchill on page 183 is reproduced with permission of Curtis Brown, London, on behalf of The Estate of Winston S. Churchill. © The Estate of Winston S. Churchill.

Every effort has been made to trace copyright holders and to obtain their permission for the use of copyright material. The publisher apologizes for any errors or omissions in the above list and would be grateful if notified of any corrections that should be incorporated in future reprints or editions of this book.

The third party copyrighted material displayed in the pages of this book are done so on the basis of 'fair use for the purposes of teaching, criticism, scholarship or research' only in accordance with international copyright laws, and is not intended to infringe upon the ownership rights of the original owners.

Glossary

al-Fatiha The first *sura* (chapter) of the Qur'an, which is recited during daily prayers.
Amir Title given to a military commander, governor or prince, or a leader.
anjuman Organization; association.
Caliph The successor of the Prophet Muhammad as leader of the *umma*.
doongah A large punt or travelling boat in colonial India.
du'a Prayer of supplication.
fatwa Juridical opinion.
Hajj Pilgrimage to Mecca. The greater of the two pilgrimages to Mecca (see also *'umrah*) undertaken during the last month of the Islamic calendar; the fifth 'pillar' of Islam.
Hajji Prenominal title given to male Muslims who complete the Hajj.
'Id Muslim religious festival.
'Id al-Adha Feast of the sacrifice celebrating the end of the annual Hajj.
'Id al-Fitr Feast that marks the end of Ramadan.
ihram The state or condition of purity Muslims must enter before performing the Hajj; also the term for the two pieces of white cloth worn by male pilgrims during the Hajj.
imam Muslim religious leader.
jama'at Community.
jheel Lake or wetland in India.
jihad Striving or struggling in the path of God.
Khalifa Caliph.
Khan Honorific title to denote a person of status, sometimes meaning ruler.
kiswah The pall that covers the Ka'ba (the cube-shaped structure inside the Sacred Mosque complex at Mecca) during the Hajj.
masjid Mosque.
Maulana Lit. 'master'; title given to a Muslim religious scholar.
mofussil In colonial India, 'the provinces', 'up-country'.
muezzin A Muslim elected to call other Muslims to prayer (anglicized from the Arabic, *mu'adhdhin*).
mufti Legal scholar.
Nizam Title of the ruler of Hyderabad in colonial India.
Ramadan Muslim month of fasting.
sa'i Lit. 'seeking' or 'ritual walking'. An integral rite of the Hajj, which involves walking and running between the hills of Safa and Marwah in Mecca.
salat Worship/ritual prayer; the second 'pillar' of Islam.
salat al-jum'a Friday prayer, congregational prayer.
sawm Fasting/abstinence during Ramadan; the fourth 'pillar' of Islam.

shahada The Islamic testimony of faith and first of the five 'pillars' of Islam: 'I declare that there is no god but God and I declare that Muhammad is His Messenger.'
Sufi A follower of Sufism or Islamic mysticism.
Sultan Ruler, king.
sura A division, or chapter, of the Qur'an.
tabligh Communication of a message or revelation; fulfilment of a mission; to preach.
tarboosh A fez.
tawaf The practice of circumambulating the Ka'ba seven times during the Hajj and 'umrah.
tonga Light, two-wheeled horse-drawn carriage used in colonial India.
umma The universal Muslim religious community.
'umrah Lesser pilgrimage to Mecca, which can be made at any time of the year.
zakat Almsgiving; the third 'pillar' of Islam.

Abbreviations

AGU	Anti-German Union
AOS	Anglo-Ottoman Society
BEU	British Empire Union
BMS	British Muslim Society (became the MSGB in 1930)
CIS	Central Islamic Society
CUP	Committee of Union and Progress
ICEI	Institution of Civil Engineers of Ireland
ICS	Indian Civil Service
LMI	Liverpool Muslim Institute
MP	Member of Parliament
MSGB	Muslim Society of Great Britain
P&O	Peninsular and Oriental
SS	Steamship
WIA	Western Islamic Association
WMM	Woking Muslim Mission

Note on quotations and spelling

To ensure that the sources retain their authenticity, all quoted material is *verbatim* unless otherwise stated. This accounts for the various spellings of the same word, for example 'Mahommedan', 'Mahomedan', 'Mohammedan', 'Muhammadan', 'Moslem' and 'Mussulman' for Muslim, and 'Quran', 'Qur-an' and 'Koran' for Qur'an. It also explains the inconsistent use of 's' and 'z' in certain words written by the same author, including Lord Headley. Spelling of Muslim names and place names, underlining, italics, capitalization and inconsistent punctuation within quotations is also *verbatim*.

Introduction

Lord Headley is a name of world-wide fame and is sure to occupy a prominent place when the future historian sits down to write out his 'History of Conversion of the British Isles to Islam'. Perhaps the British calendar may show 'St. Headley's Day' as a red-letter day and a Bank-holiday.[1]

This book examines the life and times of the fifth Lord Headley (1855–1935), an Anglo-Irish aristocrat who made international headlines in 1913 when he defied convention by publicly converting to Islam. It narrates why and how Headley chose Islam in 1913, and examines his life as arguably the public face of Islam in Britain between the two world wars. The abovementioned quote, rather optimistically proposing a 'St. Headley's Day', was published in the Indian Muslim newspaper *The Light* in 1926. It underlines Headley's reputation and standing among Muslim communities outside of Britain more than a decade after his conversion to Islam.

Eighty-five years after Headley's death in 1935, Islam is the second largest religion in Britain but, with Muslims constituting 5 per cent of the population of England and Wales, *The Light*'s prediction almost a century ago of the 'Conversion of the British Isles to Islam' is far from being realized.[2] With the resurgence of interest in Muslim heritage in the West since 9/11, there is growing recognition in Britain and further afield that Headley is an important figure in the modern history of British Islam, but he remains a marginal historical figure and there is certainly no 'St. Headley's Day' on the national calendar.

Headley's life and work has not hitherto been documented or analysed in any detail. In fact, he has been largely overlooked by scholars writing about the history of Islam in the West, Christian–Muslim relations and Western engagement with Islam and Muslims, subjects that have grown significantly over the past two decades.[3] This neglect is partly due to the fact that Headley was not, by his own admission, a scholar of Islam nor an intellectual. In Britain, Headley has been overshadowed by two British Muslim convert contemporaries: William

Henry Abdullah Quilliam (1856–1932) and Muhammad Marmaduke Pickthall (1875–1936). Quilliam was the first British-born missionary of Islam, founder of the pioneering Liverpool Muslim Institute (c.1889–1908), and a prolific public speaker and writer about Islam and Muslim issues. Pickthall was an influential Muslim political activist, as well as a celebrated writer and intellectual, whose English edition of the Qur'an has remained in print since it was first published in 1930.[4] Unlike Headley, both Quilliam and Pickthall have been, and continue to be, the subjects of critical biographies and scholarly analysis.[5]

There has not been, until now, a biography of Headley and it is only in recent years that he has appeared, usually fleetingly, in some general and academic studies of the history of Islam in Britain and the Global West.[6] This book, then, takes a historical-biographical approach to document, explain and critically assess Lord Headley's life, work and legacy. It is not, strictly, a conventional biography: after outlining Headley's life before his religious conversion, it focuses on his religious beliefs and conversion to Islam, his work as a Muslim leader in Britain and unofficial Muslim ambassador overseas, and the national and international socio-religious and political milieu in which he lived and operated between 1913 and 1935. This book thereby aims to go beyond a standard narration of Headley's life in order to show what it meant to be a Muslim convert – and, in Headley's case, a prominent one – in Britain, and how his life is significant for a broader understanding of the globalization of Islam in the first half of the twentieth century. It addresses the following core questions:

1. Who was Lord Headley and what was his life like before his conversion to Islam in 1913?
2. How did Headley encounter Islam, why and how did he convert to it in 1913, and how did Headley's contemporaries respond?
3. How did Headley negotiate Islamic prohibitions and practise Islam in Britain?
4. What did it mean to be a Muslim in a non-Muslim country like Britain between the two world wars?
5. What was Headley's role in shaping the organization, propagation, institutionalization and indigenization of Islam in early-twentieth-century Britain?
6. How effective was Headley as a Muslim leader?
7. How did Headley negotiate his personal politics and national and religious identities, especially during the First World War when the Muslim Ottoman Empire was at war with Britain and, afterwards, when the Ottoman Empire was dismembered and the office of the Caliph (the leader of Sunni Muslims) abandoned?

8. How did Headley respond to the politics of Muslims and pan-Islam, differences between Muslims, and the globalization of Islam in the 1920s and 1930s?
9. Was Headley an effective ambassador for British Muslims overseas and what kind of relationships did he have with other Muslims in the West, the British Empire and beyond?
10. What is Headley's legacy and relevance today?

Sources and methodology

Aspects of Headley's life are reasonably well documented in his many publications and contemporaneous published sources, notably newspapers, magazines, journals, books and pamphlets. Of particular value are partisan Muslim missionary publications and, especially when examining the reasons for his religious conversion, published personal testimony, both of which raise surmountable methodological issues.

The Muslim missionary publications were written and edited with an ideological bias and partly for propaganda purposes. However, as I have argued elsewhere, as long as the influences and biases of these sources are recognized, the contributions by and about Muslim converts like Headley offer rich and varied insights into the motivations for and process of religious conversion; and they also reveal much about their lives and concerns as Muslims in a non-Muslim country.[7] These sources also provide a wealth of information about the community or communities that the Muslims joined, including their philosophy, activities, the attitudes of outsiders and relationships with other faith groups as well as Muslims in other countries. Frustratingly, however, the Muslim missionary publications of the interwar period (primarily *The Islamic Review* and *The Light*), which have been central to the writing of this book, seldom contain responses or a 'right to reply' to its authors. It would be fascinating to know, for example, what Headley's fellow British Muslims really thought about his oft-repeated call for the 'Westernization' of Islam in Britain and other non-Muslim countries (see Chapter 5). Alas, in the absence of written or oral documentation, we will probably never truly know.

Some scholars of religion have cast doubt on the ability of published (and unpublished) personal conversion testimonies to illuminate the religious conversion process. For example, sociologists Brian Taylor and James Beckford have argued that conversion testimonies are almost exclusively produced retrospectively, are temporally variable and socially constructed in terms of both ideology and vocabulary.[8] Beckford found that there is a formal, public or even 'official' conception of appropriate features of the conversion experience in testimonies.[9] These arguments have weight because, like all autobiography and biography, religious conversion testimonies are constructions or reconstructions of experiences. John Lofland and Norman Skonovd have usefully shown that problems arising from the 'moulding' or 'structuring' of testimonies can be overcome, arguing that 'the conversion experience *itself* is partly molded by expectations of what conversion is about or "is like"', and consequently there is the probability of finding in testimonies a good fit between 'real' experiences and 'paradigmatic' accounts.[10] Lewis R. Rambo, whose remarkable work on conversion theory has long influenced my own approach to researching conversion and converts to Islam, has also highlighted that the writing of testimonies can be an integral part of the religious conversion experience because testimony (made and remade) serves as an opportunity to demonstrate the converts' language transformation and biographical reconstruction.[11]

In addition to the core published sources already discussed, particular insights about Headley's life and times have been gleaned from a combination of largely unpublished private and public material. I have drawn on Headley's surviving private papers and correspondence, as well as those of his close family. Insights from Headley's contemporaries have been teased out from the private papers of some of his friends and colleagues, as well as public and official papers, especially British Foreign and India Office records.

Structure

This book is broadly chronological in structure but, given its focus on Headley's life as a Muslim, weight is given to the period from 1913 to 1935. To that end, Chapters 1 to 3 examine Headley's life prior to his conversion to Islam and Chapters 4 to 9 explore his religious conversion and life and work as a Muslim public figure.

Chapter 1 outlines Headley's Anglo-Irish ancestry and conventional early life, from his school and university years to his search in the late 1870s for a profession, which led him to briefly study law before working in journalism and politics. Chapter 2 shows that Headley settled on a career in civil engineering in the early 1890s. It describes Headley's first major project, which happened to be in British India, where he lived in a Muslim-majority community for the first time and was introduced to the Qur'an. Headley returned to London engaged to be married and with the reputation of an excellent civil engineer. Chapter 3 discusses the highs and lows of Headley's life at the beginning of the twentieth century in Ireland, from an initially happy marriage, fatherhood and continued professional success to a series of personal crises that deeply affected his mental well-being and led to his incarceration in a Dublin lunatic asylum. It reveals that Headley found solace in religion but that he began to question aspects of Christian teaching, lost faith in the church, and moved towards Unitarianism. The latter reintroduced Headley to the life of the Prophet Muhammad and the religion of Islam, which he had first encountered and studied in India.

Chapter 4 details why and how Headley converted to Islam in 1913, the same year that he succeeded to the Baronetcy. It considers the context in which he rediscovered Islam by surveying the history of Muslims, Islam and Islamic missionary activity in late-Victorian and Edwardian Britain, then narrates Headley's path to formal conversion, documents private and public reactions and describes how Headley responded to his critics. Chapters 5 and 6 examine Headley's first decade as a Muslim public figure. Chapter 5 considers the period between his religious conversion in 1913 and the end of the First World War. It begins by examining Headley's leadership of British Muslims through the Woking Muslim Mission, his practice of Islam and call for its 'Westernization' in non-Muslim countries like Britain. It then explores how the First World War, specifically the Ottoman–German alliance, affected British Muslim sensibilities and relates how Headley demonstrated his loyalty to Britain, only to suffer a humiliating fall from grace when he was convicted for drunk and disorderly behaviour in 1917. Chapter 6 examines the immediate post-war period, from 1918 to 1923, first looking at Headley's personal life, including his short-lived second marriage in 1921 and bankruptcy in 1922, and then considering Headley's tentative involvement in post-war politics on behalf of British Muslims as Britain and its Allies decided the future of the Ottoman Empire. Chapter 7 focuses on Headley's Hajj, or pilgrimage to Mecca, in 1923. It narrates the sequence of Headley's Hajj and considers not only its spiritual impact on Headley as a Muslim but also its political significance, not least because the Hajj of 1923 coincided with the Allies' final deliberations about Ottoman Turkey's post-war fate. Chapter 8 discusses Headley's role as an unofficial ambassador for British Islam in the 1920s. It first maps Headley's domestic and international Muslim networks. The chapter then outlines how disputes among Muslims in Britain and overseas about the Ahmadiyya and the institutionalization of the Qadiani Ahmadi movement in England brought to the fore theological and practical questions about the nature of Islamic 'brotherhood' for Headley, which he expressed in his speeches and writings, and the attempt to build a new mosque in London. Chapter 9 documents Headley's twilight years, from 1929 through to his death in 1935. It shows that, although Headley opted for semi-retirement in the English countryside, he remained a dedicated Muslim leader and also devoted his final years to defending Muslims in the Middle East and India, and working tirelessly – but ultimately unsuccessfully – to raise funds for a London mosque.

Note

To avoid confusion with other family members, Headley is referred to as Rowland or Rowland junior throughout Chapters 1 and 2, and in Chapter 3 until the narrative reaches 1913, when he succeeded to the Baronetcy. From Chapter 4 onwards, which examines the period after he became Lord Headley, he is referred to as Headley. To further ensure clarity, Headley's wives are generally referred to throughout the text by their first names: Teresa, Barbara and Catharine.

1

A conventional start
Early years, 1855–92

Rowland George Allanson-Winn, the future fifth Lord Headley, was born in London on 19 January 1855. The British newspapers on that cold and cloudy Friday were full of reports and opinion pieces about the Crimean War, which had begun in October 1853. Britain had been drawn into the conflict with its allies France, the Ottoman Empire and Sardinia against Russia, ostensibly to check further extension of Russian power in the vast but fragile Ottoman territories. Following a series of logistical and tactical failures and mismanagement, by 1855 the war had become unpopular in Britain. Ten days after Rowland's birth, the British Parliament approved a motion for an investigation into the conduct of the war, which led to the resignation of the Conservative prime minister George Hamilton-Gordon, the fourth Earl of Aberdeen (1784–1860). The war continued for another year, but its wider concern, the so-called Eastern Question – the question of what should become of the Ottoman Empire as its subject peoples and their rulers sought autonomy or independence, encouraged and discouraged primarily by Russia, Britain and France – rumbled on for almost the entirety of Rowland Allanson-Winn's long life.[1] As is related in the subsequent chapters of this book, six decades later, after he had converted to Islam, Rowland found himself inexorably caught up in the politics of the Eastern Question and the decline of the Ottoman Empire and Turkey, which had, in 1517, declared itself the Caliph (or Khalifa), the successor to the mantle of the Prophet Muhammad and the leader of the universal Muslim community, or *umma*.

This chapter focuses on Rowland's early life. After describing Rowland's ancestry and family, it briefly documents his formative years at school and university to reveal that he led a conventional life, did well academically and excelled at sports. After university, however, Rowland struggled to settle on a career, and the period between the late 1870s and the early 1890s was marked by uncertainty and a lack of direction, compounded by the stirring of religious doubt. Rowland abandoned legal studies in favour of various professional jobs, including editorship of a newspaper and, in 1892, he attempted to become a Unionist politician in his ancestral homeland, Ireland.

Antecedents

Rowland George Allanson-Winn had a conventional upbringing. He was the eldest child of the Honourable Rowland Allanson-Winn (1816–88) and his wife, Margaretta Stefana (née Walker, 1823–71). The Winn family had risen in society during the late eighteenth century with George Winn (1725–98), who was one of the Barons of the Exchequer (judges of the court of common law) in Scotland from 1761 to 1776. In 1763, George Winn inherited the estate of a cousin in Little Warley, in the English county of Essex, and in 1776 he was created the first Baronet of Little Warley. In 1789, the first year of the French Revolution, George Winn became Tory Member of Parliament (MP) for Ripon in North Yorkshire and was rewarded for his support of William Pitt the Younger (1759–1806), who recommended his elevation to Lord Headley, Baron Allanson and Winn of Aghadoe in County Kerry, south-west Ireland, in 1797. George Winn assumed the surname and arms of Allanson by royal licence in 1777, but he used the double-surname of Allanson-Winn.[2]

The first Baron Headley was succeeded in 1798 by his eldest son, Charles Winn-Allanson (1784–1840; he curiously used the surname of Allanson *after* that of Winn), who also succeeded a distant cousin to become the eighth Baronet of Nostell in Yorkshire in 1833. With no sons to succeed him, Charles' only brother, the Honourable George Mark Arthur Way Allanson-Winn (1785–1827) had issue, but he died aged forty-two in 1827. Therefore, when Charles Winn-Allanson died thirteen years later, the Baronetcy passed to his nephew and George's eldest son, another Charles Allanson-Winn (1810–77), who became the third Lord Headley.

Although Ireland was part of the United Kingdom of Great Britain and Ireland (UK) until 1922, as Irish peers the Barons Allanson and Winn were not automatically entitled to a seat in the House of Lords. The third Lord Headley, Charles, was, however, appointed a Tory Representative Peer for Ireland in 1868. When Charles died after a long illness in 1877, he was succeeded by his eldest surviving son, Charles Mark Allanson-Winn (1845–1913), who was also appointed a Representative Peer for Ireland. To avoid confusion, the fourth Lord Headley was known in the family as Charlie Allanson-Winn.

In the early 1880s, shortly after Charlie Allanson-Winn succeeded to the Baronetcy, the family estate consisted of 12,769 acres in County Kerry (reduced from around 25,000 acres in the previous decade), valued at a modest £5,600 per year.[3] The family fortune was already in sharp decline when Charlie became the fourth Baron, and the Headleys were cash poor. Nonetheless, the estate included a large late-Georgian villa, Aghadoe House (rebuilt c.1860), described when it was built as 'a very fine building, densely shaded with trees', and set on a model farm overlooking Lough Leane (or Loch Lein) near Killarney.[4] Further estate property was located to the west of Aghadoe, at Glenbeigh on the mountainous Iveragh Peninsula. The superficial splendour of the Headley residences in picturesque Aghadoe and Glenbeigh contrasted with the poverty endured by tenants of the estate. Tensions between landlord and tenants increased during the nineteenth century because, as the *Dublin Review* noted in 1836:

> In Ireland, unlike every other country, there scarcely exists any community of interest between landlord and tenant, though in bitter irony they are called 'their benefactors' – assuredly no other relation is recognized between the one and the other than that of buyer and seller, in mercantile language; the proprietor looks upon his land as so much merchandise, from which the highest rate of profit must be extracted, and in order to do so, the tenant is kept in a state of villainage like the vassal of a feudal baron to his superior.[5]

The *Dublin Review* included an extract from a report written several years earlier by a Mr Wiggins, 'an English practical agriculturalist', as illustrative of 'what landlords, who know their own interests, may *effect*, and how easy it is to manage even the rudest and most ignorant boor by adopting kind and conciliatory measures':[6]

> Lord Headly's [sic] estate of Glenbeg [sic], situated in a wild district of Kerry, at the entrance of the Iveragh Mountains, consisting of 15,000 acres, much of which is rocky, boggy, and mountain ground, was, in 1807, inhabited by a people, to whom the bare idea of labour was offensive, and work was considered as slavery, though a robust, active, enterprising, and hospitable race of peasantry.
>
> Lord Headly resolved to cultivate their good qualities, without being at first very eager to punish their bad ones, and has succeeded in introducing a degree of improvement and cultivation, which without these effects, must have required a century. They are now well clothed, and as orderly and well-conducted as you see in any village in England. Agriculture has improved with very little sacrifice of rent or money.[7]

This English opinion piece would not have found favour among Headley's tenants, for whom the absentee Barons and their land agents were brutal, exploitative men.

In an arrogant act of defiance against his tenants and other critics, during the late 1860s, the third Baron, Charles Allanson-Winn, built Glenbeigh Towers (1867–71), a medieval-style solid stone fortress, complete with a huge three-storey keep raised on a battered platform. In his classic guide to Irish country houses, the historian Mark Bence-Jones described Glenbeigh Towers as 'a grim' building, and noted that 'the complete absence of battlements, machicolations and other pseudo-medieval features served to make the building more formidable'.[8] Charles Allanson-Winn raised funds for the project by dramatically increasing the rents on his estate, which were enforced by a tough land agent. He was not, however, happy with the final result; the cost of construction spiralled out of control and the walls leaked. Charles Allanson-Winn threatened, but probably could not afford to sue, his architect. Glenbeigh Towers was – and is still – referred to locally as 'Winn's Folly'.[9]

Charles Allanson-Winn had a very difficult relationship with his son and heir, Charlie. It was exacerbated by endless concerns about money and not helped when, in 1867, Charlie defied his father's wishes by marrying the 'almost penniless' widow, Elizabeth ('Bessie') Housemayne Blennerhassett (1846–1928), who was the daughter of a lowly Dorset clergyman.[10] When Charlie Allanson-Winn succeeded his father in 1877, the Irish 'Land War', a period of civil unrest in which tenants rebelled against absentee landlords, was gathering momentum. Although Charlie sought to settle debts and duties by selling off land when his father died, the Headley estate remained heavily mortgaged.

As the fourth Lord Headley, Charlie Allanson-Winn did little to improve relations with his tenants. Thoroughly English (born in Brighton, educated at Harrow and Oxford), Charlie spent little time in Ireland until later in life; he served with both the English and German armies, travelled widely and preferred to live at Warley Lodge in Little Warley, Essex.[11] The Lodge was part of the Baron's modest English estate, which in the early 1880s comprised 1,038 acres in Essex and 2,235 acres in Yorkshire. Consequently, in 1883, the total family estate of a little more than 16,000 acres in Ireland and England was valued at £13,388 a year.[12]

Childhood

Charlie Allanson-Winn dropped 'Allanson' from his surname in 1883. By contrast, his uncle, Rowland's father, who was born in 1817 and was a grandson of the first Lord Headley, used the surname Allanson-Winn without royal licence.[13] Granted the rank of the Baron's younger son, the Honourable Rowland senior was nevertheless heir presumptive if his nephew Charlie did not produce a son (he had one child, a daughter, when he became Lord Headley in 1877); and Rowland junior was next in line. Rowland senior and his wife Margaretta Allanson-Winn had three children after Rowland junior, all daughters: Helen Margaretta (1857–1941), Stephanie (1858–1940) and Margaretta Anne (1860–1951).

Figure 1 The Honourable Rowland George Allanson-Winn with his sisters and mother, Margaretta Stefana Allanson-Winn, Oxford, c.1869.
Source: Courtesy of Janet Webb / The Estate of the Fifth Lord Headley.

Rowland junior and his sisters were raised at the family home overlooking the prestigious Chester Square in London's Belgravia. They also had the run of the Glenbeigh estate in Ireland, which was formally transferred to their father in the 1860s. Although Rowland senior complained about lack of money, the family lived well, attended to by several domestic servants.[14] Rowland junior had a happy childhood and, though he later had a fractious relationship with his father, always recalled both of his parents with great fondness. He was educated privately in London except for a brief spell in 1868 at Westminster School, located in the precincts of Westminster Abbey. Two years later, in March 1871, tragedy struck the family when Rowland's mother Margaretta died at the age of forty-seven. Rowland had just turned sixteen. Many years later, he wrote a 'hymn' called 'The Power of God's Love', which recalled his loss:

> When Thou didst take my mother dear
> > In early life to dwell with Thee,
> I mourned her loss with many a tear,
> > And thought death gained a victory.[15]

Religion was important in the Allanson-Winn household. The family was firmly Protestant and worshipped in Anglican churches in London and Ireland. Late in life, Rowland described his parents as 'good and God-fearing people': they 'were not afraid of Him, but they feared to do anything they felt might be contrary to his wishes'.[16] Rowland was baptized in infancy, but he apparently had doubts about the church from an early age. Seventy years after his baptism, after he had converted to Islam and perhaps with the benefit of retrospective reasoning, Rowland wrote that

> from childhood's earliest days my whole nature had been in revolt against the ruthless cruelty of the Supreme Being as represented by the Christian God, an almighty and omnipotent ruler of the universe who was so like a human tyrant that he required heavy bribes before he would save one from perdition.[17]

When he reached the age of eighteen, not long after his mother's death, Rowland was expected to be Confirmed:

> Here was a definite step to be taken one way or the other. Either I was to back up my [baptism] sponsors and please my father by being 'Confirmed', or I was to obey the dictates of my own conscience and intelligence and refuse to ratify what I felt was but a figment of idolatry and superstition. It was a severe struggle, since on the one hand I had the desire to do what my father wished, and on the other I had to go in a line diametrically opposed to my own knowledge and belief.[18]

Rowland decided to 'follow the line of least resistance' and 'prevent a row and much unpleasantness'; he received his first Holy Communion at the Anglican church of St. Mary's in Putney, south-west London, in 1873.[19] Writing in 1926, he claimed:

> I have never forgiven myself for the deception I practised before God in Putney Church on that day [. . .]. I despised myself as a cur, for had I not presented myself in the House of God and stated my belief in what I well knew to be a made-up ceremony which meant nothing and could have no possible effect upon the God I loved and to whom I addressed my thanksgivings and prayers?[20]

It would, however, be many decades before Rowland's apparent disdain for the church led to his conversion away from Christianity.

University life

In February 1874, Rowland applied to take a degree in mathematics at Trinity College Cambridge. While idling away the months before going to university, he visited Oxford and there met and had a brief relationship with a young machinist called Alice Johnson. Alice became pregnant with Rowland's child.[21] It is not clear whether Rowland told his father or sisters about the pregnancy and there is, as would be expected, no direct reference to it in the surviving family correspondence.

How Rowland, barely nineteen years old, dealt with the fact that he was to become father to an illegitimate child, and whether he maintained contact with Alice during the pregnancy, is also unclear with the passage of time. He was accepted to Trinity and, financed by his father, left the family home in London for Cambridge in September 1874.[22] A few months later, on 20 January 1875 (the day after Rowland's twentieth birthday), Alice gave birth to a daughter, Laura 'Ivy' Davis, in Abingdon, near Oxford. The name of the baby's father was omitted from the birth certificate.[23] Rowland was not reconciled with Ivy for several decades (see Chapter 9).

Rowland enjoyed university. He studied moderately and had a busy social life. From a young age, Rowland had been a keen sportsman and counted among his primary recreations (in the order later given in his *Who's Who* biography) boxing, fishing, rowing, skating, swimming, fencing, shooting and golf.[24] At Cambridge, he excelled in boxing and won the university middleweights in 1876/7. Surviving letters from father to son in this period indicate that Rowland senior was

Figure 2 The Honourable Rowland George Allanson-Winn, London, c.1874. *Source*: Courtesy of Janet Webb / The Estate of the Fifth Lord Headley.

increasingly concerned that his son and heir was sacrificing academic work for sport and socializing with his friends. His anxiety increased as Rowland frittered away his allowance and accumulated a series of debts in both Cambridge and London.[25] At the beginning of his second year at Cambridge, Rowland received a cheque from his father, who implored him to 'pay off at once all you owe with the money I send you and then you will feel free'.[26] Having been assured by his son that he would focus on studying, Rowland senior felt 'quite certain you will never regret the resolution you have so wisely taken to drop things that must of necessity hinder you in your career at Cambridge. The most hopeful sign is the mistrust you have of yourself: "mistrust" being the "mother of surety".'[27]

However, Rowland strayed off course once he was back among his university friends, ignored his father's letters, neglected his health and suffered a bout of 'fever and rheumatism'. Rowland senior was extremely concerned for his son's well-being. On 10 December 1876, he wrote to Rowland: 'You have no idea what anxiety you have caused us by your long silence.' There was also a hint in the correspondence that Rowland junior might have experienced problems with his mental health that, as is related in the subsequent chapters of this book, flared up with serious consequences later in life. His father advised that 'The strong man is the well-balanced man – not the mere muscular man'.[28]

Contrary to his father's wishes, Rowland continued to devote his time to boxing. When he informed his father in April 1877 that he planned a rerun of a particular bout, Rowland senior conceded: 'you are old enough now to take your own course, only don't expect me to go along with it.'[29] In the 1877/8 year, Rowland added the university heavyweight title to his middleweight success.[30] And, to the relief of his father, he graduated with a Bachelor of Arts, Mathematical Tripos, in 1878.[31]

However, Rowland's academic and sporting success did not appease his father for long. Rowland left university unsure of his future career and spent the early part of 1879 with friends in England and Ireland. As the year progressed, Rowland senior became more agitated that his son was not making a name for himself, let alone improving the family's strained finances. In turn, Rowland attempted to fend off his father's impatience. It was a clash of the generations and both men felt vindicated by their responses to the other. For example, replying to a tardy letter received from his son, Rowland senior wrote: 'Your letters are getting more and more offensive as they are getting more childish.' He chastised his son for living 'the idle life': 'Recollect that you have spent more than 2 months now in London by yourself amusing yourself doing nothing at all if not doing worse [. . .] – and in my house and at my expense.' He warned him that 'I have means of knowing things you know not of'.[32]

Carving a career

Rowland initially resisted his father's attempts to influence his choice of career. Refusing to go out to India as a respectable junior civil servant, he briefly took up private tutorial teaching in London. Rowland's sister Margaretta wrote despairingly to him in April 1879:

> Papa is dreadfully worried and more and more trying. One feels that one must be as patient as possible for he has so much to bother him. What makes it so hard is that most of it is caused by himself. He is very anxious about you and is I feel sure beginning to think that he has treated you badly, that prays on his mind a good deal, then there is no money and all together our affairs are in a nice mess. We can't manage to marry money, for rich people never like us, so there is nothing to do but to wait and hope for better times.[33]

Relations between father and son were temporarily bridged when, later in 1879, Rowland decided to follow in the footsteps of his great-grandfather, the first Baron Headley, by training to become a barrister. George Winn had entered Lincoln's Inn (one of the four Inns of Court of London to which barristers in England and Wales belong) in 1744, and he was called to the Bar in 1755. Rowland's application to Lincoln's Inn was successful, and he was admitted in November 1879.

Correspondence between Rowland and his father in the early 1880s indicates that the former lacked confidence in law, and there is little sense in the letters or in his later reflections on life that he genuinely anticipated a legal career. Nonetheless, delighted that his son was pursuing a respectable and financially lucrative career, and keen to encourage him, Rowland senior wrote to congratulate his son every time he had a modicum of success with the many law exams.[34]

Once at Lincoln's Inn, however, Rowland began to harbour thoughts of a career in politics. This again echoed the life of his great-grandfather, who had been Tory MP for Ripon. Rowland was, like his father and forefathers, a staunch Conservative and Unionist, committed to the preservation of the Union between Great Britain and Ireland. Ultimately, paternal encouragement was not enough to keep Rowland at Lincoln's Inn and, towards the end of 1882, he left London for Salisbury. At Salisbury, he took up the position of editor of one of Britain's oldest provincial newspapers, the *Salisbury and Winchester Journal*. Founded in 1729, the *Journal* had shifted from a Whig to a neutral political stance and eventually took a pro-Unionist position.[35] How Rowland was appointed to the job in 1882 with no prior experience is unclear, though his family background probably influenced the newspaper's board of directors. For his part, it seems probable that Rowland considered the job as a stepping-stone towards the political career he desired. Already in late 1882 some apparently well-placed friends were preparing to find him a constituency in which to stand in a future general election. His father was characteristically anxious, telling Rowland that 'your advisors or seconders may be quite in Earnest and good and influential men', but also warning that his 'back' might not be 'strong enough to sustain them'.[36]

Within a year of joining the *Journal*, Rowland had fallen out with its proprietor and his boss, James Bennett. In December 1883, Rowland wrote to his father informing him that he would be leaving the *Journal*; Rowland senior replied on Christmas Eve: 'I am greatly afraid there has been some misunderstanding or quarrel between you especially after your telling me [Bennett] was so fidgety as to be almost unbearable sometimes.'[37] The relationship between father and son again collapsed with a bitter correspondence between London and Salisbury. Rowland senior wrote:

> I think I never knew a young man so void of what is called tact as you are. When you want to get anything done you first cherish suspicion of the person you apply to and then set about abusing and insulting him in unmeasured terms. [...] I think by this time you must look back on your letter with some regret and shame. Even if I had been the cruel and artful and wicked father you make me out it would not entitle you to forget to whom were writing. [...] I am too old and experienced to be humbugged by undeserved unworthy suspicions.[38]

Only Rowland senior's side of the London–Salisbury correspondence has survived. He claimed that his son had accepted an annual allowance of £200 on the condition that he 'gave up theatricals' but then Rowland junior had renaged on the agreement and threatened to wreak his 'full vengeance' upon his father by seeking 'a theatrical employment or anything which turns up which I think you would dislike most, and moreover to make you still more unhappy I will marry who I choose – and the more you dislike my choice all the better'.[39]

Rowland returned to London and also travelled to Ireland during 1884 and 1885. He considered settling permanently on his father's Glenbeigh estate to revive the family fortunes there. He was, however, dissuaded by his father, who warned him that an English landowner was not safe in the Nationalist (anti-Unionist) stronghold of County Kerry and, moreover, argued that the boggy and sea-battered Glenbeigh estate was almost worthless: 'It seems destined that this old baronetcy – this fine old family, should be despised by the successors to it and die out.'[40]

Resigned to the reduced status of his family, Rowland's father encouraged him to get 'a Secretary-ship to some nobleman or gentleman or M.P.'[41] This paternal pressure led to another dispute between father and son. Rowland was, at the time, in contact with a near-contemporary, George Herbert, the thirteenth Earl of Pembroke (1850–95), who had been Under-Secretary of State for War for Tory Prime Minister Benjamin Disraeli (1804–81). Pembroke sent a letter to Rowland care of his father's London address in October 1885. Rowland was furious that his father took two weeks to forward the letter, during which time Rowland senior wrote directly to Pembroke in an effort to secure a job for his son. Rowland junior rejected the idea of becoming a secretary, and instead restated his plan to run the Glenbeigh estate. His father wrote angrily from Glenbeigh:

> As to your assuming the Agency of my property here it is quite preposterous. It requires the immediate exercise of all that tact and experience and all diplomatic art [that] can be brought to bear on it. The latter is an art in which you certainly do not speak.[42]

Ireland and Westminster

It is quite remarkable that Rowland repeatedly sought to settle in County Kerry in the early 1880s, not least because relations between his cousin Charlie, the fourth Lord Headley, and the impoverished tenants of the Headley estates reached a new low. Frustrated with non-payment of rents in Ireland (rents in England did not cover costs), Charlie Allanson-Winn had attempted to evict many tenants during 1882 and 1883. This caused a bitter dispute between landlord and tenants that was replicated across Irish estates in this period. The press reported in spring 1886 that Lord Headley's tenants were still striking against 'exorbitant rents', and that the conflict had 'deprived him of the principal source from which he derived his income'.[43] In fact, his position was so dire that, in April 1886, Charlie Allanson-Winn was declared bankrupt, with gross debts of almost £46,000: 'The announcement of the bankruptcy has furnished society with a sensation, although the baron himself has not for some time been in very general request in social circles.'[44]

The English press turned firmly against Charlie, Lord Headley. In a report cabled from London and reprinted internationally, it was noted that, despite the non-payment of rents, Lord Headley 'continued to live in extravagant style at foreign watering places, and to occupy swell lodgings in the West End during the London season'. Further, 'Baron Headley has not set foot in Ireland for many years, and his wife and young daughter have been compelled to live a solitary life of misery, amid splendor at Arghadoe [sic] House, objects of the sympathy of the entire community'.[45]

The 'bankrupt baron' was 'a typical absentee Irish landlord; fond of sporting events and addicted to high play at cards':

> More than once he has tried to make his tenants pay the proportion of interest on the mortgages against his estate which their holdings represented in addition to enforcing prompt payments of rent, in order to provide funds to enable him to lead a luxurious life abroad. He has scarcely spent a penny in Ireland since he succeeded to his title and is now in hiding. Court officers are searching for him everywhere, but thus far have been unable to serve notices upon him.[46]

While Lord Headley's fortunes slumped, in spring 1886 Rowland achieved some financial security by accepting the position of private secretary to a popular Conservative politician, Frederick Seager Hunt (1838–1904). Hunt was a successful businessman and head of the wine and spirit merchants Seager Evans and Company, famous for its 'Seagers Gin'. Hunt was also a founder member of the Primrose League, which was established in 1883 to spread Conservative principles across the UK.[47] He was elected Conservative MP for the London district of Marylebone West at the general election of 1885, which the Liberals won under William Ewart Gladstone (1809–98) with his commitment to Irish Home Rule, or self-government for Ireland within the UK. Rowland joined Hunt prior to the general election of July 1886 when, in a dramatic reversal of the previous year's election, Robert Gascoyne-Cecil, the third Marquess of Salisbury (1830–1903), formed his second Conservative government in alliance with the Liberal Unionist Party, thereby ending a long period of Liberal dominance in Parliament. Hunt was re-elected MP for Marylebone West in 1886 (and again in 1892).[48] Rowland was jubilant at the changed political landscape, not least because the failure of Gladstone signalled the electorate's lack of support for Irish Home Rule.

After the 1886 general election, however, economic and political turmoil spread across Ireland. In County Kerry, the ongoing dispute between Lord Headley and his tenants culminated in violence throughout the winter of 1886/7 that directly implicated Rowland's father as landlord of the Glenbeigh estate. The new disturbances coincided with the beginning of the 'Plan of Campaign' (1886–91), a strategy organized by Irish Nationalist politicians to reduce the rents of tenant farmers burdened by poor harvests. At Glenbeigh in October 1886, Rowland's father attempted but failed to evict more than fifty tenants for non-payment of rent.[49] Matters came to a head at the end of January 1887 when the Glenbeigh land agent and 'emergency bailiffs', flanked by scores of police officers, effected many forced evictions over several days.⁵⁰ The events at Glenbeigh were widely reported across the UK, especially in the pro-Home Rule press:

> They went first to Patrick Reardon's at Droum, in a wild glen three miles beyond Glenbeigh. His rent was four pounds ten shillings, and he had nothing wherewith to pay. He told the agent he could not pay, and was ordered out of the house at once, as it was to be burned. He had scarcely got out his furniture when the emergency [bailiff] men fired the roof, and after it was burned, pulled down the walls.⁵¹

On the evening of 25 January 1887, the Mayor of Cork convened a public protest meeting:

> A series of resolutions was adopted protesting against the barbarous and inhuman evictions at Glenbeigh; calling upon the Government to suspend all such unchristian proceedings until they make inquiry as to whether the victims of such cruelties were in a position to meet the demands of their unscrupulous taskmasters; and by a third resolution an influential committee was appointed to receive subscriptions towards the relief of the evicted.⁵²

A few days later, the *Illustrated London News* featured an engraving of the dire scene at Glenbeigh on its front page. Entitled 'The Rent War in Ireland: Burning the Houses of Evicted Tenants at Glenbeigh, County Kerry', the image depicted burning property, and bailiffs and police battling with the tenants as their wives and children looked on in horror.⁵³

Rowland junior wrote a robust defence of his father's actions in a letter published in the London *Times* and other newspapers. He argued that, since taking possession of the Glenbeigh estate, his father had been 'practically deprived of his rents' but had 'always spent a large proportion of what he received upon the property':

> Draining, reclaiming waste lands, planting, and building have all provided labour and so improved the condition of the poor tenants, many of whom are masons, carpenters, &c [sic]; and I may mention incidentally that the castle [Glenbeigh Towers], facetiously alluded to as 'Winn's Folly', cost £8,000, most of which went into the pockets of the tenants.⁵⁴

Some newspapers empathized with the Allanson-Winns. According to the *Aberdeen Journal* in June 1887, 'We have all heard enough of the so-called hardships to the tenants in Glenbeigh':

> In regard to Glenbeigh many of the tenants were several years in arrears. Mr Head, Mr Allanson Winn's agent, has published a statement showing that the

arrears amounted in all to £6177, and that the proprietor generously offered to remit four-fifths of the amount – that is £5312 – on condition of the tenants paying a year's rent, which amounted to the extraordinary sum of £865! But the tenants, at the command of the [pro-tenant Irish National Land] League, refused to get rid of their debt of £6177 by the payment of £865; and the parish priest was so indignant, as well he might, that he called his people 'poor slaves' for their conduct, and announced that he would never interfere between landlord and tenant again. Thus does the story of 'oppression' collapse when the facts are calmly investigated.[55]

Rowland and his father wisely avoided Ireland while the dispute rumbled on, but they attempted to calm the situation through the press. In February 1888, their new land agent at Glenbeigh, D. Todd Thornton, informed readers of the London *Times* and *Kerry Evening Post* that 'the gross rental of the [. . .] estate, before the reduction of 35 and 40 per cent was offered the Glenbeigh tenants, would not pay the interest on the money expended by the Hon. R. Allanson Winn's (the present owner's) predecessors in improving the tenants' holdings'.[56]

Boxing

In May 1888, Rowland's father died suddenly at home in London.[57] Since Charlie, the fourth Lord Headley, had only one child, a daughter, Rowland junior became heir presumptive. Rowland continued working for Seager Hunt, but he also pursued other interests. For example, he accepted a commission from an old Cambridge friend, Ernest Bell (1851–1933), to write a short guide to boxing. The son of the London publisher George Bell (1814–90), Ernest Bell edited the cheap and popular 'All-England Series of Athletic Sports' books published by his father's firm. Rowland set to work on *Boxing*, which was published in 1889.[58] He used the introduction of the book to extol the virtues of a masculine sport like boxing and its benefit to the nation. This was timely because, despite the advance of an aggressive imperialism in the 1870s and 1880s, British confidence had been shaken following defeat in the First Boer War (1880–81) and the siege of Khartoum, Sudan, which ended with the death of its former governor-general and a British national hero, Major-General Charles Gordon (1833–85):

> [N]o Englishman should condemn this healthy exercise, which calls forth to such a marked extent those two great national qualities – pluck and endurance. Many an English boy, by nature inclined to be soft and effeminate, has been completely changed by hearing of deeds of daring. His mind has been seized by a

desire to emulate some unusual effort of activity or courage, and to improve the strength and endurance of his own body. The child's moral tone has undergone a change for the better – has received a fillip in the right direction – and he may grow into a good, sturdy, upstanding Britisher, able to lead a charge in battle, or defend himself by personal effort when occasion demands.[59]

Boxing was well received by the critics. The *St. James's Gazette* thought that 'Mr R. G. Allanson-Winn [...] deals with his subject in a lively, not to say racy, style'.[60]

The success of *Boxing* led to a second commission from Ernest Bell, for a guide to weapons of self-defence. Rowland wrote and illustrated most of the book but, 'not having leisure to take in hand the whole of the work myself', he called upon an old law student friend, Clive Phillipps-Wolley (1853–1918), to contribute a chapter.[61] The 'chatty little book' was published as *Broadsword and Singlestick* in 1890.[62] Undoubtedly with an eye to his family's problems in Ireland, Rowland wrote in the introduction:

> Unfortunately there are individuals, possibly in the small minority, who regard anything like fighting as brutal or ungentlemanly. In a sense – a very limited sense – they may be right, for, though our environment is such that we can never rest in perfect security, it does seem hard that we should have to be constantly on the alert to protect that which we think is ours by right, and ours alone.[63]

While the *St. James's Gazette* argued that the authors 'give a sufficient list of weapons with which to dispose of a rough' and considered the case of the umbrella as a weapon 'a revelation', it criticized Rowland for neglecting 'the use of a stone in a pocket-handkerchief, which has been known to be used with effect'.[64] The *Scotsman* thought it to be 'an excellent practical handbook, the directions being plain and brief'.[65] Both *Boxing* and *Broadsword* were included in a seven-volume edition of the 'All-England Series' edited by Ernest Bell in 1890.[66] The two books were reissued several times during Rowland's lifetime, and remain in print today.

The 1892 general election

Although Rowland had modest success with his first two books, he continued to harbour political ambitions. After seven years working in Whitehall as a private secretary, and without his father to discourage him, Rowland actively sought a constituency seat to contest. He inevitably looked to Ireland where he was a Justice of the Peace and also became, in 1891, High Sheriff for County Kerry.[67]

When a general election was called for July 1892, Rowland was selected as Irish Unionist Alliance candidate for Kerry South, the constituency that included Glenbeigh and Aghadoe. The Irish Unionist Alliance was founded in 1891 to oppose Home Rule for Ireland and, though aligned to both the Conservatives and the Liberal Unionists, its MPs took the Conservative Party whip at Westminster. Rowland's decision to contest Kerry South was symbolic; he knew that he had no chance of dislodging the incumbent Irish National Federation MP, Denis Kilbride (1848–1924), even though the Nationalists had recently split into two rival factions. Five years earlier, Kilbride had stood unopposed when he took Kerry South from a Nationalist colleague in a by-election. Kilbride was considered a hero by many in Ireland after being evicted from a sub-tenanted holding in 1887 by his absentee landlord, the fifth Marquess of Lansdowne and sixth Earl of Kerry (1845–1927), whose Irish estate exceeded 120,000 acres.

Rowland was almost as absent from Ireland as Lansdowne and his cousin Charlie, Lord Headley. Rowland visited Glenbeigh in this period, but was more often to be found in London at his lodgings in Duke Street, Westminster.[68] Like other Unionists, he attempted to rally support for the Conservatives in England rather than canvas in Ireland. One of his first speeches after selection was at a Primrose League meeting in London when he substituted for his boss, Frederick Seager Hunt. Rowland praised the Conservative government and policies that had, he said, directly benefited 'the wage-earning classes'. However, he cautioned against 'any grandmotherly legislation that tends to cramp and confine the powers and freedoms of an individual, for it seems to me as unfair to force an able-bodied Englishman to work only eight hours a day when he wanted to work for say ten hours'.[69] On Ireland, he explained:

> I myself have been associated with the Irish people, for whom I have a great affection (hear hear.) Yes, they are a queer lot, but I love them in spite of their faults; I cannot but love them (cheers.) On reading the appalling accounts of the cold-blooded murders and mutilations, one used to be rather ashamed of belonging to that country. Now all that is to a great extent changed, thanks to a proper administration of the law.[70]

He then rounded against Gladstone and advocates of Home Rule:

> [Y]ou can take it from one who knows what he is talking about, that as soon as the Home Rule Bill becomes law, Civil War will break out in Ireland. The Home Rule split shows that the self-restraint and tact necessary for proper government is not possessed by the men to whom, if Mr Gladstone's [Home Rule] Bill becomes law, the offices of the State would be entrusted.[71]

Ireland must, he argued, remain part of the UK: 'we have got our own [. . .] glorious Empire purchased by the blood and treasure of our ancestors and handed down to us by them as a precious legacy. Let us hang on to that Empire, Liberal Unionists and Conservatives together.'[72]

Throughout May and June 1892, just weeks before election day, Rowland remained in England and addressed more Primrose League meetings, primarily on the subject of Ireland.[73] Introducing Rowland at a 'packed' meeting in Westgate-on-Sea, the chairman Colonel Jones said that 'a gentleman who could stand up for his country and the Government in such a hot-bed of so-called nationalism as Kerry [. . .], and fight for what he (the speaker) must call the forlorn hope, if perchance, he might win a seat in the interests of law and order, was worthy of their most hearty thanks and all the support it was in their power to give him'.[74] The local press summarized Rowland's speech:

> [I]t was a well-known fact that, given Home Rule, Ireland could not in any given time, or indeed in any time at all, of herself raise a force sufficient to protect her own shores. We should still have to protect her with our forces, and that meant that we must tax her to pay expenses, and taxation without representation was a thing never heard of. Was Ireland to have two sets of members? One body sitting at Dublin and the other at Westminster, and probably fighting one against the other. What was the capital of Ireland? (A voice: 'Belfast.') He was quite right.[75]

Rowland finally left England for Ireland in mid-June, when Parliament was dissolved. He immediately wrote a manifesto letter to 'Friends and electors of South Kerry', which was published in the Unionist *Kerry Evening Post*:

> My family has for many years past been connected with Kerry, and my own feelings of affection for those amongst whom many of the happiest years of my life were passed, are well known to those whose acquaintance and friendship I am proud to possess.
>
> These are what may be called personal and family qualifications, without which I should not consent to contest this division, and it may be advisable that I should at once tell you what I think of Home Rule.
>
> In my opinion it would be most unwise to attempt any sort of separation from Great Britain. The management of Local Affairs is one thing, splitting up the United Kingdom into fragments is quite another.
>
> England has for many years past done all she can do to further Ireland's best interests, and Ireland has a larger representation in Parliament, in proportion to her population and wealth, than any other division of the Kingdom; and the Irish Tenant class possesses advantages which cannot be claimed by the same class in England, Scotland, or Wales.

[. . .] If I could see any advantage to this Country, I would support Home Rule to-morrow, and it is only through the firm conviction that Separation would only bring disaster to Ireland and disgrace to the United Kingdom, that these views are advanced by me.[76]

While the *Limerick Chronicle* thought Rowland's case was 'strong, as might be expected from a candidate with a double surname', the Nationalist press and politicians were not at all sympathetic, and reminded the electorate that Rowland's father had been responsible for the violent evictions at Glenbeigh.[77] Rowland sought a right to reply to his many critics via the newspapers, claiming in a letter published on 6 July that, 'at the time of the Glenbeigh evictions the management of the estate was not in my hands, and [. . .] neither myself or my [land] agent, Mr D. Todd Thornton, had anything to do with those evictions'.[78] The *Kerry Evening Post* considered the claims made against Rowland to be 'disgraceful' and it maintained that 'Mr Winn is deservedly popular at Glenbeigh'.[79]

Rowland attended a major Unionist convention in Dublin and then returned to Glenbeigh in early July 1892. He held a series of hustings events in and around the parish. The *Irish Times* noted that 'the size of the divisions he is contesting is so great that his hands are more than full. There are eleven polling districts, some of them being fifty miles apart'.[80] One of the first meetings was 'in a field close to Beaufort House', to the west of the constituency. The *Kerry Evening Post* reported that 'About 250 people attended, and though there was a little attempt at interference in the way of "booing," the speaker was able to hold his audience for three quarters of an hour, and to answer several questions to the apparent satisfaction of his questioners.'[81] The following day, Rowland addressed a smaller crowd at Caragh Lake, Glenbeigh:

> The weather was against a large attendance, but those who were present gave a most attentive hearing to the speaker, who enlarged chiefly on those methods, of which he approved, for improving the condition of the people and increasing the flow of capital into the country.[82]

On 10 July, Rowland held a widely reported hustings event on the Glenbeigh estate which was attended by his tenants. The *Irish Times* noted that Rowland's 'successful and popular' agent, D. Todd Thornton,

> exposed the attempts of certain mischievous persons who had sought to implicate Mr Winn with the 'Glenbeigh evictions', and urged the tenants not to be led away by those advisers who, for their own ends, incorrectly represented the state of affairs, but to vote for the candidate and to assist the great cause they had at heart – the cause they intended to fight for over and over again.[83]

Rowland then took the stage:

> As they all knew, he had nothing to do with those evictions. He was anxious to walk in the footsteps of his ancestors, who had for generations spent their best energies and large sums of money in the improvement of their estates in different parts of Kerry. As instances of really good landlords, he mentioned his great uncle Lord Headley, his uncle the late Lord Headley, and his late father, all of whom had done their utmost to improve the condition of the tenants on their estates.[84]

The Unionist press admitted that Rowland experienced some heckling from the audience, but concluded that he had delivered a 'lucid' speech 'in which he had dealt with the political situation and upheld the cause of the Union'.[85] Polling for Kerry West and East was concluded before the electorate voted in Rowland's constituency of Kerry South. The Unionist candidates in both Kerry West and East were roundly defeated by Nationalists. Nevertheless, on the eve of polling in Kerry South, the local *Evening Post* ran an optimistic opinion piece which proclaimed that there was 'much support' for Rowland:

> This week he has had a most successful meeting at Glenbeigh – the scene of the evictions which his opponents would cast in his face, but which charges he so truthfully refuted. If promises are kept he ought to make a good fight at the polls, and if not elected should feel gratified at the fact that he was able to show that Unionism was not dead in Kerry.[86]

After a hectic month of campaigning, the promises of support were not realized and Rowland polled a mere 86 (3.6 per cent) of the 2,407 votes cast in Kerry South. The incumbent MP, Denis Kilbride, retained his huge majority with 2,096 (87 per cent) votes (and he went unopposed at the subsequent general election, in 1895).[87] Rowland wrote a letter for publication in the *Kerry Evening Post* in which he thanked those who had supported him 'against overwhelming odds'.[88] He partly attributed 'the smallness of the Unionist minority' to 'apathy and inactivity', encouraged by 'the most prominent professing Unionists in the Kenmare district [who] abstained altogether from voting, or in any way assisting their cause'. Moreover, in one of his first public comments that touched on matters of religion, he argued that the defeat was 'chiefly to be accounted for by the active part taken by the Roman Catholic priests, without exception, throughout South Kerry'.[89] As a Protestant Anglican, Rowland was wary of the influence of Catholic priests in the local community. In the short term, Rowland's experience in Ireland in 1892 and for several years afterwards merely reinforced his commitment to Protestantism, tied as it was to the politics of the Union, in which he had been raised.

Although the divided Nationalists did well in Ireland in 1892, Salisbury's Conservatives won most seats in the UK, but not an overall majority. Gladstone managed to form a minority Liberal-led government and therefore became prime minister for the fourth and final time in August 1892. Somewhat ironically for Rowland, Gladstone relied on Irish Nationalist support to form his government. Rowland had signed off his defeat letter in the *Kerry Evening Post* with a defiant promise that he would 'fight again'.[90] In reality, he was weary of party politics and desperately in need of money. By mid-summer 1892, Rowland had decided on a new career path well away from politics that precipitated his swift return to London and, shortly afterwards, voyage to India.

2

Imperial engineer, 1892–1900

Following inevitable political failure in Ireland, Rowland Allanson-Winn returned to London. Disillusioned with party politics and with a degree in mathematics, he began a short engineering course at King's College London. Rowland was fortunate that, at the end of the nineteenth century, civil engineers were in demand not only in the UK but across the vast British Empire.[1]

This chapter examines Rowland's professional career as a civil engineer. It relates how Rowland took on his first engineering job in British India and considers the impact of working in that country on his professional and personal life: he successfully oversaw a major road project in the Muslim-majority princely state of Jammu and Kashmir, where he also encountered Islam for the first time and met his future wife. The chapter ends by discussing Rowland's return to the UK in the late 1890s, when he married and, capitalizing on his achievements in India, he made a name for himself as a distinguished civil engineer and expert in coastal erosion.

Jammu and Kashmir

Rowland was introduced to the successful civil engineer Charles Spedding (1857–1925) in London in 1892. Spedding was director of a prominent India-based firm, Spedding and Company, which he had established in Lahore in 1884.[2] The introduction to Spedding was possibly made by Rowland's former boss, Frederick Seager Hunt MP, who was partly educated in India and had business contacts in that country.[3] Although he had been formally studying engineering for a very short time, Rowland did not hesitate to accept Spedding's invitation to join him in India as an assistant engineer. Rowland and Charles Spedding left London together on the Peninsular and Oriental (P&O) steamship SS *Thames*, on 8 September 1892.[4]

The journey from London via the terminus port of Brindisi to Bombay (the main landing stage in India for ships from the West) took a month by passenger liner in 1892. Rowland recalled years later that, while the SS *Thames* was anchored off Aden, 'diving-boys were swimming all around the ship, when, all of a sudden, a shark appeared and snapped off the leg of one of the poor little chaps'. Rowland helped bring the boy onto the ship, 'and our doctor looked after the injury and tied up the stump'.[5]

The rest of the journey was uneventful and Rowland arrived at Bombay on 2 October 1892.[6] According to the popular *Handbook for Travellers in India and Ceylon*, published in London the previous year, 'A trip to India is no longer a formidable journey or one that requires very special preparation. The Englishman who undertakes it merely passes from one portion of the British Empire to another.'[7] This might have been true for those privileged travellers who flitted between luxury hotels in the major cities and towns, but Rowland was bound for what was known in the Anglo-Indian slang of the day as *mofussil*, or 'the provinces', 'up-country'. At Bombay he took the three-day express train north to Rawalpindi in the Punjab. From there, he journeyed by *tonga* (a light, two-wheeled horse-drawn carriage) for some 200 miles to Srinagar, the capital of Kashmir and what was likely his first direct experience of a Muslim-majority region.[8]

Rowland's home for the next four years was to be in the state of Jammu and Kashmir, known as the 'happy valley' because it was a popular resort for the British in India. It was also called the 'northern bastion of India' since it is located mostly in the Himalayan mountains on 'the high roof of the world', then the borderline for the empires of Britain, China and Russia.[9] Since 1857, India had been ruled by the British Crown but the vast country comprised two types of territory. When Rowland arrived, there were eight major provinces of British India and a handful of minor provinces directly administered by the British viceroy and governor-general of India, and nearly 600 princely states (also called 'native states') nominally ruled by local princes, princesses or chiefs under the suzerainty of the British Crown.

For almost fifty years prior to Rowland's arrival, Jammu and Kashmir had been a united princely state of the British Empire in India. Following the defeat of the Sikhs in the First Anglo-Sikh War of 1845–6, the state was ruled by the Hindu Dogra Rajput dynasty until the Partition of India in 1947. When Rowland entered Jammu and Kashmir in the early 1890s, its ruler was Maharaja Pratap Singh (1848–1925). The Maharaja ruled over a huge region of more than 80,000 square miles with only two sizeable towns (Jammu and Srinagar),

9,000 villages and a total population of around 2.5 million people. But it was, as one contemporary guidebook stated, 'a country with diverse races, who speak different languages, profess different religions, and have different customs and manners'.[10] This pluralism was the inevitable result of a long history of different dynastic rulers, shifting national borders and religious traditions, most notably Buddhism, Hinduism, Islam and Sikhism. However, the majority religion in Jammu and Kashmir was Islam: the first regular Census of 1891 recorded that more than three quarters of the population were Muslim (of whom 95 per cent were Sunni and 5 per cent Shi'i[11]), followed by minority communities of mainly Hindus (concentrated in Jammu province) and Sikhs.[12]

Most Muslims in Jammu and Kashmir were descendants of Hindus who had converted to Islam under Muslim rule during the fourteenth and fifteenth centuries. For John Collett and Ashutosh Mitra in their *Guide for Visitors to Kashmir* (1898): 'That the Muhammadans in Kashmir are the descendants of Hindus converted to Islam is corroborated by the fact that the members of the two religions live on very amicable terms, and that the Muhammadans have not the same religious zeal that characterizes their co-religionists elsewhere.'[13] As the British imperialist writer E. F. Knight (1852–1925) proposed in his 1893 book *Where Three Empires Meet*:

> The observers of neither faith have cause to boast of the religion of their forefathers. The ancestors of most of these people were converted backwards and forwards [. . .] according to successive dynasties. They are now neither good Hindoos nor good Mussulmans. One result of this is that fanaticism is seldom displayed, except, of course, when Shiahs and Sunis [sic] meet – those Nonconformists and High Churchmen of Mahomedanism.[14]

Jammu and, especially, Kashmir (the British often referred to the princely state as, simply, Kashmir) had long captivated the Western imagination because of its dramatic natural terrain.[15] The British government's official *Imperial Gazetteer of India* considered that the state 'may be likened to a house with many storeys. [. . .] There are valleys, and occasional oases in the deep cañons of the mighty rivers; but mountain is the predominating feature'.[16] Collett and Mitra wrote:

> There is, perhaps, no land under the sun which has received such praise in prose or rhyme as the valley of Kashmir. And, indeed, it is very beautiful – 'an emerald of verdure enclosed in a radiant amphitheatre of virgin snow'. The valley, which is peopled by a primitive type of the Aryan race, is intersected by a beautiful meandering river, and is covered with luxuriant fruit trees and fragrant flowers, with majestic chinars and silvery poplars. Behind all stand the majestic snow-clad mountains.[17]

Before the 1890s, Jammu and Kashmir had few passable roads and it was instead traversed on foot through arduous mountain passes and rivers. This began to change with the construction of major routes contracted by the Maharaja and Britain. Rowland's employer, Spedding and Company, was the pre-eminent contract engineering firm in Jammu and Kashmir at the end of the nineteenth century. Since Rowland left little account of his years in India and his correspondence from this period has not survived, the numerous accounts of Jammu and Kashmir written by his contemporaries help set the scene. One of these, E. F. Knight, journeyed from London to India in February 1891 with Charles Spedding. Spedding had just completed the construction of the Jhelum Valley road, a feat of civil engineering that cut through the mountain sides along the course of the Jhelum River for 200 miles between the Punjabi village of Kohala and the large town of Baramulla in Kashmir. The former road was, according to Collett and Mitra, 'barely more than a path, and was rough and steep, being in no wise [sic] practicable for wheeled traffic'.[18] Knight travelled along Spedding's new route and considered it to be 'the only road practicable for wheels in the whole of this country'. Spedding had, he continued, 'overcome all the extraordinary natural difficulties which this mountainous district poses to the engineer. It is spoken of by competent judges as being one of the finest mountain roads in the world.'[19]

Knight wrote that the end of the road, Baramulla, was 'a typical little Kashmiri town, with narrow dirty streets, thronged by a dirtier and not particularly picturesque population'.[20] However, he praised the town's architecture and its famous roof gardens:

> The houses are built of sun-dried brick, with the woodwork of eaves, doors, and lattices more or less artistically carved. The gabled mud roofs are densely overgrown with long grass interspersed with bright flowers. I had often read of the roof-gardens of Kashmir, and now knew what was meant. On looking down from above on a Kashmir town this almost universal custom produces a pleasing effect, even the tops of the mosques and Hindoo temples being thus converted into gardens and tiny fields, over which, in the summer days, the birds and butterflies hover in numbers.[21]

The Baramulla–Srinagar road

When E. F. Knight visited Kashmir in 1891, the Jhelum Valley road ended at Baramulla, some thirty-two miles from the capital at Srinagar. Like many travellers, Knight proceeded to Srinagar by boat, 'up the sinuous Jhelam and across the Woolar Lake'.[22] The boat journey took twenty hours in 1891. Eager to improve transport, commerce and communication, in 1893 the Maharaja gave Spedding a contract to extend the Jhelum Valley road from Baramulla through the Kashmir valley to Srinagar in the east. Despite his inexperience, Rowland was employed to supervise the construction of the new road. It was a pivotal position for an ambitious and complicated project that carved through some thirty-three miles of what the *Imperial Gazetteer of India* described as 'a continuous avenue of poplars', parts of which were more than 5,000 feet above sea level.[23]

Figure 3 The Honourable Rowland George Allanson-Winn with young servant, Kashmir, 1893.
Source: Courtesy of Janet Webb / The Estate of Fifth Lord Headley.

Before work could begin on the road in autumn 1893, Rowland found refuge from the summer heat at Gurais (or Gurez) in the high Himalayas, to the north of Baramulla. The colonial newspaper *Homeward Mail from India* noted in August:

> This comparatively unknown but beautiful valley has recently been the halting-place of a great many Cashmere visitors, who have preferred its dry and bracing air to the damper, if more fashionable, atmosphere of Gulmarg [south of Baramulla]. Among those who have pitched their camps in the cool forest glades which everywhere abound may be mentioned:– [. . .] Mr. and Mrs. Mitchell[24] and Mr. Allanson-Winn. The valley is now looking its best, and picnics are constantly taking place, the golf links, laid out by Mr. W. Mitchell, who is himself one of the best players in Cashmere, prove a great attraction to those visitors who are fond of the game.[25]

Construction of the Baramulla–Srinagar road began in earnest in early October 1893 when, the Indian *Pioneer* newspaper related, 'Mr. [Allanson-]Winn started a large number of sub-contractors on the earthwork, employing Kashmiris and Poonch men chiefly on the banks and Pathans on the heavy cuttings.' The following year, 'the masonry was put in hand, and brick-burning was commenced all down the line, the earthwork and collections of soleing [*sic*] and metal being simultaneously carried on'.[26] It was gruelling work and, throughout, Rowland, assisted by servants, lived under canvas in the Kashmir valley. For two years, he and his workmen pitched tents beneath the 'magnificent chinar trees' at Pattan, one of the historic capitals of the valley and conveniently situated halfway between Baramulla and Srinagar.[27]

As Rowland later admitted, he faced 'almost every conceivable difficulty' constructing the road.[28] Progress was hampered by massive landslides and floods along the route. For instance, the *Homeward Mail from India* reported in August 1894 that Srinagar had

> narrowly missed a catastrophe equal to that of last year [when it was devastated by floods]. Although rather early for a heavy flood, the rain that fell almost continuously from Monday, June 18, till Friday the 22nd, raised the level of the river to such a height that house-boats could not pass below the bridges. The Munshi Bagh [area] was partly inundated, and the first bridge, which alone stood the flood of last year, was pronounced unsafe and closed to traffic. Mr. Tickell, the engineer-in-charge, was ill at Gulmarg at the time, but Captain Cupper, who was acting, deserves the credit of having saved the European station. With the assistance of Messrs. Nethersole and Allanson Winn, he kept a regiment of coolies at work night and day, driving in stakes and piling up sandbags to strengthen the embankment.[29]

Besides flooding, progress on the road was also, according to the *Pioneer*, 'interfered with by the opposition of certain native officials, and it is only fair to say that a considerable loss of time was occasioned by frivolous and vexatious objections to necessary work'. The 'interference' continued into 1895, and only 'gradually died away as the work approached completion'.[30] Rowland alluded to the construction of the Baramulla–Srinagar road, or perhaps an earlier Spedding project, in a lecture to the Institution of Civil Engineers of Ireland in 1901:

> The primary intention of those constructing roads [. . .] has always been to provide an easier and quicker means of communication between two places than the natural conformation of the ground affords. [. . .] How often have the most important conditions been lost sight of altogether. [. . .] There is a story told of one of the Eastern magnates who employed [a] European engineer to make a road from an important town at the foot of a range of mountains over a lofty pass, and then on to another town some miles away in the plain at the other side of the range. The engineer pegged out his zigzag up to the pass, and then down the other side, taking a gradient in both cases well suited to the expected traffic. He then, as there were no obstacles of any kind, took a perfectly straight line from the point of leaving the foot of the mountains to the town to be reached. In this he was quite correct, but the potentate who came to inspect the work was much displeased, and said the straight line was not pretty, and that he insisted upon having the zigzags across the plain so as to be in harmony with the zigzags over the mountain range![31]

The *Pioneer* described other problems and delays. For example, in 1895, large parts of the road surface 'kicked up and much of the work had to be gone over again at considerable extra expense'. The next year, one of the steam rollers used to finish the road surface 'came to grief' and was 'placed quite *hors de combat* by a collision caused by the carelessness of one of the drivers'.[32] Finally, on 30 October 1896, the *Pioneer* reported that, three years after construction began, 'the final inspection of this important work took place and the road was formally handed over to the State Engineers by Mr. R. G. Allanson-Winn, of the firm of Spedding and Co., who has had charge of the construction from start to finish'.[33] The completed road included 167 bridges and culverts forged across the valley. According to the *Pioneer*, 'The total completed earth-work has run up to 14,000,000 cubic feet, and a very large portion of this amount is in heavy banks across jheels [lakes, wetlands] or rice fields.'[34]

The chief medical officer for Kashmir, Dr Ashutosh Mitra, described the new road as he found it in 1897:

> The *tonga* road from Baramulla to Srinagar is now complete, but many travellers will prefer to change the jolting of the hill carriage for the more gentle and

agreeable motion of a boat. The new road is nearly 33 miles long from the Agency road, Baramulla, to the Dudhganga bridge, Srinagar. The alignment is partly on the old foot-path, but for the most part it winds round the toes of the lower Kharewas, or takes a straight line across the many *jheels* which are met on the line. Three and a half miles from Baramulla is the village of Dilna, where Dhanjibhoy and Co. have built stables on the left hand side of the road. Passing Sangrawan and Phutka, Choorah, eight miles from Baramulla, is reached. Here the Ningal river is spanned by three brick arches, and the two next bridges of importance cross the Choorah and Bulgam streams. After Bulgam (10 miles) the road takes a turn to the right through Rhinji, Tarpur, Khamayar, and Phalalan, till Pattan is reached. This is the half-way stage between Baramulla and Srinagar, and here may be seen two excellent types of ancient Hindu temples in a very fair state of preservation. Passing the 16th mile at Puttan, the road takes a sharp turn to the left and crosses the Hanjvera *jheel* and bridge. About two miles further on is the village of Singhpura, and beyond that the bridge at Haratrat. The road now turns to the right again, and Meerghund, about 24 miles from Baramulla, is reached. Here there is a small rest-house. Sportsmen will find some excellent snipe and duck shooting on the extensive *jheel*. A couple of miles further on is Lawapura, from where the old road branches off to Gulmarg. The only other place of interest before Srinagar is reached is Chak, where the post horses are changed for the final stage. Passing Shalteng and Zankoot, where there is also some capital duck shooting, the Srinagar race course comes in view, 32 miles from Baramulla, and then Dudhganga bridge and poplar avenue leading to the new Amira Kadal. The rows of poplar trees are quite a feature of the road. The trees also serve the useful purpose of affording protection where the bank is steep and dangerous to *tongas* and carriages.[35]

Courtship in Srinagar

Having fulfilled his contract, Rowland rested in Srinagar. Also known as the 'City of the Sun', Srinagar was the summer capital for both the Maharaja and the British Resident (the appointed government official for the region) and their retinues. *The Imperial Gazetteer of India* described Srinagar as a 'quaint, insanitary city', and E. F. Knight wrote that 'it appears a pleasing place at first sight and worthy to be the capital of a great State, but the traveller is somewhat disillusioned when he leaves the waterside to penetrate the narrow streets'.[36] Situated between the two banks of the Jhelum River, in the 1890s Srinagar had a population of around 100,000, divided between what Knight called 'the native town' and 'the European quarter': 'No European is permitted to take up his quarters in any portion of the native town, and he is forbidden even to enter it by night.'³⁷ Knight thought the European quarter 'a pleasant colony', with all the trappings of genteel English society:

> Here are the Residency, the British church, the English library, the hospital, and of course the inevitable polo and cricket ground, golf links, race-course, and rowing club. [. . .] The Jhelam, where it flows through the European quarter, presents quite a lively appearance. Gay house-boats and capacious family doongahs [large punts, travelling boats] line the shore, and when the heat of the day has passed the water is covered with rowing-boats, whose occupants are men in flannels and girls in Thames-side summer dress.³⁸

The European quarter in Srinagar had very little accommodation and, by the 1890s, it was struggling to cope with a growing number of European visitors. Collett and Mitra found that 'There are no dak bungalows [government staging houses] or hotels. Travellers must, therefore, be prepared to live in boats or tents. House-boats are very comfortable to live in, but their number is limited'. A small row of brick houses was set aside for permanent residents, and a camping ground for 'married visitors'. Most tourists and the many 'bachelors' who worked in and around the town had to pitch their tents in a designated area.³⁹

As Charles Allen noted in his classic oral history of the British 'Raj', the social and racial divisions between Europeans and Indians evident in the major cities 'were even more clearly marked' in the provinces:

> Each district had as its focal point the Station, consisting of 'the cantonment where the military personnel lived and worked, the civil lines where the civilians such as the ICS [Indian Civil Service] and canal people and the police and forest officer and so on lived, and then the city, which was just a mass of small shops and rather smelly drains and was very densely populated'.⁴⁰

Conversely, Allen continued, attitudes towards 'the natives' could be less severe 'up country' when Europeans had to work in close proximity to Indians, as was the case on the Baramulla–Srinagar road project.⁴¹ We will never know precisely what kind of relationships Rowland had with his Kashmiri servants or the hundreds of Indian labourers who built the Baramulla–Srinagar road. It is likely that he was quite detached, not least because he was a white British man of some professional standing who did not speak the languages of the men he lived and worked closely with for several years. But we do know that Rowland became interested in the religion of many of these men. He recalled later that, while working in Kashmir, he read an English edition of the Qur'an given to him by 'a friend'.⁴²

That Rowland took an interest in Islam was unusual for a Westerner, though perhaps he was affected by the same sense of spirituality felt by some of Charles Allen's oral history subjects: 'The Hills had an atmosphere that "stirred the imagination, something almost verging on the religious".[43] This was especially the case in Kashmir with its majestic mountains, mighty rivers, dramatic valleys and exotic flora and fauna. As Allen continued, 'Part of the magic lay in the sounds; the doves, the barbets and the cuckoo, sounding "even more beautiful than it does in England". There were the sounds of water, "a sort of pulsating coming up from the valleys below, the sound of the river rising as pulsating waves of air".[44]

The architecture and visible archaeology of the Kashmir valley increased the spiritual atmosphere for Westerners. Buddhist and Hindu temples nestled alongside Islamic mosques and tombs. Collett and Mitra's *Guide for Visitors* pointed out that, in Srinagar,

> on the right bank of the river [Jhelum] is a famous mosque called Shah Hamadan. It is built of cedar, and is very elaborately carved; there is a golden ball on the top; this finial is used on all the mosques in Kashmir. It is described as being 'a remnant of a Buddhist Tee, very much altered, but still not so very unlike some found in Nepal'. [...] Opposite this mosque, on the other side of the river, is a very fine ruin in limestone of a noble mosque, called the Pathar *masjid* [mosque]. [... Nearby] is a very old and interesting building called Badshah. It is the tomb of Kashmir's greatest ruler, Zein-ul-ub-din, who was the patron of art and literature, and who introduced the manufacture of shawls. [...] Not far from this tomb [...] is a very fine and peculiarly constructed building, the Jumma *masjid*. [...] It is the principal mosque in Srinagar, of wooden architecture – a style which is regarded as an indication of decadence and decrepitude.[45]

It was in Srinagar, in 1895 or 1896, that Rowland met his future wife, Teresa St Josephine Johnson (1871–1919). Teresa's grandfather had been an ordnance officer for the British East India Company and her father, William Henry Johnson (1833–83), started his working life with the Great Trigonometrical Survey, which attempted to measure the entire Indian subcontinent with scientific precision. William Henry Johnson conducted numerous surveys in the Punjab Plain, and in 1853/4 made what was described as 'his first considerable ascent of the Snowy Peak near the Néla pass' in the north-western Himalayas.[46] In 1855, Johnson joined the Kashmir Survey and led many outstanding surveys across Jammu and Kashmir.

In 1862, Johnson began surveying from Leh in Ladakh to the Chinese frontier. Three years later, he accepted without leave from the Government of India an invitation from the Muslim Khan[47] of Khotan in Chinese Turkestan (present-day Hotan, in Xinjiang) to enter his territory and fix its position on the Survey. According to the explorer and geologist Lieutenant-Colonel Henry Haversham Godwin-Austin (1834–1923), Johnson was 'the first European traveller who had penetrated so far beyond our frontier and returned in safety; Adolphe Schlagintweit [1829–57], the first who attempted this perilous journey having been murdered in 1857'.[48] Speaking at the Royal Geographical Society in London in 1866, Major-General Sir Henry C. Rawlinson (1810–95) hailed Johnson's journey to Khotan as 'most remarkable', and the Society later presented Johnson with a gold watch in recognition of his many achievements.[49] However, as Peter Hopkirk notes, all Johnson received from his employer was 'an official rebuke for crossing into Khotan without permission from his superiors'.[50] Shortly after returning to India, Johnson retired from the Survey and accepted the post of governor and joint-commissioner of Ladakh offered him by the then Maharajah of Jammu and Kashmir, Ranbir Singh (1830–85).

Rowland's future wife, Teresa, was the youngest daughter of William and Anne Johnson. She was born in Akhnoor, a Himalayan foothill town of the Jammu district, in February 1871.[51] When she was baptized almost three years later, the family was living at Leh, the old capital of the Himalayan kingdom of Ladakh, the 'land of the high passes'. Teresa had not quite turned twelve years old when her father died at the age of fifty in February 1883. A great deal of mystery surrounds the circumstances of William Johnson's premature death. The official cause of death was given as pneumonia, and he was quickly buried in the Church of England Cemetery at Lahore.[52] However, Lieutenant-Colonel Godwin-Austin, who worked with Johnson in Kashmir in the 1850s and 1860s and wrote his obituary for the Royal Geographical Society in England, noted that his former colleague died 'under most melancholy circumstances, being fully persuaded that he had been poisoned'.[53] Godwin-Austin felt that Johnson 'must have been a valued and trusted servant of the Maharajah, and his position must have been one most difficult to fill without creating great jealousy, and, no doubt, many enemies'.[54]

After her father's death, Teresa remained with her mother and siblings in Kashmir, settling in Srinagar. At the age of just sixteen, in September 1887, Teresa married John Cooke, a paymaster and retired Major in the British army.[55] Like Teresa, John had been born in India, in the British cantonment of Deesa. John Cooke was a widower when he met Teresa, and twenty-eight years her senior.[56] Teresa gave birth to a son, Cyril Norman, in Srinagar on 14 April 1892.[57] The couple had no other children and the fate of John is unknown; he either died in the early 1890s or Teresa left him for Rowland.[58]

Rowland was sixteen years Teresa's senior. There is no record of their courtship in India and they did not marry until 1899. What is clear is that, with the Baramulla–Srinagar road successfully completed by the end of 1896, Rowland made plans to leave India early in the New Year. In the meantime, he began writing a new, substantial (384-page) illustrated book about boxing, also called *Boxing* and published in 1897 as part of the 'Isthmian Library' series by A. D. Innes and Company of London.[59] Rowland dedicated the book to his 'cousin and brother bruiser Charles, Lord Headley, as a slight mark of my appreciation of his manly instincts and love of all true sport'.[60] Like its predecessor of the same name, *Boxing* was reasonably well received by critics

Figure 4 The Honourable Rowland George Allanson-Winn (left) demonstrating a boxing position, *c*.1890s.
Source: Courtesy of Janet Webb / The Estate of Fifth Lord Headley.

in the general press. The London *Graphic* thought that Rowland had assumed 'the position of an old and tried coach who has seen many boxers taught and many learn, and who knows just the little points where they go astray or where a hint may be valuable'.[61] The sporting newspaper *Referee*, however, was more critical, arguing that Roland had conflated 'boxing with gloves and scrapping with the raw "uns"'.[62]

Return to England and Ireland

Rowland left Bombay on the P&O steamer, SS *Oriental*, on 9 January 1897 and landed at Brindisi at the end of that month.[63] Like other privileged travellers, he opted to continue his journey to London by railway, thereby avoiding the rough winter seas in the Bay of Biscay. It is likely that Teresa and her son Cyril left India with Rowland on the SS *Oriental* in January 1897: a 'Mrs Norman Cooke and child' were listed as passengers; 'Norman' was Cyril's middle name.[64] It is difficult to imagine how Teresa felt on leaving rural India, probably for the first time (and never to return), and landing in the unfamiliar and busy metropolis of London.

Rowland wasted little time in London. Buoyed by his professional success in Jammu and Kashmir, he went to Ireland to further his career. He actually had little choice as the family fortune had declined under Charlie Winn, the fourth Lord Headley. Like his money-obsessed father, Rowland was sensitive to this and, shortly after his return to Ireland had a serious argument with Charlie when he discovered that the latter had sold off some of the Headley family silver plate. Along with jewellery, furniture and other effects, the Headley plate had been bequeathed by the third Lord Headley to his successor 'to devolve as heirlooms with his Irish estate'. As 'tenant in tail' (one entitled in possession or on the death of the fourth Lord Headley to an entailed interest in the estate), Rowland sought an injunction to prevent his cousin from selling or parting with other family heirlooms that he expected to inherit.[65]

While the dispute between Roland and Charlie rumbled on in 1897, Rowland set about furthering his engineering career in the UK and, in the autumn, he briefly returned to India without Teresa.[66] In India, he had become interested in the science of soil and water erosion and the practical solutions for taming the vast Kashmiri rivers.[67] Rowland pursued this interest back in Glenbeigh, which was apt because, as he wrote in 1906, his family had 'lost nearly 100 acres of land on the shore of Dingle Bay [Glenbeigh], in Co. Kerry, since 1842' due to coastal erosion: 'The advance of the sea in those sixty-odd years has been in many places as much as 1,100 feet, and good pasture and building sites alike have been engulfed in the insatiable maw of the restless Atlantic.'[68]

Rowland recognized that the problem was endemic across other parts of the UK: 'the position at Glenbeigh is every whit as hard as that which is complained of at any place in Yorkshire, Norfolk, Suffolk, and Essex'.[69] He started speaking and writing about the subject, proposing civil engineering solutions for coastal protection as it affected both Ireland and especially eastern and southern England. In 1897, he advised the trustees of the Glenbeigh estate 'as to the best means to adopt in dealing with the very rapid encroachment of the sea on the southern shore of Dingle Bay, at a point where a road and houses were in immediate danger'.[70] He knew the foreshore at Dingle Bay well, and over the next year directed the construction of a series of 'slanting groynes' which quickly accumulated shingle and 'retained all along the toe of the cliff, which soon became completely protected from the sea, even at the highest tides'.[71] Later in 1898 he was commissioned to install a series of low groynes to protect the coast around Glenbeigh. He expected that the groynes 'will be the means of saving to the estate 600 acres of building and valuable pasture land, which is now in the greatest danger'.[72]

In June 1899, with the works at Glenbeigh nearing completion, he read a paper on 'Foreshore Protection' at the prestigious Society of Engineers in London. The paper was published in the Society's *Transactions*, awarded its Bessemer Premium prize and reported widely in the national and provincial press.[73] Rowland also tentatively re-entered public life for the first time since his election defeat in 1892 as he called for the establishment of a single government department devoted to 'scientific enquiries and investigations' of coastal defence.[74] He presented the idea at a meeting of the British Association at Dover and in a letter published in several English and Irish newspapers, including the London *Times*; the proposal was swiftly dismissed by the Board of Trade as too expensive.[75] Rowland saw out the year and the nineteenth century by quietly marrying Teresa at Kensington Parish Church in west London.[76]

3

Troubles, 1900–13

This chapter explores what was to be a turbulent first decade of the twentieth century for Rowland Allanson-Winn. It describes the highs and lows of Rowland's life, from an initially happy marriage and home life as well as professional success in Ireland to a series of personal crises that profoundly affected his mental health and well-being. It shows that, even in the depths of despair, Rowland found solace in religion and, while his belief in God did not waver, he lost confidence in the church and aspects of Christianity. It describes how, by the time Rowland succeeded to the Baronetcy in January 1913, he was nominally a Unitarian. However, a close examination of Rowland's short book of poems and verses, entitled *Thoughts for the Future* (1913), indicates the fifth Lord Headley's growing admiration for the Prophet Muhammad, which led to his realization that Islam was a valid and viable alternative to Christianity.

'A man of many parts'

There is every reason to assume that Rowland celebrated the arrival of the twentieth century with the same optimism espoused by the British press on the first day of January 1900. Although Britain was again at war in South Africa (the Second Boer War, 1899–1902), the London *Daily Telegraph* encouraged its readers to enter the new century

> with high hearts and confident hopes, and use to each other on this memorable morning none but words of good cheer and of pleasant omen, since to be of courage and cheerful spirit is the heritage of Englishmen, and since they cannot look back upon the glorious past of their race and nation without such thankfulness to Almighty GOD as may well inspire them with trust in His favour and protection in the long future which must still be reserved for this our Imperial breed.[1]

The early years of the twentieth century were, on the whole, good for Rowland. In June 1900, he reached an agreement with his cousin Charlie, the fourth Lord Headley, over the disputed family heirlooms, and their relationship improved.[2] The Census of Ireland, conducted on 31 March 1901, records Rowland at the age of forty-six settled with Teresa, aged thirty (and heavily pregnant), in their first home at Sorrento Road in Dalkey, an affluent coastal suburb of Dublin. The household also comprised Cyril, who had taken the surname 'Winn' and was listed in the Census as Rowland's stepson, and an English domestic servant.[3] Rowland and Teresa's first child, Rowland Patrick (who, to avoid confusion, was known in the family as 'Paddy') was born in Dalkey on 22 May 1901, closely followed by Charles in 1902 and Thomas ('Tommy') in 1903. To accommodate their growing family, Rowland and Teresa moved a short walk from Sorrento Road to a larger house at Coliemore Road, which overlooked the sea.

Rowland's professional life thrived as his family expanded. He opened a consulting office at South Frederick Street in Dublin. His reputation as an expert in coastal protection increased through many more lectures and articles on the subject. In 1900, the Royal Scottish Society of the Arts in Edinburgh awarded him a Silver Prize for his paper, 'The Sea as a Constructive Agent'.[4] An illustrated article in which Rowland advocated a system of groynes in vulnerable coastal areas was published in both the British and American editions of *Pearson's Magazine*, and abstracted for newspapers as far away as New Zealand.[5] In 1901, Rowland was elected to membership of the Institution of Civil Engineers of Ireland (ICEI). His first lecture for the Institution, entitled 'The Constructive Power of the Sea', was awarded a Mullins Silver Medal by the ICEI Council.[6]

In spring 1901, Rowland's firm completed the installation of groynes to prevent flooding in Youghal, County Cork, in the far south of Ireland. (The local authorities commissioned him to extend the work in 1902.) His lecture about the project was also awarded a Mullins Silver Medal.[7] Having studied and battled the destructive North Atlantic Ocean in south-west Ireland, Rowland travelled to the United States in autumn 1902 to examine its impact on that country's north-east coast, in the area around New York City and New Jersey. While in the United States, he gave an illustrated lecture at the American Society of Civil Engineers.[8]

Rowland also found time to rework his previous books on boxing and self-defence to produce a final volume on the subject, entitled *Self-Defence*, which was published in London in 1903.[9] The following year, the influential newspaper *Irish Builder* described Rowland as 'a man of many parts, a champion middle-weight boxer in his day at Cambridge, a distinguished globe-trotter, an editor and excellent *raconteur*.¹⁰ Along with a busy family life, Rowland was a magistrate for County Kerry, managed the estate at Glenbeigh, and flitted between the east and the west coasts of Ireland and his London club (the 'Oxford and Cambridge'). Rowland had become a confident and popular public speaker on the subject of civil engineering, and a collection of his papers was published in London in 1904.¹¹ He also took on further engineering commissions, including the installation of a system of chain cable groynes for the protection of sea walls at Barnageeragh, north of Dublin.¹²

In 1905, the Board of Commissioners of the busy port at Arklow in County Wicklow, to the south of Dalkey, advertised for an engineer to design and supervise an extension of the south breakwater of Arklow Harbour. The Board received more than one hundred replies, but unanimously appointed Rowland engineer for the project in March 1906.¹³ It was a significant commission and, in September, his company took borings at the site in advance of submitting final designs to the Board, which were accepted in October 1906.¹⁴ However, as the *Irish Builder and Engineer* reported the following April,

> a Government Department sent down an engineer, who, with singular want of professional good form, submitted designs upon a wholly different basis, and, of course, this new scheme was put forward free of charge to the local authorities, and was duly adopted, or, possibly, some might say, forced upon them.¹⁵

Professional opinion tended to concur that Rowland was treated harshly by the Arklow Harbour Board of Commissioners. The Board refused to pay Rowland his full fee for work already carried out and, after much wrangling, referred the matter to the government in Dublin. Rowland's correspondence with the Commissioners was published in the *Irish Builder and Engineer* in spring 1907: 'I have been put to a great deal of trouble, and have been much disappointed through no fault of my own.'¹⁶ Supported by the civil engineering press and colleagues, Rowland stood his ground and refused a cheque from the Board which amounted to less than the contractually agreed remuneration: 'As I recently pointed out to the Government, if Irish consulting engineers, living in this country and spending their earnings here, are to be treated with such scant courtesy and want of fairness by Government Departments, it will be necessary for many of them to emigrate to other lands.'¹⁷ The Commissioners eventually agreed to settle the matter by paying Rowland the contracted fee, and he formally resigned from the project: 'In now tendering my resignation I wish to record my regret that there should have been the slightest semblance of friction, which I think you allow I did my very best to avoid.'¹⁸

Despite this very public professional setback, Rowland was elected to the Council of the ICEI in 1906, and he was re-elected in 1907. With a new business partner, a Mr King, he moved the offices of 'Allanson-Winn and King, Civil Engineers' to the prestigious address of College Green in Dublin city centre. The *Irish Builder and Engineer* therefore voiced its 'surprise' when, in 1906, the UK government announced a Royal Commission on Sea Coast Erosion that comprised not a single member from Ireland. 'Mr. Allanson-Winn has', it noted, 'made practically a life-study of this important question, as is shown by his learned and exhaustive papers on a very difficult question.'[19] This was underlined the following year when Rowland was commissioned to write a 'Special Article' for the London *Times* about 'accumulations of sand and shingle for the protection of the coast'.[20]

Crisis

The *Times* article was one of the final pieces Rowland wrote about coastal erosion. By all accounts, it was the death of his son Tommy, at the age of just one in 1904, that triggered a turn in his good fortune and a series of crises that peaked between 1908 and 1912. Rowland loved children and, estranged from his illegitimate daughter Ivy Davis (Chapter 1), he was forty-six when his first legitimate child, Paddy, was born. He doted on all of his sons and always wrote about them with genuine warmth and affection. Rowland was, of course, devastated when Tommy died and kept in his personal papers a photograph of Teresa cradling two-month-old Tommy in 1903 (Figure 5). This was, of course, little comfort to Rowland in the short term, and he fell into the habit of drinking heavily to dull the pain of his bereavement. After Tommy's death, Rowland wrote a 'hymn' called 'God's Chastening', which expressed his anguish:

WHEN Thou didst take my darling son
    To dwell above with Thee.
His little life had scarce begun,
    But meant so much to me.

[. . .]

This sorrow took my rest away.
    And brought me near to death;
Only thy mercy let me stay
    To do more work on earth.[21]

Figure 5 Teresa Allanson-Winn with Tommy Allanson-Winn, Dalkey, Ireland, 1903. *Source*: Courtesy of Janet Webb / The Estate of Fifth Lord Headley.

Teresa was pregnant when Tommy died, and she gave birth to a boy, John, in October 1904. Another son, Owain, was born in 1906 and a daughter, Anne ('Annie'), in 1908. Annie, however, died at birth. Grief-stricken, Rowland again turned to alcohol but he also sought and found some solace in religion. However, after the death of Annie, his nerves were shattered. From 1908 onwards, he managed to keep his business afloat but he stopped writing and dropped his public lecture commitments.

The toxic combination of grief, stress and alcohol led to a deterioration in Rowland's mental well-being. Eventually, as he admitted in a letter to his cousin Charlie, Teresa had him 'quite unnecessarily' committed to a local hospital to recuperate. It would seem that Rowland's hospitalization *was* necessary, but unsuccessful in the long term: he was readmitted with 'nervous strain' on at least two more occasions before 1911.[22]

The deaths of two children inevitably put a strain on Rowland's marriage. Teresa also found it difficult to cope with her husband's unpredictable mental health and, ultimately, looked elsewhere for companionship. She initially found it with Joseph Alexander Hunter, a Church of Ireland clergyman. Two years Teresa's junior, Hunter was recently married and also lived in Dalkey.[23] According to Rowland's account in letters to Charlie (we do not have Teresa's perspective), Hunter had 'got into my house, smoked my best cigars and then, under the pretence of giving "spiritual advice" gave a good many kisses [. . .] to my wife'.[24] When Rowland discovered Teresa's affair with Hunter in spring 1911, he 'turned her out of the house and put her in [the] charge of some poor friends in Dublin – paying for her maintenance out of my own pocket'.[25] Rowland was explicit about the turn of events in his hymn, 'God's Chastening':

> Foul lust and base ingratitude
>   Broke up my little home,
> And broke my heart – in solitude
> I went to Thee alone.[26]

As the hymn indicates, Rowland continued to look to God for guidance. However, the distress and shame of Teresa's affair and her leaving the family home exacerbated Rowland's troubles.

The second national Census of the new century was conducted on Sunday 2 April 1911. The change of circumstances in the Allanson-Winn household since the first Census just a decade earlier was quite remarkable. The 1911 Census recorded seven people in residence at number 30, Coliemore Road, Dalkey. But, conspicuous by their absence were both Teresa *and* Rowland. Cyril 'Johnson Winn' was, at the age of just eighteen, 'head of family' and therefore responsible for his four half-brothers and two domestic servants.[27] Cyril was working as a mercantile marine, and so the servants presumably cared for the Allanson-Winn children. Meanwhile, on Census day in 1911, his mother Teresa was living at a boarding house in Rathmines, a suburb on the south side of Dublin and around nine miles from Dalkey; and Rowland was one of 751 patients on Ward 10 of the male section of the Richmond and District Lunatic Asylum in Dublin.[28]

The Richmond Asylum had been established almost a century earlier to address the unmet needs of the mentally unwell in Ireland. When Rowland arrived there on 6 March 1911 (a month before Census day), the asylum was still one of the largest residential institutions of any kind in Ireland and it was very overcrowded. Disease spread rapidly among the patients, leading to an above-average death rate, and alcohol abuse was rife.[29] The 1911 Census reveals that Rowland was sent to the asylum after suffering from a prolonged bout of 'mania' that had begun in January of that year.[30] Rowland was regarded as a 'lunatic', which the law adviser to the Richmond Asylum admitted had a 'very wide' legal definition 'and would seem to include any feeble-minded person'.[31]

Consequently, Rowland was incarcerated not only alongside men with similar depressive conditions but with many more who had learning difficulties.[32]

Rowland was naturally desperate to leave the asylum. The few surviving letters that Rowland wrote from Ward 10 show that he pinned all his hopes on his cousin Charlie, Lord Headley, to get him out as quickly as possible. On 3 May 1911, two months after he had arrived at the asylum, Rowland argued in a letter to Charlie that he was incarcerated 'on an illegal and malicious Committal Warrant – without examination or any reason whatever!!'[33] According to Rowland, 'I was "run in" on the 6th of March by means of a trick and was not allowed to see the Warrant or ascertain what I was accused of!!'[34] Although he denied it in one letter, Rowland inferred in others that his estranged wife was implicated in his incarceration: 'I have never been a case for any Asylum, only for Hospital at Killarney [. . .] and since then I have been merely tricked by my wicked ungrateful bitch of a wife who ought to be put in a sack with that bloody b– of a parson [Joseph Hunter] and burnt first and then drowned or vice versa.'[35] Whether or not Teresa was involved, it was one of Rowland's household servants – a nameless 'hysterical little Bitch' – who actually turned him over to the authorities (though by June 1911, he claimed to Charlie that the servant was 'on her knees and only just realizes what awful trouble her lying information has caused me').[36]

Rowland stated that the magistrate's charges against him were twofold: first, 'restlessness' and, second, 'assaulting my second son Charles Rowland'. He was emphatic that there were 'no other charges whatsoever'.[37] He assured Charlie that 'Having been perfectly quiet and having drunk nothing stronger than cyder [sic] or stout or beer for nearly four years past I was absolutely sober and collected'.[38] Rowland recalled that he was taken from his home by the Dalkey Police 'on pretence that they wanted me at the Police Station to sign a Warrant to commit a man who had assaulted a child. They refused to show me any document and took me off to the Four Courts Bridewell'.[39] Rowland was himself a magistrate; he was incredulous that a fellow magistrate had 'committed me to a living tomb!!' and 'That such things sh[oul]d be possible in a presumably civilized country "beats all" as they say.'[40]

Rowland claimed that he was kept by the Dublin Police 'without food or water for days' and that they had refused 'to supply me with soap water and towel so that I was compelled to wash my hands and face in the pan of the W.C.' He said that he had endured 'a brutal assault by two large constables who tried to throttle me on the plank bed', but appears to have dropped that allegation by the time he was released from the asylum.[41]

In the first surviving letter to Charlie, dated 3 May 1911, Rowland wrote that he expected to leave the asylum in a matter of days: 'I shall then hope to be "top dog" and will bring a very pretty little action for damages against the miscreants who have put me to all this loss of time and caused me to be absent from home for <u>two months</u>.'[42] He wrote defiantly on 6 May that 'I'm certainly not going to sit down calmly under the stigma and disgrace of <u>insanity</u>.'[43] He admitted to Charlie that this was his third time in an 'asylum', but argued that 'three Asylums don't make a lunatic any more than 8 visits to the Reptile House at the Zoo turn a man into a Cobra or a Rattle-snake!'[44] However, the doctors on Ward 10 disagreed with their patient, and Rowland remained at the Richmond Asylum. On 8 June, a desperate Rowland asked Charlie to obtain from the asylum authorities 'a Form of Application for the Discharge of a Patient': 'I am quite sick of being in here all through the Summer and it is really most cursed hard luck considering that I've done nothing whatsoever to deserve it.'[45] But Rowland's pleading was unsuccessful, and he was not released until 27 July 1911, almost five months after being admitted to the asylum.[46]

Rowland returned to Dalkey and resumed family life, but now without his wife and the mother of their four sons. He told Charlie, Lord Headley, in May 1911 that Teresa's lover, Joseph Hunter, had 'deserted' her, 'poor wretch, and she now, too late, regrets her folly. It has been a sad business for me as we have never had any scandal <u>like this</u> in our family.' He conceded, 'Of course I must get rid of her as I can never take her back, the deception being too <u>cruel</u> and <u>heartless</u>.'[47] With Teresa banished from the family home and living in Rathmines, Rowland took charge of the children.

In line with convention, Rowland and Teresa did not divorce, nor was their separation ever made public. It is unclear whether they met again after 1911. Teresa moved a short distance from the boarding house in Rathmines to Donnybrook, another district in south Dublin. She died in a Donnybrook nursing home in October 1919 at the age of forty-eight.[48] One of Rowland's granddaughters recalled decades later that, though she did not meet Cyril, her father Charles (later, the seventh Lord Headley) told her that Cyril was 'rather downtrodden' in the Allanson-Winn household.[49] During the First World War, Cyril moved out of the Dalkey family home to live with his mother in Donnybrook. After serving with the British army in France, Cyril returned to the merchant navy as Cyril Allanson-Winn and eventually settled in England, where he appears to have remained in close contact with Rowland.[50]

Figure 6 The Honourable Rowland George Allanson-Winn with his sons at Margate, c.1912.
Source: Courtesy of Janet Webb / The Estate of Fifth Lord Headley.

Thoughts for the Future, Muhammad and Islam

Settled in Dalkey in 1912, Rowland described the recent past as a time 'of very dreadful persecution and suffering', when 'the hand of death was very near, and this world with its pleasures and pains had ceased to interest me very much'.[51] It was, he continued, 'a time when I knew that my feet were on the borderland and I longed to cross the boundary and learn the truth'.[52] Rowland's faith in God sustained him through his protracted period of crisis. In turn, he wrote many more 'hymns of praise and gratitude' and a few 'verses' after the death of Tommy. Curiously, he never referred to Annie or her death in any of his writings. Mostly written 'at sunrise', the hymns and verses flowed 'after I had been mercifully delivered from the most terrible dangers and passed unharmed through vicissitudes and trials which must have ended fatally but for my absolute trust in God's protection and His good providence'.[53] The danger felt horribly real: one hymn referred to 'The frequent walks through

Death's dark vale'.⁵⁴ However, as another, entitled 'The Revelation of God's Protecting Care', explained:

> To feel Thy care, to know Thy love –
> Flashed from the starry realms above,
> Binds me to Thee with sweetest ties
> And wafts my spirit towards the skies.⁵⁵

Another, 'On Delivery from Human Peril', confirmed:

> Thou gavest me courage in the strife,
>   And didst my power uphold,
> When sordid devils sought my life
>   With horrors manifold.⁵⁶

It is striking that Rowland's faith in God increased at the time of his incarceration in the Richmond Asylum. There is little sense of a struggle regarding his faith in Rowland's surviving correspondence from this period. However, a curious undated short 'Note to Self' on a scrap of paper in Rowland's distinctive handwriting lodged with his private papers suggests otherwise:

> Keep this note – as I may have to refer to it. I hope it will convince you of the exceeding inaccuracy of your reasoning and how your doubts may be salved. Is it not worth a struggle to become 'Sons of God and [illegible] with Christ'! All sciences are difficult as you know. Why should the science of living be easy? The older you get the more a riddle will life become to you till you feel more a child in the hands of an Invisible Parent, and you will have to fight for your faith and on your knees many a time – with the only weapons at your command which you now know. If you will not put on your armour you will be beaten in the fight and without the girdle you will be beaten in the race of life.⁵⁷

The note ends with a reminder to 'vid: Isai: 50.10', or 'see the Book of Isaiah, chapter 50, verse 10': 'it will tell you how to proceed when you "walk in darkness and have no light" and when you die you will, can, never get any other help.'⁵⁸ The Old Testament passage that Rowland referred to exhorts that they who trust in God will be helped by Him.⁵⁹

As he recovered from illness and the traumatic events of the past few years, in 1912 Rowland assembled a collection of his own hymns and verses for publication. The twenty-five pieces he settled on are solemn and moving, mostly about his grief following the deaths of his parents and his son Tommy. The collection underlined that he found peace and sanctity in God, but it also revealed publicly for the first time his struggle to accept fundamental aspects of contemporary Christianity. The small pocketbook of sixty-four pages was published in London in the summer or autumn of 1913 with the optimistic title *Thoughts for the Future*.[60] By the time of its publication, Rowland had succeeded his cousin Charlie as the fifth Baron Headley, the eleventh Baronet of Nostell and the fifth Baronet of Little Warley.[61]

Protective of his church-going sisters and other family members, the new Lord Headley (hereafter referred to as Headley) had his little book published semi-anonymously, with only the author's partial initials, 'A.W.' for 'Allanson-Winn', embossed in gold on the green cloth covers. *Thoughts for the Future* affirmed Headley's lifelong belief in God, who had, he wrote, 'given me His loving protection and kept my human frame from all harm ever since earliest childhood'.[62] But it also indicated that he had moved from what he later called 'the strict and narrow forms of the Low Church party' to Unitarianism.[63] It is not clear whether or not Headley formally became a Unitarian; rather, he later said that since he was not convinced by Christianity, he came to *consider* himself to be a Unitarian.[64] Unitarianism was a haven for those Victorians and Edwardians with unorthodox religious views, and a common choice for the several hundred Britons who eventually converted from Christianity to Islam in this period. Most famously, the Liverpool solicitor William Henry Quilliam converted from Methodism to Unitarianism and then to Islam in the 1880s, and took the Muslim name Abdullah.[65] Quilliam was the first Briton to publicly propagate Islam in his homeland, and he established the Liverpool Muslim Institute (LMI) with a dedicated Muslim prayer room in 1889. The LMI closed in 1908, a few years before Rowland/Headley took a serious interest in the religion he had first encountered in India, but, as is related later in this book, he came to know and work closely with Quilliam in London during and after the First World War.

Unitarianism encouraged enquiry through reason and, crucially, it enabled Headley to consider Muhammad alongside Christ, Krishna, Buddha and others as a *teacher* about God. But, in a break from Unitarianism, by the time *Thoughts for the Future* was published, Headley recognized Muhammad, Moses and Christ as *prophets* of God. He wrote in the short introduction to *Thoughts for the Future*:

> My love for God is a thing apart, inexplicable to my finite human mind, and known only to the dear Father who made me and gave me the power to Praise Him unceasingly. I believe that, great as is my reverence for Moses, Christ, and Mahomet, and all the inspired saints and prophets, had there been no such revelation to mankind, I should love and praise my dear Father in Heaven *just the same*.[66]

For Headley, monotheism, or the belief in one God, was 'older than the hills', but

> the surprising thing is that human beings with brains and intelligence should have been so foolish as to allow dogmas and the tricks of sacerdotalism to obscure their view of Heaven and their Almighty Father, who is *always approachable* by each one of His creatures, whether human or saintly (*i.e.*, partly Divine). The key to Heaven is *always there* and can be turned by the humblest or most miserable human being without any help from Prophet, Priest, or King.[67]

Headley had good reason to be afraid of his family's reaction as he *publicly* recalled childhood doubts about the church and its teaching:

> The dogmas of the Christian Church – I care not whether Roman Catholic or Protestant – have repelled me ever since earliest childhood, and I don't know whether my boyish distrust of the creed as laid down by St. Athanasius was less strong than is my contempt today for the man who lays down the law from a pulpit and consigns millions of his fellow-men to everlasting perdition because they don't agree with him.[68]

Headley proposed an antidote in Islam. Somewhat idealistically, he recalled the Muslims he had met in Jammu and Kashmir twenty years earlier:

> After over forty years of thought and prayerful effort to arrive at a correct view, the dominant idea in my mind is that the whole fabric of so-called religion is of man and not of God. I must also confess that visits to the East have filled me with a very deep respect for the simple faith of the Mahomedans, who really do worship God all the time and not only on Sunday, like so many Christians. Their beautiful trust in their Almighty and Merciful Creator, who is never absent from them for a moment of the day or night, awakens feelings of the keenest sympathy in my heart. I love to join in the devout praise of the earnest Mussulman because I know he is genuine; there is no pretence about him when he takes off the little bit of carpet from his horse's back and prostrates himself before his Maker. This happens several times every day from sunrise to sunset, and in his devout and happy mind he is present with God Himself. There has been no need of priestly aid; he has found the Mercy Seat alone and without any help from any outside source whatever.[69]

Headley concluded the introduction of his book with a quote from 'that saintly man', the British soldier and sometime governor-general of the Sudan, Charles Gordon, who was killed during the Siege of Khartoum in 1885 (see Chapter 1): 'Gordon said of the Mahomedans: "I do not see the sect of Pharisees among the Mussulmans. Whatever they may think they never assume, as our Pharisees do, that A and B are doomed to be burned; and you never see the very unamiable features which are shown by our Pharisees".'[70]

The opening poem, the longest in the collection, is entitled 'Religion'. It confirmed Headley's belief in monotheism without intercession and his respect for a line of prophets that ended with Muhammad as the final *messenger* of God. In short, the poem supports the Islamic testimony of faith – the *shahada* – which is the first of the five 'pillars' of Islam.[71] The opening verses are as follows:

DEAR Father, my religion is
    The sacred one of Love,
Which leads me by the straightest path
    To Thy sweet Home above.

I do not look aside or feel
    The need of human aid,
For 'Thou art with me everywhere',
    As Prophets great have said.

No prophet, priest, or human king
    I need when I approach;
To Thee alone my songs I sing,
    No other thoughts encroach.

In every blade of grass I see
    Thy sacred, loving hand;
In every thought that comes to me
    Behold the Promised Land.

Stern Moses gave us Thy commands,
    Which Thou didst send to Him;
They showed Thy true and just demands
    And kept us from all sin.

Then gentle Christ with spirit sweet
    Sang the glad song of Love;
The Sermon on the Mount did greet,
    And point to Heaven above.

He gave the prayer, Divinely taught,
    Which begs deliverance from
The tempter's power and evil thought
    Which from deep hell does come.

Then Mahomet, Thy chosen Son,
    Inspired by fire Divine,
Laid down the law, the greatest one,
    Which must for ever shine.

> THAT THOU ALONE MOST MERCIFUL
> OUR FATHER DEAR DOST REIGN,
> AND THAT WE MUST ALL TIME THROUGHOUT
> FROM OTHER GODS REFRAIN.[72]

In addition to his own hymns and poems, Headley added a short excerpt from the *Arabian Nights*. By way of introduction, he noted that 'It is wonderful how absolute faith and trust in God banishes all fear and makes the most dreadful conditions not only bearable, but even beautiful'.[73] He repeated his admiration for 'the spirit of faith which animates the average Mahomedan' and demonstrated his growing understanding of the faith of Islam:

> Call it madness, call it fanaticism, or what you will, the fact of the real presence of God is the essence of the creed of the faithful followers of Moses, Christ, and Mahomet; is the chief reason why they have no fear of death or hell, which hold out such terrors to many of us highly civilized Westerns.[74]

In one of the last hymns in *Thoughts for the Future* that again acknowledged and praised 'Moses, Christ, and Mahomet', Headley added a footnote after the word 'Mahomet': 'It is impossible to be a good Mahomedan without being a good Christian. Why are they at war?'[75] He returned to this question in a prose piece, 'Why Contention between Sister Religions?', at the very end of the book. Tellingly, Headley concluded:

> The Mahomedans have the advantage of us, for the idea of a Heaven without women is unthinkable to them. They know that as God has provided this most precious gift on earth, so He will continue to provide that priceless gift in Heaven. After all, it seems but reasonable that a man should be more happy living for ever in Paradise with his dear wife and the women he loves than sitting for ever on a cloud in the company of uncharitable persons of more than questionable morals and intolerant religious convictions and fanatical dogmas.[76]

The religious themes expressed in *Thoughts for the Future* – of Christianity corrupted by 'dogma' and 'sacerdotalism', the 'simplicity' of Islam and 'sincerity' of Muslims, and the oft-overlooked reality of Christianity and Islam as 'sister faiths' – would characterize Headley's explanation and defence of Islam for the rest of his life.

4

Conversion to Islam, 1913

Unconvinced by Christianity, Headley considered himself to be a Unitarian by 1913. This chapter explores why and how he converted to Islam at the end of that year, and examines reactions to his religious conversion. While Headley's knowledge and experience of Muslims and Islam in India in the 1890s contributed to his shift towards that faith, they do not explain his religious conversion two decades later. To help understand the reasons for and reactions to Headley's conversion, this chapter first considers the context in which he discovered – or rediscovered – Islam by surveying the history of Muslims, Islam and Islamic missionary activity in late-Victorian and Edwardian Britain. It then narrates Headley's path to formal conversion and the public announcement in November 1913 that he had converted to Islam, documents private and public reactions to that news and, finally, shows how Headley responded to his many critics.

Islam and Muslims in late-Victorian and Edwardian Britain

On his return to the UK from India, Rowland was preoccupied with family life and work, but he continued to question theological and practical aspects of Christianity. Whatever religious doubts he might have had, however, it was not common for a Christian to formally convert to Islam in Britain before the First World War. Negative nineteenth-century attitudes towards Muslims and misunderstanding about Islam persisted into the new century, which meant that Islam was typically stigmatized in Edwardian popular culture. Islam was linked in the British public imagination to the Ottoman Sultan and Caliph, Abd al-Hamid II (1842–1918), whose autocratic rule between 1876 and 1909 was contrasted with parliamentary democracy in Britain and encouraged a belief that the Ottoman Turks embodied unjust, despotic, backward and incompetent Muslim governance.

While Benjamin Disraeli, the two-times British prime minister (in office 1868 and 1874–80), advocated a pro-Turkish policy as a bulwark against Russian ambitions in the East, his political rival, William Ewart Gladstone, who was four-times prime minister between 1868 and 1894, famously lobbied for the expulsion of the Ottoman Turks from Europe. In 1876, the year that al-Hamid II was proclaimed Sultan-Caliph, Gladstone referred to the Turks as 'the one great anti-human specimen of humanity', a description that had salience in Britain well into the twentieth century.[1] Influential Christian Evangelical apologists also made good use of newspapers, magazines and journals to denigrate the character and conduct of the Prophet Muhammad as a demonic, heretic impostor, and to discredit his religion as sensual yet violent, hostile, intolerant and fraudulent.[2]

Ironically, the Western Christian missionary campaign required the study of other religions to displace them. This led to better knowledge and more widespread discussion about Islam in particular. Colonization, exploration, emigration and immigration also improved knowledge and debate about religions, and introduced diverse images of Muhammad and interpretations about Islam based on authentic Muslim sources.[3] Some scholars, such as F. D. Maurice (1805–72) and Reginald Bosworth Smith (1839–1908), adopted more sympathetic and conciliatory approaches to Muhammad and Islam within a framework of Christian theology. They recognized Muhammad as a sincere and true prophet of God and argued that, given its Abrahamic roots, Islam was not an enemy of Christianity but, rather, a 'sister faith'.[4] This was echoed and expanded upon by Muslim scholars and defenders of Islam who visited or settled in Britain in the late-Victorian and Edwardian period. Prominent among them was the Anglophile judge and Muslim leader Syed (or Saiyid) Ameer Ali (1849–1928), who emphasized that Islam was the final stage of Abrahamic religion and was therefore *superior* to 'incomplete' Christianity.[5]

Headley was unquestionably influenced by men like Boswell Smith and Ameer Ali. However, it was certainly not expected in 1913 that a British peer of the realm would contemplate Islam as a viable faith, let alone formally convert to it. Indeed, although there had been a Muslim presence in Britain since at least the sixteenth century, few Britons converted to Islam on British soil prior to the foundation of Abdullah Quilliam's Liverpool Muslim Institute in the 1880s (Chapter 3).[6] Quilliam probably converted overseas, during a short trip from his hometown Liverpool to Morocco in *c*.1882, but he did not publicly announce that he was a Muslim until 1887.[7]

The few other Britons who converted to Islam in the nineteenth century and returned to the UK were similarly reluctant to make their religious beliefs public.

Possibly the first British convert to Islam who returned to Britain a Muslim and continued to practise his faith was the Honourable Henry Stanley (1827–1903), who converted to Islam in India in 1859.[8] Ten years later, in 1869, Henry Stanley became the third Baron Stanley of Alderley with a seat in the House of Lords. He was, therefore, the first and, prior to Headley's conversion, only British Muslim peer. Despite – or perhaps because of – his influential position, Stanley was, however, a fairly discreet Muslim public figure and a very private man. Stanley's Cheshire country estate was not far from Liverpool, but it is unlikely that he visited Quilliam or the LMI. Stanley died in 1903 and his Muslim funeral and burial in Cheshire was led by the imam (Muslim religious leader) to the Ottoman Embassy in London.[9] That the Ottoman imam conducted Stanley's funeral is curious because, by the early twentieth century, many funerals for Muslims in Britain were led by Quilliam in his capacity as Shaykh al-Islam of the British Isles, an honorific title reputedly conferred by the Ottoman Sultan-Caliph in 1894. As Shaykh al-Islam, Quilliam was effectively the supreme authority on Islam in Britain and the leader of British Muslims.[10]

Quilliam and his LMI were a magnet for the many Muslims from across the world who passed through the port of Liverpool in the late-nineteenth and early-twentieth centuries. The LMI was also the institutional base for around 300 predominantly white Britons who converted to Islam between its foundation in the late 1880s and closure in 1908.[11] Quilliam personally encouraged and enabled the majority of those conversions to Islam. Most converts were local to the Liverpool area and the remainder were scattered across the UK and the British Empire. At the beginning of the twentieth century, Britain governed more than half the world's Muslims (including eighty million in the Indian subcontinent alone) and, like Headley, some converts worked in India and other British colonies, where they were directly exposed to Muslims and Islam as well as other religious and cultural traditions.[12]

In 1897, a German academic estimated that there were 2,700 Muslims living in the UK, compared to 2,600 in France and 800 in Italy.[13] The number of Muslims in the UK swelled in the early years of the twentieth century with the arrival of temporary visitors such as students, seafarers, traders, intellectuals, diplomats, tourists, lawyers and other professionals, some of whom settled permanently. Quilliam travelled across urban Britain to meet many of the nascent Muslim communities and their leaders, and he documented their activities in his weekly newspaper, *The Crescent*. The greatest concentration of Muslims was in London, a city that Quilliam visited regularly. In the mid-1890s, for example, he enthusiastically reported the activities of a South African-born Muslim, Mohammed Doulie (1846–1906; also known as Dollie), who organized Islamic prayers and celebrated religious festivals at a temporary mosque in his home near Regent's Park.[14] In September 1896, Quilliam also reported in *The Crescent* that a group of Muslims, including some of the Queen's Indian attendants at Windsor Castle, celebrated 'Id al-Adha (feast of the sacrifice celebrating the end of the annual Hajj, or pilgrimage to Mecca) at Britain's first purpose-built mosque, located to the south-west of London in the town of Woking, Surrey.[15]

The Woking mosque had been built by the Orientalist and traveller Gottlieb Wilhelm Leitner (1840–99), who retired to England after a successful career in India.[16] Leitner shared the view of liberal Christian scholars like F. D. Maurice and Reginald Bosworth Smith that Islam was a 'sister faith' of Judaism and Christianity. He concluded a public lecture in London in 1889 by 'expressing a hope that the day will come when Christians will honour Christ more by also honouring Muhammad. There is a common ground between Muhammadanism and Christianity, and he is a better Christian who reveres the truths enunciated by the Prophet Muhammad.'[17]

The mosque at Woking formed part of Leitner's Oriental Nobility Institute, which he established in 1884 'for Oriental scholars, including those natives of India of good family and position who desire to keep their caste and religion whilst residing in this country for official or professional purposes'.[18] Leitner accepted a donation from Begum Shahjahan (1838–1901), ruler of the Indian princely state of Bhopal, to build the mosque.

Despite his sympathetic interpretation of Islam, Leitner insisted that the growing Muslim community in nearby London request his permission to access the mosque, and that its use was restricted for prayer. In a letter to the *Pall Mall Gazette*, he stated:

> I extended its use to Mahommedans generally in this country, in order to enable them to practise their own religion as established, not to convert Englishmen to Islam, or to introduce new doctrines into that faith, or to promote any political or religious propaganda, or to celebrate the generally unhappy marriages between Mahommedans and Englishwomen. [. . .] The mosque is proof of British toleration, especially to our Mahommedan fellow-subjects, and, as such, must be used in that grateful and reverential spirit which is characteristic of Orthodox Mahommedans of good birth, but which is sadly wanting in some of the youths that come to this country.[19]

Quilliam responded sarcastically:

> What a piece of fulsome cant! The existence of an ornamental structure in the back garden of a person's house into which a limited number of worshippers are allowed to enter by favour only is a proof of toleration![20]

As a pan-Islamist and staunch defender of the Ottoman Sultan-Caliph, Quilliam also reported in *The Crescent* the political activities of London-based Muslims that Leitner alluded to in his *Pall Mall Gazette* letter. Like Quilliam, they were agitated by Britain's wavering support for the Ottomans and anxious about the future of the Caliphate (or Khilafat, the office or government of the Caliph) and decline of the *umma*. In 1903, the Indian Muslim lawyer and scholar Abdullah Al-Mamoon Suhrawardy (1870–1935) revived the London branch of the Anjuman-i-Islam (established in 1886), an international pan-Islamic organization.[21] He renamed the London branch the Pan-Islamic Society, with the primary aim to 'safeguard and represent all Islamic interests of as many Muslim peoples and countries as possible without any distinction of sect or colour or race or country'.[22] In 1907, it became the Islamic Society and, in 1910, the Central Islamic Society (CIS). By 1913, the Society had around 300 members, mostly Indians, but also Egyptians, Turks and some Britons, including Quilliam, who had left Liverpool in 1908 and eventually settled permanently in London with a new identity. Masquerading as Professor or Dr 'Henri M. Léon' (or sometimes 'de Léon'), Quilliam continued to defend and promote Islam, but he devoted more of his time to scholarly interests such as philology (see Chapter 8).[23]

The Pan-Islamic/Islamic Society was not intended to be missionary-focused, but Suhrawardy facilitated conversions to Islam and mentored new converts including a young Londoner, Bertram Khalid Sheldrake (1888–1947), whom Quilliam met along with Suhrawardy and other members of the Society in London in 1906.[24] Sheldrake subsequently became the London correspondent for *The Crescent* and, in 1912, a vice-president of the CIS. Acutely aware of the religious and social needs of London's growing Muslim community, Suhrawardy sought to buy the mosque at Woking, which had fallen into a state of disrepair following Leitner's death in 1899. Suhrawardy proposed to purchase the mosque directly from Leitner's son, Henry Leitner (1869–1945), but failed to secure adequate financial backing.[25]

Khwaja Kamal-ud-Din, the Ahmadiyya and the Woking Muslim Mission

In October 1912, a year before Headley's religious conversion, an Indian Muslim lawyer, Khwaja Kamal-ud-Din (1870–1932), arrived in London on legal business. Kamal-ud-Din was a convert to the Ahmadiyya Movement in Islam, which was founded by Hazrat Mirza Ghulam Ahmad (1835–1908).

Following a series of visions which drew upon the Islamic belief that a Messiah and a Mahdi ('guided one') would come to lead Muslims against the unbelievers, Ahmad personally assumed both roles. Ahmad saw himself as the Messiah for Christians and the Mahdi for Muslims. In 1889, he inaugurated the Ahmadiyyat, or Ahmadiyya community, in his hometown of Qadian in the Punjab. Ahmad accepted the allegiance of followers who affirmed standard matters of Islamic belief and practice, but contrary to majority Sunni and Shi'i understandings of Islam, refuted the idea that Muhammad was the final prophet of God and swore allegiance to Ahmad as the divinely appointed Messiah and Mahdi.[26] Consequently, some Muslims regarded (and still regard) the Ahmadiyya to be a heretical movement outside the fold of Islam.

Ahmad and the Ahmadiyya were one of many responses to the Indian Muslim rallying cry of 'Islam in danger'[27] and the call after the 1857 Rebellion (or 'Mutiny' against British rule) for Islamic reform and revival that favoured an Islam based on primary sources.[28] However, Ahmad's response was radical: while he supported the British Raj (he preferred Christian over Sikh rulers), in the 1880s Ahmad gained a reputation for rigorously defending Islam in disputations with Christian missionaries.[29] There was little that was doctrinally challenging in Ahmad's criticisms about Christianity: he raised concerns about the authenticity of the Gospels, refuted the Trinity and Atonement as beliefs that had nothing to do with the teachings of Jesus, and emphasized that Islam was the final revelation and a living faith.[30] However, unlike his contemporaries, Ahmad took the attack to the many Christian missionaries in the Punjab, challenging them through his robust defence of Islam and, in the 1890s, with his claim that he had special favour from God.[31]

Ahmad founded the Ahmadiyyat in order to revive and promote Islam in a way which, he believed, was consonant with how Muhammad would have wanted to see Islam in the modern era. Ahmad sought to prove that Islam rather than Christianity was the most complete religion and better suited for progress at the dawn of the twentieth century by showing that Europeans and Americans, particularly from the elites, were turning to Islam.[32] Consequently, in 1892 a special meeting of the Ahmadiyyat agreed to propagate Islam and promote the welfare of new converts to Islam in Europe and America.[33] An Ahmadi mission to England, the centre of the British Empire, was inevitable when Ahmad recalled a vision in which he saw himself

> standing on a minaret in London and elucidating the truth of Islam in a very argumentative discourse in the English language. After this I caught a large

number of birds that were sitting on small trees. They were of white colour and of about the size of a partridge. I inferred from this vision that though I myself would not go to England, [. . .] my writings would be circulated among those people and many upright Englishmen would fall prey to the charms of Islam.[34]

Kamal-ud-Din joined the Ahmadiyyat in 1893. He became intimately involved in its activities, gaining the reputation of a fluent public speaker and champion of Islam. In 1901, Ahmad's ambition of a European mission came closer to reality with the establishment of the Anjuman Isha'at-e-Islam, the Ahmadiyya's central body for the propagation of Islam. Kamal-ud-Din stated that its 'primary task' would be 'the dissemination of Islamic teachings in the English language', and he was appointed editor of a new English-language journal, *The Review of Religions*. In a sign of solidarity with Ahmad and the Ahmadiyyat, Quilliam as well as Sheldrake and several other British Muslims contributed to *The Review of Religions* before the First World War.

Kamal-ud-Din went to England in 1912 in his capacity as a lawyer rather than as an Ahmadi missionary, but he decided to abandon his legal career and settle in London to defend, explain and propagate Islam. He received the blessing of Ahmad's successor and the first Caliph of the Ahmadiyyat, Hakim Nur-ud-Din (1841–1914) in Qadian. By October 1912, Kamal-ud-Din had found premises for Muslim students to assemble for *salat al-jum'a* (Friday or congregational prayer), which he led as the imam.[35]

When the court case which had brought him to England was settled in December 1912, Kamal-ud-Din began formal proselytizing and missionary activity. Although he was inspired by Ahmad and backed by the Ahmadiyyat, Kamal-ud-Din downplayed the differences between Ahmadis and other Muslims, and instead promoted a more ecumenical faith. He was familiar with the British and their social and cultural mores, and therefore made good use of public meetings and lectures, 'at-homes', gatherings at restaurants and hotels, as well as the press and magazines to explain Islam. He addressed Muslim student societies and Islamic groups, and also reached out to non-Muslims by talking at metropolitan Oriental and literary circles, and at meetings of unorthodox but broadly sympathetic faith groups such as Quakers, Spiritualists, Theosophists and Unitarians. Kamal ud Din was not antagonistic towards Christianity or Christians and, having studied at a Christian college in Lahore, he was able to elucidate the similarities between the 'sister faiths', compare and contrast the Qur'an and the Bible, and justify Islamic religious and social codes and practices. Like Ahmad, Kamal-ud-Din also argued that the British were more benign than other potential rulers, and he asserted that Indian Muslims were loyal to the Crown and Empire. He soon made a name for himself in England as a lucid, moderate defender of and teacher about Islam and Muslims.

In January 1913, Kamal-ud-Din led *salat al-jum'a* for a small group of London Muslim students at the abandoned mosque in Woking.[36] This was possible thanks to the efforts of Ameer Ali and allies who, in 1910, had established a London Mosque Fund with the aim of constructing a mosque and Islamic cultural centre in the capital. In spring 1912, Ameer Ali and two executive committee members of the London Mosque Fund, the Indian politician and sometime vice-president of the Council of the Secretary of State for India, Abbas Ali Baig (1859–1932), and the Orientalist, Professor Thomas Walker Arnold (1864–1930), made a formal agreement with Henry Leitner that secured Woking mosque and an adjoining building, the Sir Salar Jung Memorial House (or Hall), for the use of Muslims in England.[37]

In February 1913, Kamal-ud-Din drew on his experience of editing *The Review of Religions* to produce from his home at Richmond, south-west London, the first issue of a monthly journal, initially called *Muslim India and Islamic Review* (it was renamed *Islamic Review and Muslim India* in 1914, and became *The Islamic Review* in 1921). From the outset, the journal was intended to counter and correct misinformation and misunderstanding about Islam and Muslims in Britain and also affirm Indian Muslim loyalty to the British Crown. Kamal-ud-Din argued in the first issue that 'an average Londoner is more ignorant of the Islamic world than many Englishmen are of the Arctic zone', and he insisted that Indian Muslims 'have always believed in the British Raj as a blessing to India. We do believe that our community is better off under the present regime'.[38]

The *Muslim India* included extracts from Ahmad's writings and speeches, and those of other prominent Ahmadis such as the scholar Maulana[39] Muhammad Ali (1874–1951), whose English translation of the Qur'an was announced in the *Islamic Review* in 1915 and later sold at Woking mosque.[40] Contributors to *Muslim India* in 1913 included prominent Indian political writers such as Maulana Zafar Ali Khan (1873–1956) and Mohamed Ali (1878–1931), and two British Muslim converts previously associated with Quilliam's LMI: John Yehya-en-Nasr Parkinson (1874–1918), who had been LMI vice-president, and Frank Djaffar Mortimore, who had lectured at the LMI and written for *The Crescent*. Mortimore gave his 'Impressions of Islam' in the July 1913 issue of *Muslim India*:

> I must readily admit that it is with some reluctance that a person changes his religion, and particularly so in England, where there seems to be an atmosphere

of antipathy to other faiths, naturally imbued from the cradle of Western teaching.[41]

When, in August 1913, Kamal-ud-Din accepted an invitation from Abbas Ali Baig to move into the Memorial House at Woking and take charge of the mosque, he did so precisely to help address the problem that Mortimore and other Muslim converts expressed. Kamal-ud-Din anticipated that the mosque would become the centre of Muslim missionary activity in Britain and provide religious and social support for Muslims, including converts. Encouraged by Baig, Kamal-ud-Din established the Woking Muslim Mission (WMM) and, in a sign of Ahmadi support, he was joined by the first of many professional missionaries from Qadian, Chaudhry Fateh Muhammad Sayal (also known as Fateh Muhammad Sial, 1887–1960).

In terms of proselytizing, Kamal-ud-Din's priority was to introduce non-Muslims to a straightforward and liberal Islam, *not* the Ahmadiyya. A written oath of allegiance and printed 'Declaration Form' for new converts omitted any mention of the spiritual leader of the Ahmadiyyat.[42] Kamal-ud-Din had already facilitated a few conversions to Islam prior to settling in Woking by, to quote him directly, 'simply [laying] a true, plain, unvarnished account of Islam before the people, and [leaving] their own hearts and consciences to do the rest'.[43] His first British convert was Fátima Violet Ebráhim, whose Indian Muslim husband had invited Kamal-ud-Din to their home in late 1912. Ebráhim told a correspondent in India the following year that Kamal-ud-Din returned frequently to her house and, in turn, she and her husband visited Kamal-ud-Din at his home for *salat al-jum'a*, 'when after praying he used to preach'.[44] Ebráhim noted that 'Kamal-ud-Din has studied Christianity and therefore he is better able to make comparisons as to what is said in [the] Bible on different subjects and how Al-Koran treats the same subject, thereby proving how superior Islam was to Christianity'.[45] She found his 'logical arguments in favour of Islam and his comparisons of Islam and Christianity [...] most interesting and convincing. [...] My eyes were beginning to open in favour of Islam and gradually I found that I was Moslem at heart'.[46]

While Kamal-ud-Din and Sayal were making steady progress in England, all was not well within the Indian Ahmadiyyat, which formally split into two groups in 1914. The division was the result of disagreement within the Ahmadiyyat about who should succeed Mirza Ghulam Ahmad's successor, Hakim Nur-ud-Din, when he died in March 1914. Pre-existing divisions within the Ahmadiyyat led to the formal establishment of the 'Lahori' and 'Qadiani' groups, each named after its respective geographical base.[47] Kamal-ud-Din aligned himself with the more liberal Lahoris, who believed that Muhammad was the final prophet but recognized Mirza Ghulam Ahmad as a reformer of the faith. However, Kamal-ud-Din's assistant, Chaudhry Fateh Muhammad Sayal, allied with the Qadianis, who believed that Ahmad was a prophet and that his successors had the gift of prophecy.

Kamal-ud-Din continued to promote a more mainstream Islam through the WMM, and Sayal left Woking to establish a Qadiani *jama'at* (community) and mission in south London (see Chapter 8).[48] In line with Ahmad's strategy, Kamal-ud-Din and other missionaries who joined him at Woking from Lahore focused on educating and converting Britons to Islam. Despite the bitter disagreements between Ahmadis in India and their division into two groups, Kamal-ud-Din always presented the Islam as propagated from Woking as what he called 'non-sectarian' and, despite his clearly stated position on British rule in India, apolitical.

Kamal-ud-Din's propaganda exploited Edwardian insecurities, brought about by unparalleled industrial conflict and social discord over issues such as Ireland and women's suffrage.[49] He recognized the decline in church membership, but was sensitive to the fact that it did not necessarily imply any diminution of the search for stable and absolute systems of belief and practice. Kamal-ud-Din and his staff proffered Islam as a secure, progressive, rational, tolerant moral force in the face of increasing materialism and secularity. They promoted a liberal and syncretic form of what might be described as Anglo-Islam.[50] The Qur'an was referred to as the 'Islamic Bible' and the mosque the 'Muslim Church', which welcomed non-Muslims.[51] Potential converts were constantly reminded of the Qur'anic principle, 'There is no compulsion in religion',[52] that they pledged their allegiance to Muhammad and all other prophets *including Jesus*, and converted to Islam rather than the Ahmadiyya. Reviewing the work of the WMM, the influential Anglican missionary H. U. Weitbrecht Stanton (1851–1937) argued with some justification that 'the form of Islam which is propagated in the Woking mission is very far from being the accepted orthodox kind'.[53] He said that Kamal-ud-Din was an Ahmadi, part of a movement which, in his view,

> represents an endeavour to reconcile Islam to a certain extent with modern thought, so as to turn the edge of the chief objections to it on the part of Christians. Islam is represented as the religion of toleration and as being the rational form of religion best suited to the enlightenment of the 20th century. The idea of the Fatherhood of God, which is utterly contrary to the teaching of Mohammed, is frequently brought in. Polygamy is represented as temporary and partial, as a concession to the needs of human nature. The existence of slavery in Islam is bluntly denied.[54]

Headley's path to conversion

The precise details have been lost over time, but Headley certainly heard about Kamal-ud-Din in the first half of 1913. After succeeding to the peerage earlier that year, Headley had moved into Aghadoe House in Killarney, but shortly afterwards it and other parts of his Irish estate were put up for sale to settle the previous Baron's debts.[55] The sale of estate property and the turbulent politics of Irish Home Rule encouraged Headley to settle permanently in England with his four young sons. It was a wise decision since, in 1912, an Irish Home Rule Bill introduced by the UK government paved the way for the Government of Ireland Act 1920, which, amid violence and bloodshed, partitioned the country and anticipated Home Rule in both the north and south of Ireland. Headley bought a comfortable house called Ivy Lodge in St Margarets, near Twickenham in the south-west London suburbs and very close to Richmond, where Kamal-ud-Din lived until the summer of 1913.[56] Despite his leaning towards Islam, Headley does not appear to have attended any of the many meetings organized by Muslim groups in London, such as the CIS, before he heard about Kamal-ud-Din.

In September 1913, Kamal-ud-Din eagerly reported to one of the Ahmadi Urdu newspapers, *Badr*, that he had received a letter from 'a Lord belonging to a most exalted family', and he sent a copy of the letter to Hakim Nur-ud-Din in Qadian. Headley, at this stage still referred to anonymously in Kamal-ud-Din's regular reports and letters to India, told the missionary that he had been reading copies of *Muslim India*. He asked to meet Kamal-ud-Din because 'I have become in my heart a follower of that great Prophet', but he said that he was unable to 'accept Islam openly'.[57] The main obstacle appears to have been Headley's family, especially his church-going sisters who did not approve of Islam.[58] There followed a rather frenzied correspondence (now lost) between Headley and Kamal-ud-Din, who reported to another Ahmadi newspaper, *Paigham Sulh*, that 'It is hardly six weeks since I met him and he has written me 32 letters. [. . .] Four times I have been his guest and twice he has been my guest.'[59]

By November 1913, Headley had also read an English translation of one of Mirza Ghulam Ahmad's lectures, published as *The Teachings of Islam* (1910) and presumably given to him by Kamal-ud-Din. The latter reported to *Badr* that Headley was 'wonder struck' by the lecture: 'He wrote to me saying that this book presents such a lofty code for humanity that he does not consider himself worthy to be a Muslim. What a great understanding!'[60] Evidencing what he called Headley's 'zeal' for Islam, Kamal-ud-Din quoted from one of the letters:

> I believe that not one drop of blood needs to be shed in order to give people the honour of accepting Islam. I am sure that the time is not far away when people, seeing its beauties, its simplicity and its world-wide attraction of truth, will join the fold of this religion of God in large numbers. It is my heart-felt desire also to see His Majesty King George V become a Muslim, and I wish to see all sincere persons of a pure nature in the British empire following the teachings of the Arabian Prophet.[61]

As Headley discovered more about Muhammad and Islam, he quite quickly moved towards formal conversion. However, in October 1913, Kamal-ud-Din noted some concern:

> The Lord is under a misconception, may God deliver him from it. He writes that he has started preaching Islam gradually within his family so that when he announces his acceptance of Islam he brings others with him. Unfortunately this is a self-delusion. But now is not the time, nor does my position in relation to his position, allow me to say to him that it is a delusion. Anyhow, he has started talking about this to his sisters in a mild way.[62]

The October 1913 issue of *Muslim India* contained an extract from Headley's recent book, *Thoughts for the Future*, entitled 'How to be Free from Fear and Grief' and signed semi-anonymously by 'A. W.' The article affirmed Headley's admiration for the spirit of Islam and 'the fact of the real presence of God' among Muslims, which, as Kamal-ud-Din had taught him, created a fearlessness of death.[63] The next issue of *Muslim India* (November 1913) included a short unsigned article, probably written by Kamal-ud-Din, entitled 'Method of Preaching Religion as Given in the Quran'. It reiterated the WMM's now familiar position: 'Conversion, as our Book says, should come out of free choice and spontaneous judgement, and never be attained by means of compulsion, or even persuasion.'[64] The subsequent pages contained two consecutive articles written and signed 'Headley', which effectively and publicly confirmed his conversion to Islam.

In the first article, called 'Simplicity in Religion', Headley again embraced Islam as a simple, monotheistic and, above all, classless faith without leaders or bodies bidding for temporal power. Islam, he argued, was

> free from sacerdotalism with its attendant dogmas and greed for power, [so] we must concede that the government of a nation or empire would go on more smoothly if such a peaceful religion were universally adopted. [. . .] The spirit of Islam soars far above petty jealousies and the racial distractions of East and West.[65]

He was adamant that

> a study of the Koran will reveal the fact that there is nothing antagonistic to previous revelations – Mahomet's instructions, as laid down in the book completely back up the Bible teaching, extending them to suit the requirements of the time.[66]

Headley claimed in his second article, 'The Religion of the Future':

> Though my gratitude for God's favours and loving care has been profound from my earliest youth, I cannot help observing that within the past few years, since the pure and convincing faith of the Muslims has become a reality in my heart and mind, I have found happiness and security never approached before. Freedom from the weird dogmas of the various branches of Christian Churches came to me like a breath of pure sea air, and on realising the simplicity, as well as the illuminating splendour, of Islam, I was as a man emerging from a cloudy tunnel into the light of the day.[67]

Headley's point regarding 'happiness and security' was important. As was related in Chapter 3, the years and months immediately prior to Headley's conversion were difficult for him. Headley had started a new life in England and, though he continued to battle with depression for the rest of his life, Islam gave him 'happiness in misery and strength when the forces of evil seemed about to overwhelm me'.[68] A few months after his religious conversion, Headley wrote a new poem called 'After the Battle of Life':

> Dear Father, I can praise Thee now,
>   The lengthy struggle o'er,
> Again repeat the oft-told vow
>   And thank and love Thee more.[69]

Headley ended his 'Religion of the Future' article for *Muslim India* by quoting one of his own poems that endorsed the revelations of Moses, Jesus and Muhammad, also originally published in *Thoughts for the Future*. He added that the poem was written 'by one who was always at heart a follower of Mahomet, though at the time of writing he was almost entirely ignorant of the main features of Islam'.[70] Indeed, it was only *after* meeting Kamal-ud-Din and being guided by him that, within three or four months, Headley recognized Islam to be a viable alternative to Christianity. Reflecting later on his first encounters with Kamal-ud-Din, Headley said that he had been 'much impressed' with the missionary's 'quiet dignity and gracious manner', and bowled over by his explanation of Islam as a simple, non-sectarian and tolerant faith.[71]

Moreover, Islam offered Headley – and many of Kamal-ud-Din's other British converts – an antidote to the perceived political and social ills of late-Edwardian society mentioned earlier.[72] Despite his break from convention in matters of religion, Headley was and remained a politically and morally conservative man. He was a staunch monarchist and patriot who, as is related later in this book, did not look favourably on groups such as the Suffragettes and Suffragists, Irish Nationalists and Socialists, who threatened to destabilize the existing social order. Headley admired Kamal-ud-Din's patriotism and loyalty to the British Crown and Empire and, as is evident from his first written reflections about Islam quoted earlier, he was comforted by Kamal-ud-Din's claim that Islam would not merely arrest the drift towards atheism but also make the country easier to govern.[73] As 'a plain Englishman with sons who will some day have to be provided with wives', he was also keen to believe that Islam would counter 'moral degeneracy' in British society and facilitate a 'return to that Early Victorian modesty':

> I love modesty in a woman and, though it is the fashion to laugh at the Easterns for keeping their women veiled and secluded from the vulgar gaze, I think they are to be admired for wishing to shield and protect what they hold so sacred. [. . .] Some of the modern costumes for women are, to my mind, far worse and more suggestive than absolute nudity.[74]

At the end of 1913, Headley wrote that Kamal-ud-Din had been 'a veritable living concordance, and has patiently explained and translated portions of the Koran which did not appear quite clear to me'.[75] As missionary, mentor and friend, Kamal-ud-Din facilitated Headley's conversion to the faith he had directly encountered in India in the 1890s.

Public conversion to Islam

The Egyptian writer and political activist, Dusé Mohamed Ali (1866–1945), devoted a short chapter of his memoirs, written late in life and shortly after Headley's death, to the circumstances of the latter's public conversion to Islam and Kamal-ud-Din's involvement.[76] In 1913, Ali was living and working in London as founding editor of *The African Times and Orient Review*, and he was also a vice-president of the CIS.[77] He had recently met Kamal-ud-Din and they were on good terms. Twenty years later, however, Ali publicly accused Kamal-ud-Din of being 'somewhat dictatorial in his manner' and concluded that he was 'an aggressive rather than a persuasive missionary'.⁷⁸ Ali's recollections must, therefore, be read with some caution, but his description of Headley's conversion is important as it is the only known surviving 'insider' account.

According to Ali, Headley and Kamal-ud-Din continued their discussion about Islam in early autumn 1913,

> until one day Kamal ud-Deen hurried into my office, oozing perspiration and excitement, to inform me that Headley had embraced Islam. A few evenings later he called at my flat to say that Headley had put his decision to embrace Islam in writing and joyfully produced the document.⁷⁹

On Saturday 15 November 1913, Ali, Kamal-ud-Din and Headley attended a CIS function held at the cosmopolitan Frascati's restaurant in central London. Addressing the audience of mainly Indian Muslims and 'a sprinkling of Egyptians and one or two Turks' and converts including Sheldrake, Kamal-ud-Din 'complained that his work was greatly hindered by the slackness of his professing co-religionists'.⁸⁰ He then read out a portion of Headley's letter that confirmed his intention to become a Muslim.

Ali alleged that Kamal-ud-Din had not secured Headley's permission to publicly announce his conversion. Headley, on the other hand, told the press the following day that 'When the [Central] Islamic Society asked me to their dinner the other night, I was only too pleased to be able to go and tell them how deeply was my attachment to their religion.'⁸¹ Indeed, he gave a short speech at the event which was reproduced in *Muslim India* in December 1913. Headley quoted extensively from one of Kamal-ud-Din's lectures, which suggests that his speech was scripted in advance and that he had anticipated Kamal-ud-Din's announcement.⁸² He praised the aims and work of the CIS and said that he hoped to be elected as a member of the Society. Headley also 'wished it to be known that he will make it his very sacred and delightful duty to explain to all his friends what, according to his lights and intelligence, he believes constitutes the faith of Islam'.⁸³

Ali noted that 'There was a full representation of the London and Provincial press present and each one copied [Kamal-ud-Din's] letter'.⁸⁴ He claimed that Kamal-ud-Din was shocked the next day to find the newspapers 'filled with sensational news' of Headley's conversion.⁸⁵ Indeed, the news spread like wildfire. It made the front page of the next day's edition of the *New York Times* ('Irish Peer turns Moslem') and was widely reported in the daily newspapers in Britain and across the world on Monday.⁸⁶ The London *Times* announced

Headley's religious conversion in its 'Court Circular' section, the official record of the British aristocracy.[87] Ali wrote:

> The quite unknown Lord Headley suddenly became front page news and Kamal ud-Deen, who knew what he had done but was in a blue funk because of the wide publicity which was accorded his indiscretion, rushed to my flat at 8.30 a.m. to solicit my advice. I told him to go at once to Lord Headley and inform him of the circumstances and apologize for the indiscretion.[88]

Ali's biographer, Ian Duffield, suggests that Ali might have exaggerated his role, 'yet it seems plausible that with [Ali's] large experience of Britain and the British, Khwaja Kamal ud-Din would have used him as a confidant.'[89] Ali said that he was 'creditably informed' that 'although Lord Headley stormed, upon the reassurance of his sister and the unexpected notoriety he had inadvertently secured, he was rather pleased with himself'.[90] Contrary to Ali's rather dramatic account, it seems unlikely that there was any tension between Headley and Kamal-ud-Din, and they forged a close personal relationship that lasted until the latter's death almost two decades later. A few days after the public announcement, Kamal-ud-Din reported to *Paigham Sulh* that he had

> fulfilled the long-cherished, heart-felt wish of Lord Headley that I spend a night at his house. What affection, what friendship, and what eagerness to serve! He set up my bedroom himself, lit the fire, made the bed. When I rose in the morning and was about to start prayer, he appeared in his night garments bringing me tea and grapes. Before I used the bathroom, he checked the hot and cold taps himself, in the manner of a servant.[91]

Reactions

Dusé Mohamed Ali's claim that Kamal-ud-Din panicked after the CIS meeting might contain an element of truth because, as was highlighted in the *Muslim India* of December 1913, news of Headley's conversion 'created a unique interest, which has travelled from London into the four corners of the world'.[92] Kamal-ud-Din could not have predicted the international interest generated by the public announcement of Headley's religious conversion.

Ali was correct in stating that Kamal-ud-Din 'proceeded to make capital of this "conversion" among his co-religionists in India where the conversion of a real-life British nobleman to Islam caused the Indian Muslims, especially Kamal ud-Deen's sect, to feel rather proud of their fellow countryman's achievement'.[93]

Headley's conversion was a coup for Kamal-ud-Din personally and for the nascent WMM. Kamal-ud-Din immediately contacted Hakim Nur-ud-Din in Qadian, noting that 'God has changed the fortunes of Islam by granting us just one man. Whatever Lord Headley says, it is splashed in the newspapers the next day. People now want to listen to lectures on Islam.'[94]

A week after the CIS function, a special public meeting of Ahmadi Muslims was held in Lahore to celebrate Headley's conversion. *Paigham Sulh* reported the event:

> Even before the appointed time, Muslim brethren started arriving in crowds, and by the time of the opening of the proceedings the Ahmadiyya mosque and the adjoining marquee were entirely full. Besides Muslims of all sections of society, followers of other religions were also present in large numbers.[95]

The meeting, which was also described in the colonial press, endorsed a resolution put forward by the philosopher, poet and politician Muhammad Iqbal (1877–1938): 'A telegram of congratulations should be sent on behalf of the Muslims of Lahore to the Right Honourable Lord Headley, through Khwaja Kamal-ud-Din of the Woking Mosque, England, on his acceptance of Islam.'[96] For Iqbal:

> The biggest cause of the decline of the Muslims is the neglect of the task of the propagation of Islam. Thank God that the man who first recognised this shortcoming is Khwaja Kamal-ud-Din, who has sacrificed all worldly interests to take this great work upon himself. It is, therefore, our duty not to neglect to help him in any way, and we must not let the question of Ahmadiyyat stand in the way of this noble work, for our God, our Prophet and our Scripture is the same.[97]

Importantly, those gathered at the meeting agreed that 'a campaign for funds be launched among the Indian Muslim population for the Islamic mission of Khwaja Kamal-ud-Din. A trust should be created, having Ahmadis and other Muslims as members, to receive the contributions, and the funds should be spent to support Khwaja Kamal-ud-Din.'[98] Iqbal and several other prominent Muslims were duly elected as founder members of the Isha'at Islam (Western Countries) Trust.[99]

For the Ahmadi journal *The Review of Religions*, which Kamal-ud-Din had formerly edited, Headley's conversion was a sign that 'There has begun an awakening to Islam in the West. The gloom which Christian misrepresentation had spread over the West has begun to disappear and people are becoming more and more alive to the truth of Islam.'[100] Back in Britain, a buoyant John Yehya-en-Nasr Parkinson wrote a rallying article for *Muslim India* which encouraged Muslims in Britain and elsewhere to support the WMM: 'The flag of Islam has been planted in the heart of England, keep it there.'[101]

Kamal-ud-Din reported in *Muslim India* that, soon after Headley's conversion was made public, several people, including 'three highly respected members of the nobility', had followed him into Islam. The WMM office was, he claimed, 'flooded nowadays with inquiries about Islam'.[102] Once the news about Headley's conversion broke, Kamal-ud-Din and Sayal (who was still at Woking in 1913 and early 1914) gave interviews to the press, and circulated copies of the November issue of *Muslim India*, which contained Headley's first signed essays about Islam, to journalists and other potential influencers and allies.

The newspapers referred to Headley's conversion as 'a bolt from the true blue of conformity' and concurred that it had created 'a mild sensation'.[103] However, the British press was generally less critical of Headley as a Muslim than it had been towards Quilliam and the LMI community in the late-nineteenth century, when issues such as the Eastern Question and the virulent but struggling Christian missionary endeavour in Islamic lands made Muslims in the West particularly vulnerable to attack.[104] The *Guardian* newspaper, for example, considered Headley's conversion to be a 'lamentable error', but tempered its criticism:

> We have no doubt that many a prayer for Lord Headley will go up from humble Christian hearts that he may return to the way of truth; and unquestionably that is the proper attitude of mind towards a profoundly regrettable incident. We need not characterise it in severer terms.[105]

A provincial newspaper in the United States astutely noted that 'Whereas in olden times an apostacy of this kind would have been punished as an atrocious crime, it is nowadays regarded in the light of a harmless eccentricity, denoting some abnormality of a possibly brilliant mind.'[106] A columnist for the *Leeds Mercury* wrote with tongue in cheek:

> I have been looking up the authorities to see what would have been done to Lord Headley by our fiercer and certainly more Christian forefathers. [. . .] Opinions amongst the learned seem to differ as to whether his Lordship ought to be burned alive at the stake, hanged, drawn and quartered, or merely beheaded. [. . .] As it is, the whole thing is very uninteresting. Nobody cares very much whether Lord Headley is a Moslem or a Persistent Pessimist or a Shaker.[107]

The press did, however, find Headley's conversion to Islam interesting. Notably, in their initial coverage, some newspapers picked up on points made by Kamal-ud-Din and Sayal and attempted to explain Islam and correct common errors about that faith. They were not wholly successful and tended to focus on contentious matters such as polygamy. The *Daily Sketch*, for example, argued that 'The religion, of course, recognises no form of priesthood, believing in direct communication with the Deity. [. . .] Polygamy is allowed by creed, but no member is allowed to have more than four wives. In England there are very few members of the religion with more than one wife.'[108]

The *Daily Sketch* characterized Headley as 'a grey-moustached, handsome man, with a fine intellectual forehead and good features, while his habit of smiling when he talks gives him a happy appearance'.[109] For Mohamed Ali, editor of the Indian Muslim separatist weekly newspaper *The Comrade* of Delhi, who happened to be in London in autumn 1913, Headley was 'not at all the kind of morbid man that one often associates with people who are generally converted from one faith into another, often through intellectual caprice'.[110]

Thanks to Kamal-ud-Din, there was initially some confusion about the British Muslim Lord's background. Although Kamal-ud-Din had known Headley for some months by November 1913, he wrongly believed that Headley was a member of the House of Lords, and told journalists that 'A few more conversions in the House of Lords and the House of Commons [. . .] would be the best thing for our rule in India that could possibly happen.'[111] This misunderstanding was compounded by a careless journalist who mistook Headley for his cousin Charlie, the fourth Baron Headley, who had sat in the Lords. The journalist filed his report with a London press agency, and it was quickly distributed worldwide. The *Arkansas Gazette* headline 'English Peer, Once a Prospector Here, Turns Moslem', accompanied by a photograph of Charlie Winn (who had, indeed, attempted to settle his debts by prospecting in North America), was typical of initial newspaper reports overseas and in Britain:

> Since the death of the late Lord Stanley of Alderley [in 1903 . . .] the British House of Lords – supreme tribunal of the Empire – while boasting of a Buddhist Earl, in the person of Lord Mexborough, has had no Moslem peer to represent in its councils a religion professed by nearly 100,000,000 lieges of the British crown. This role will henceforth be filled by Lord Headley.[112]

Back in London, the *Pall Mall Gazette* wrote that 'in view of the large Oriental interests of the Empire, there is a certain fitness in having the Faith of Islam represented in the House of Lords'.[113] The *Jewish World* agreed, adding that 'For ourselves, we only wish it were well and strongly represented in the House of Commons too.'[114] Representing an equally marginalized faith group in Britain, the *Jewish World* felt that

There is a very widespread tendency in these 'tight little islands' – as the Aliens Act [of 1905[115]] and the spirit which inspired it prove – to forget that England is not the British Empire, and that while the home population is comparatively homogenous in race and creed this does not apply to the Empire at large. The British Empire is a conglomerate of many faiths and peoples; and if the presence of Mussulman peers in Parliament keeps that fact before some of our insularly-minded fellow-countrymen it will be a point gained.[116]

Responses

Headley personally gave numerous interviews the day after his conversion was made public, and he also wrote a series of articles and letters during November and December 1913 that sought to explain and clarify his reasons for converting to Islam. But first he confirmed his identity. He emphasized that, unlike his cousin Charlie, he was not a Representative Peer in the Lords and, since he no longer had any 'inclination towards politics', he was 'not likely ever to seek election'.[117] He told the *Pall Mall Gazette* rather pointedly that 'My late cousin and myself had very little in common, and only agreed in our love for field sports.'[118] However, he further confused the press by announcing his Muslim name, Saifurrahman Shaikh Rahmatullah Farooq, which he said meant 'Sword of the Most Compassionate; a Chief or Leader; Grace of God; and One who Separates Right from Wrong.'[119] The international Catholic newspaper, *The Tablet*, sarcastically commented:

> As Lord Headley, the Mahometan neophyte, has been given a name novel and even alien to English ears, his friends are in some difficulty about their manner of addressing him in the future. But there is a way out of the difficulty which unites the old nomenclature with the new. One of the new appellations means a sword. Then, suggests a correspondent, why not Lord Be-headley?[120]

Headley admitted that his Muslim name was complicated for the native English speaker:

> I did not give it to myself, and it certainly seems rather long to the Western mind! But, for all that, it is a very beautiful Eastern name [. . .]. I am very proud of this name, though I cannot say it quickly at present. In Europe I shall be satisfied to be called Headley or, as I much prefer it amongst my intimate friends, Rowland.[121]

Indeed, he generally went by the name Lord Headley, Headley or 'Al-Farooq'.

Having attempted to clarify his identity, Headley was quick to deny rumours that Kamal-ud-Din or others at Woking had coerced him to convert to Islam:

> It is possible that some of my friends may imagine that I have been influenced by Mohammedans; but this is not the case, for my present convictions are solely the outcome of many years of thought. [. . .] Even my friend Khwaja Kamal-ud-Din has never tried to influence me in the slightest degree [. . .] he [has shown] the true spirit of the Muslim missionary, which is never to force or even persuade.[122]

In the spirit of Kamal-ud-Din, the cornerstone of Headley's argument for Islam, which he maintained for the rest of his life, was that the *original* teachings of Judaism, Christianity and an 'unchanged' Islam were 'sister religions, only held apart by dogmas and technicalities which might very well be dispensed with'.[123] Besides, Christianity originated in 'the East':

> How is it that we do not complain about the nationality of Christ, who we must believe was a swarthy Asiatic? His mother, the Virgin Mary, was an Asiatic, and Moses and nearly all the inspired prophets were Easterns. The Holy Prophet Mahomet was, like the others, an Eastern, and was given his instructions from on high: the Holy Koran contains the Word of God like the Bible and other inspired works, and confirms the Bible and previous revelations.[124]

Explaining his conversion to Islam, Headley confidently reaffirmed his commitment to *Christian* principles:

> In publicly identifying myself with the Mahommedan faith I am not departing in any way from the beliefs I have held for the last twenty years. [. . .] I have taken no active steps to renounce membership of the Church of England, in which I was brought up, nor have I gone through any ceremony proclaiming my formal adoption of the Mahommedan faith, but the religion is the creed I hold.[125]

Echoing views already expressed in *Thoughts for the Future* and articles for *Muslim India*, Headley explained that centuries of corrupt sacerdotalism and sectarian bigotry had rendered organized Christianity unfit for the new century:

> It is the intolerance of those professing the Christian religion which more than anything else is responsible for my secession. I was reared in the strict and narrow forms of the Low Church party. Later I lived in many Roman Catholic countries, including Ireland. The intolerance of one sect of Christians towards other sects holding some different form of the same faith, of which I witnessed many instances, disgusted me. You never hear Mahommedans speak concerning those of other religions as you hear Christians talk of one another. They may feel very sorry that other persons do not hold the Mahommedan faith, but they

don't condemn them to everlasting damnation because of a differing belief. The purity and simplicity of the Mahommedan religion, its freedom from dogma and sacerdotalism, and the obvious truth of it make a special appeal to me.[126]

He added:

The earnestness and sincerity of the Mahommedans, too, are greater than anything I have ever seen on the part of Christians. The ordinary Christian man puts on religion on Sunday as a respectable habit because he thinks it is right, and possibly because his father and his grandfather before him always honoured Sunday with the same observance. When Sunday is over his religion is discarded for the rest of the week. With the Mahommedan, on the contrary, there is no distinction between Sunday and any other day. He is always thinking of what he can do in God's service. Although I have accepted the Mahommedan faith, I am still a Christian in so far as believing in Christ and following the teachings of Christ. The Mahommedan faith, although people generally do not realise it, recognises the teaching of all the prophets – Moses and Christ as well as Mahomet.[127]

Headley's more vocal critics in 1913 and the following year sought to expose his arguments as the ravings of a fanatic or romantic idealist. There was, indeed, an idealism – and naivety – in Headley's thinking and writing, especially in the immediate days and months after his conversion. Idealism is, perhaps, an inevitable attribute of a religious convert, especially to a maligned religion like Islam in the West, in order to justify conversion to oneself and others, and to present the new faith as an improvement on the abandoned religion. In a letter published in the *Daily Mail*, a 'lecturer in Arabic in London' argued that Headley was wrong to condemn Christian intolerance of other religions:

If a Moslem in any really Moslem land were to do as Lord Headley has done and announce his conversion to Christianity his life would not be worth a day's purchase, and his death would be justified by the express teaching of the Koran. Such is Moslem 'toleration'; converts are only allowed to live where the strong arm of Christian justice can protect them.[128]

Headley conceded that 'there are fanatics in all religions', but wrote:

To refute the idea that true Moslems would murder a brother so foolish as to renounce the faith of Islam, I may quote one line which appears in the Holy Koran immediately after one of the most beautiful and impressive passages in the Book: 'Let there be no compulsion (no violence) in Religion.' No true Moslem would have any feelings but of deepest pity and sorrow for a deserter from the fold presided over and tended by our Gracious Shepherd and King.[129]

Headley further explained his actions in a succinct article entitled 'Why I became a Mohammedan', which was published in the London *Observer* newspaper at the end of November 1913.[130] The article was swiftly reprinted in many other newspapers, magazines and journals, including some important Muslim publications such as Mohamed Ali's *The Comrade* of Delhi and, in an Arabic translation, the Egyptian Salafi[131] magazine *al-Manar* ('The Lighthouse') of Cairo, which was founded and edited by a leading exponent of Salafism, Muhammad Rashid Rida (1865–1935).[132] Headley began the article by admitting, 'It is not to be expected that any decided step can be taken out of the beaten track of every-day custom without attracting attention', but he claimed that 'there has never been any desire for notoriety or publicity on my part'.[133] However, 'in this case, if my action is the means of making people tolerant and broad-minded, I am quite prepared to put up with every kind of ridicule and abuse'.[134] After all,

> We Britishers are wont to pride ourselves on our love of fair play and justice, yet what can be more unfair than condemning, as so many of us do, the Mohammedan faith without first attempting to find out even so much as an outline of its tenets or the meaning of the word Islam?[135]

Like Mirza Ghulam Ahmad and Kamal-ud-Din before him, Headley singled out the Trinity as a prime example of 'the somewhat narrow tenets of the various Christian churches', removed from the 'original teachings' of Jesus:

> [T]he Athanasian Creed [. . .] treats the Trinity in a very confusing manner. In this Creed, which is very important and deals conclusively with one of the fundamental tenets of the 'Churches', it is laid down most clearly that it represents the Catholic faith, and that if we do not believe it we shall perish everlastingly; then we are told that we *must thus think of the Trinity* if we want to be saved – in other words, that a God we in one breath hail as merciful and almighty in the next breath we accuse of injustice and cruelty which we would not attribute to the most bloodthirsty human tyrant. As if God, Who is before all and above all, would be in any way influenced by what a poor mortal 'thinks about the Trinity'. I have never thought very much about the Trinity, as it is so confusing and does no good.[136]

Elsewhere, Headley attacked the concepts of Atonement as being unnecessary in Islam 'because God can *directly* and instantly forgive transgressions when we ask Him with true repentance'; Salvation, which Islam did not deny 'to those who do their duty to God and their neighbours, whatever they may think on other subjects' (i.e. 'the atonement, a belief in the Divinity of Christ, the sacraments, and the Trinity'); and Intercession, which was not recognized in Islam, 'because we feel that, belonging to God, we are ever in His hands at every moment of the day or night'.[137]

In concluding his *Observer* article, Headley supposed that 'There are thousands of men – and women too, I believe – who are at heart Muslims, but convention, fear of adverse comments and a desire to avoid any worry or change conspire to keep them from openly admitting the fact.' Having 'taken the step' of converting to Islam, Headley emphasized that he was not simply 'just the same in my beliefs as I was twenty years ago' but he considered himself 'a far better Christian than I was before'.[138] This was possibly a conscious twist on the argument of the founder of Woking mosque, Leitner, who, as was related earlier, suggested that 'he is a better Christian who reveres the truths enunciated by the Prophet Muhammad'. The *Pall Mall Gazette* wrote:

> It says something for [Headley's] broad-mindedness that he does not propose to sever his connection with the English Church. There are many in this country who have no room in their lives for one religion. The man who can find room for two is to be congratulated, both on his largeness of view and his adaptability to varying requirements.[139]

Headley explained in a letter to the *Pall Mall Gazette* that it was wrong to assume that he had *two* religions:

> I have only one – surrender and submission to God, and beneficence to all His creatures – for this is the meaning of the word 'Islam'. It seems to me that Christ also taught this, which explains why it is impossible to be a good Mahommedan without also being a good Christian.[140]

Although Headley said that, after his religious conversion, he was 'nearly buried under letters from all parts of the world', many of them castigating him for his actions, surprisingly few were published in the general press.[141] An exception was a letter from a Mr Davidson in the *Aberdeen Press and Journal*:

> Lord Headley, in becoming a convert to Mahommedanism, has, I think, acted as a fool would do. This conversion or perversion one way or another is of small importance until he becomes a new creation in Christ (he is only in his nonage in Spiritual matters yet). When that great transaction takes place he would, in my opinion, no more think of taking his present step than turning cannibal.[142]

The Christian press and a number of clergymen were similarly critical of Headley's conversion. The *East and the West*, a journal published by the Society for the Propagation of the Gospel in Foreign Parts, commented that 'We could wish that during these twenty years he had studied the teaching and practice of Mohammedans more carefully than he has done', and castigated Headley's conception of Muslim tolerance of other religions as, quite simply, wrong.[143]

For the Reverend Berlyn of Fulham in west London, Headley's statements 'prove that he has not yet grasped the elementary fact of what essentially constitutes a Christian':

> A Christian is not necessarily a man who does his duty to God, or man, nor need he necessarily be kind, beneficent, or even socially moral. Though he lacks all these virtues he is yet 'more of a Christian' than the best Mohammedan who ever lived. A *good* Christian of necessity possesses these virtues, but his being Christian depends neither upon the possession or admiration of them any more than his religion is made perfect by them alone. The Christian religion stands for far more than the mere possession of virtues. A man, whether he be good or bad, is only a Christian if he has been 'born again', that is to say, if he has been through the Sacrament of Baptism. [...] At the same time it is necessary to point out that for the same reason no one who *has* been baptised can ever be anything else, however much he may desire it or however unworthy he may be.[144]

As usual, Headley replied to his critic:

> I affirm that you can be a most excellent follower of Christ's teaching and obey it in the spirit without ever having heard of baptism or the Lord's Supper, and without believing in the Divinity of Christ or the Trinity. Surely, it is far more important to carry out in your life those divine precepts enjoined by Christ than to rely on a mere form like baptism for salvation? The one is the spirit, the other the letter. [...] I feel sure that half the people who outwardly profess these opinions merely do so for appearance sake. [...] To my mind the real Christian is the man who tries to show it in his life by obedience and submission to God and endeavouring to do his duty to his neighbours, and by avoiding anything of the nature of a lie.[145]

Writing in the evangelical *Moslem World* journal, H. U. Weitbrech Stanton concluded:

> It is sufficiently obvious that a nominally Christian Deist who is ready to swallow the historical contradictions of Islam, has but a very short step to take in order to become a Moslem; and having already emptied the Christian faith of its specific content, he may regard himself, as Lord Headley professes, to be still a Christian after he has embraced Islam.[146]

By contrast, the Reverend S. E. Chettoe of Hendon, north London, told reporters that 'glaring inconsistencies were so apparent in the lives of many professing Christians that he was not surprised that those who looked on the outside should embrace the Mahometan religion'.[147]

Headley described himself in 1913 as having 'a strong comic vein in my nature, and it is so strong at times that it leads to my annoying, whilst harmlessly amusing, my friends'.[148] It was, he said, 'in the spirit of comedy' that he published in the December issue of *Muslim India* a letter from a Christian who asked 'How can you, a guilty sinner, be happy and at home with a Holy God?' Headley replied:

> With regard to 'guilty sinners', I must ask you to speak for yourself – if you are one such unfortunate – and associate with others like yourself, pray allow me to inform you that I am *not* particularly guilty, and I don't like being with 'guilty sinners' at any time – I avoid them carefully.[149]

Headley found the negative response from friends and relatives less easy to mock and shake off. He admitted in his *Observer* article published just a week after his conversion was made public that 'I am quite aware that many friends and relations now look upon me as a lost soul and past praying for.'[150] One friend told a *Daily Sketch* reporter that 'Lord Headley is the last man in the world I should have thought of as turning Mussulman'.[151] Headley's relatives were more problematic, and he later admitted that 'members of my family came to me with expressions of the gravest concern because I had deserted the religion of my fathers, and they assured me most positively that salvation was impossible for me now that I had taken the terrible step'.[152] He also argued years later (and with the benefit of much reflection) that 'since I had never believed in the baptisms and creeds of the Christian religion as being *necessary to salvation*, it can hardly be argued that I deserted a Faith which never appealed to my intelligence or my heart'.[153]

The few surviving letters to Headley from his sister Helen Allanson-Winn are generally warm and affectionate, but she was firm in matters of faith and religion. When Headley tried to persuade her to read the Qur'an, she wrote: 'I don't think I want to read it, the simple religion as set forth by our <u>Divine Saviour</u> Christ is enough for me'. She continued:

> [A]s to the <u>miracles</u>, who but a fool could doubt them for one moment when our lives are miracles and we are surrounded by them on all sides: our difficulty lies in being so <u>unspiritual</u>; we can't believe if we can't see with the carnal eyes, the <u>spiritual eyes</u> being blind so often and our faith nil.[154]

Headley replied to his sister (though his side of the correspondence has not survived) and Helen, in turn, wrote again to concede that 'I know exactly what you mean re: the Koran and I hate to be narrow minded and don't think we <u>are</u>:

and I never condemn anything without knowing something about it and should never say that Mahomed was "an imposter" nor do I "hate the Jews", God's chosen people.'[155] Headley's sisters came to accept – or at least tolerate – their brother's conversion to Islam. While his middle sister, Stephanie, had married into the respectable Maryon-Wilson family of Eastbourne, Sussex in 1886, Helen and Margaretta were spinsters and they remained very close to Headley, who helped to provide and care for them for the rest of his life.

5

Muslim peer of the realm
The first decade, I: 1913–18

Despite the negative responses to his religious conversion discussed in the previous chapter, Headley felt excited to be a convert to Islam associated with the new Woking Muslim Mission at the end of 1913. He was nearing the age of sixty, but appears to have been spiritually and physically energized by converting to Islam, and relished his newfound position as a Muslim public figure. This and the following chapter examine Headley's first decade as a Muslim. The present chapter considers Headley's leadership of British Muslims, his practice of Islam and repeated calls for the 'Westernization' of his religion to ensure its survival in the West. It then explores how the First World War, specifically the Ottoman–German alliance, affected British Muslim sensibilities and relates how Headley demonstrated his loyalty to Britain, only to suffer a humiliating fall from grace when he was arrested and convicted for drunk and disorderly behaviour.

British Muslim leader

Headley converted to Islam at a particularly turbulent point in history. Increased militarization, economic uncertainty and regional conflict during 1913 threatened the stability of Europe.[1] For Muslims like Headley, events in the Balkans were especially alarming as they precipitated the dissolution of the Ottoman Empire and threatened the survival of the Caliphate. Two Balkan Wars between 1912 and 1913 saw countries such as Bulgaria, Greece and Serbia, which had significant ethnic populations under Ottoman rule, defeat the Ottoman Empire. The Ottoman Sultan-Caliph, Abd al-Hamid II, was deposed by liberal reformers popularly known as the Young Turks in 1909 and replaced by his brother, Mehmed V (1844–1918), who was largely a figurehead with little political power. In the midst of the First Balkan War (October 1912–May

1913), some of the Young Turks overthrew the remainder of the old guard in the Ottoman cabinet and brought the Committee of Union of Progress (CUP) to power.[2] The CUP leaders exercised absolute control over the fragile Ottoman Empire, and edged towards supporting the belligerent German emperor, Wilhelm II (1859–1941).

On 31 December 1913, the London *Daily Graphic* concluded, 'With every opportunity of doing otherwise', the past year had nevertheless 'spared us Armageddon'.[3] War was by no means inevitable in 1914. Headley, for one, was optimistic as the New Year dawned. On 5 January 1914, he penned a poem that extolled the virtues of Muslim fraternity, and sent it to Kamal-ud-Din for publication in the newly named *Islamic Review and Muslim India*:

> It had been said we could not meet,
>   Or join in prayers for further grace–
> Together reach Thy mercy seat–
>   Or mingle praise in the same place.
>
> O Heavenly Father, Thou hast shown
>   To us, Thy loving faithful sons,
> How brotherhood has quickly grown
>   Insep'rable while time still runs.
>
> In all the ages of the past,
>   In all the future years to come,
> Thy Name alone can bind us fast,
>   Whilst we can say, 'Thy Will be done.'
>
> Great Allah, Lord, our God our King,
>   Who knowest what for us is best,
> We praise Thy Name and loudly sing
>   The fusion of the East and West.[4]

Embraced by the nascent Woking Muslim community and immediately called upon by the British and international press to speak for Islam and Muslims, Headley found himself at the beginning of 1914 a *de facto* British Muslim leader. This was, of course, entirely feasible in a decentralized religious tradition like Islam which, as Headley was keen to point out, lacked priestly hierarchy. But, in a class-based society such as Britain, status mattered and Headley's aristocratic title gave him authority and a public voice that Kamal-ud-Din and the Ahmadi leadership in India welcomed. It followed that Headley did not – and never claimed to – represent the many Muslims in Britain who were not directly connected with the London-centric WMM, including long-established and broadly working-class Arab and Yemeni communities primarily in port towns and cities such as South Shields, Glasgow, Cardiff, Hull and Manchester.[5]

Shortly after his religious conversion, Headley attended *salat al-jum'a* at Caxton Hall, the WMM's temporary central London meeting place. After prayers, Headley rose to address the congregation and 'was greeted with loud cheers and the clapping of hands, but one of the leaders of the community [. . .] called for silence and impressed upon the worshippers the necessity for preserving a reverential attitude'.[6] Convinced that Islam had a place and a future in the West, Headley said that he had 'great hopes of the spread of their faith, the simple, purified, and dignified religion of Islam', especially in Britain.[7] Kamal-ud-Din reported to Hakim Nur-ud-Din in Qadian:

> After returning home, I said to Lord Headley: 'Look, I say to you one thing – God has chosen you for a great work here. You cannot thank God sufficiently for that. You are the *Bashir* (giver of good news) and *Nazir* (warner) for your people. Your people will come to you, and not to me, to ask and learn about Islam. If you present before them a wrong picture of Islam, by your actions, your ways, your conduct, then it would be you, not me, who would be responsible before God.' I said this on Friday evening when I was at his house. The next morning at 6 a.m. he came to my room and said: 'Your words entered into my heart like electricity. Undoubtedly I shall be responsible before God if my people do not see the true picture of Islam. . . . What will happen when you go back to India?'[8]

Kamal-ud-Din agreed to teach Headley the Qur'an 'from beginning to end'. Since Kamal-ud-Din was busy at Woking, it was agreed that he would stay at Headley's house in St Margarets between Tuesday evening and Friday evening, then return to Woking until the following Tuesday.[9]

Kamal-ud-Din was confident that Headley 'will himself be a preacher and missionary of Islam in every sense'.[10] Indeed, just a month after his public conversion, Headley apparently devoted 'six to seven hours every day propagating Islam by letter and correspondence'.[11] He knew well from his years working in Westminster and Salisbury the power of the press, the written word and images. He arranged to have a portrait photograph taken with Kamal-ud-Din to help 'dispel Rudyard Kipling's notion that "East is East and West is West and never the twain shall meet", and show that the Prophet of Arabia has brought together the East and the West'.[12] The photograph was circulated widely and printed as a frontispiece in the February 1914 issue of the *Islamic Review* (Figure 7).

Headley's relationships with Indian Muslims like Kamal-ud-Din raised eyebrows in London society. However, the press was more concerned about

Figure 7 Lord Headley with Khwaja Kamal-ud-Din, November 1913. This image was first published in *Islamic Review and Muslim India* in February 1914 with the caption 'East Meets West in the Unity of Islam'.
Source: Courtesy of Ahmadiyya Anjuman Isha'at Islam Lahore (UK).

Headley's loyalties as a Muslim in Britain. Like Lord Stanley of Alderley, Abdullah Quilliam and other British Muslims before him, Headley was suspected of having 'abandoned' his allegiances to the British monarch and Britain in favour of the Sultan-Caliph and the Ottoman Empire.[13] As one provincial English newspaper commented in 1913, 'Mohammedans, it may be recollected, of whatever nationality, owe spiritual allegiance to the Sultan of Turkey.'[14] Headley sought to quash these fears, stating publicly in late 1913 that 'Nothing could be more ridiculous than that', for he 'was still, and he hoped he always would be, a most loyal subject to the King'.[15] In an unsigned article for the December 1913 issue of *Muslim India*, Headley further emphasized:

> I would not, *could* not, as a loyal supporter of the Crown and Constitution, put my hand to the plough with such confidence if I had the slightest fear that the increase in the number of those who profess Islam, which I hope to live to see, would be likely to make the subjects of His Majesty anything but loyal and law-abiding. The true believer puts his love for God, and his earnest desire to benefit every one of God's creatures, so far above any thoughts of worldly advancement that he is the last person in the world to advocate rebellion against properly constituted authority.[16]

Headley continued to dispel rumours about his Muslim loyalties into early 1914, and he successfully shifted the discussion back to one about the faith and practice of Islam as he understood it. He gave many press interviews, wrote short articles for newspapers and magazines, and contributed more poems and essays to the *Islamic Review and Muslim India*. Headley did not pretend that he was 'a religious teacher'; indeed, he later opined that 'I labour under the great disadvantage of not being an Arabic scholar'.[17] His initial articles for *Muslim India/Islamic Review* were generally succinct, well written and sincere. However, the content quickly became repetitive as Headley emphasized again and again that, although Islam and Christianity were 'sister faiths', Christianity had been corrupted by 'dogma' and 'sacerdotalism', while Islam remained 'simple', 'tolerant' and free from 'priestcraft'. Headley argued that he did 'not wish to *attack* any religious belief of Christianity', but rather, he blamed the church and denounced its clergy for effecting changes that he believed had led to dogmatic teaching, corruption, dispute and, ultimately, sectarianism.[18] Early issues of the *Islamic Review* also republished lengthy exchanges of letters between Headley and Christian adversaries, including the clergy.[19] Headley's thinking and arguments as set out in the pages of the *Islamic Review* were occasionally muddled and he sometimes deferred to more learned people to help him untangle complicated theological issues.[20] That said, the exchanges (and Headley remained an inveterate writer of letters to the end of his life) generally helped him to refine his thoughts and better understand Islam, especially in relation to Christianity.

A Western Awakening to Islam

Headley's lasting tangible legacy is arguably his extensive body of writing on Islam and Muslims in the West. Much of this appeared in *Muslim India/Islamic*

Review: he contributed around eighty articles, poems and letters to that journal, and at least one piece every year between 1913 and 1930. Some of his articles were republished as occasional papers for the Woking Muslim Mission's 'Tract Series', to help promote Islam and educate new or potential Muslims.[21] He also went on to write three books about Islam, ostensibly based on material originally published in *Muslim India/Islamic Review*. Since he was not a scholar of any religion or religions, they are by no means consistent in quality. Indeed, the first book he published after his conversion, *A Western Awakening to Islam*, does not do him justice as a writer about Islam, but it nevertheless sealed his position as a Western Muslim leader. His longest book on the subject, it mainly comprises expanded essays written for *Muslim India* in late 1913 and early 1914. Headley hastily assembled and edited the book during 1914, and it was published by Phillips of London less than a year after his public conversion to Islam.

Headley's *A Western Awakening to Islam* is a defence and uncritical explanation of Islam intended for a Western, English-speaking audience. It includes two convoluted chapters about women and Islam ('Wherever women are alluded to in the Qur-an the greatest respect and reverence is enjoined')[22] and, oddly, transcripts of two lectures written not by Headley but by Kamal-ud-Din. The most original parts of the book focus on the *practice* of Islam in 'the West' (he was primarily thinking about Europe and especially Britain), and include Headley's attempt to make a case for what he called the 'Westernization' of Islamic practice so that the ordinary working man or woman could understand and adhere to fundamental Islamic rituals and prohibitions. Headley explained that, to start with, Muslims had to correct misunderstandings about Islam prevalent in Western societies:

> [I]t will probably be advanced that Eastern ideas do not blend with Western ideas, and there can be no 'fusion', so to speak, and that to attempt to govern the nations of the West whilst an Eastern religion was recognised and influenced men's minds and actions would be quite incongruous and out of the question. Well, in reply, the writer wishes to point out that for nearly two thousand years every country in Europe has been governed under the religions of the East – *i.e.*, Jewish and Christian. [. . .] There is a great similarity between the characters of the [Abrahamic] leaders as anyone will find out on inquiring into Muhammad's life. Also a study of the Qur-an will reveal the fact that there is nothing antagonistic to previous revelations – Muhammad's instructions, as laid down in the Book, completely back up the Bible teachings, extending them to suit the requirement of the time.[23]

He continued:

> For years past one of my chief thoughts has been how can the Muslim faith be 'Westernised' so as to bring it into practical touch with the nations of Europe? Or, in other words, How can we Westerns apply ourselves so as to gain a better comprehension of what Islam really means?[24]

We have seen that Headley's thinking about Islam was strongly influenced by Kamal-ud-Din, who maintained that only a practical and flexible approach to Islam would guarantee its development and survival in the West. Dusé Mohamed Ali indicated in his memoirs that Kamal-ud-Din took this approach too far: Ali alleged that Headley told Kamal-ud-Din in 1913 that 'he liked bacon and eggs for breakfast and was partial to his whiskey'. According to Ali, Kamal-ud-Din advised Headley that 'it did not matter for the present if he had a little bacon for breakfast and took a nip or two of whiskey, provided he did those things in moderation'.[25] Whether or not Ali exaggerated the story, in his *A Western Awakening to Islam*, Headley argued:

> The difficulties which seem to exist are chiefly those due to ceremonials. The actual spirit of Islam is far above all these minor points, but it must not be forgotten that the true disciple of the Holy Prophet love to follow – to the letter, as far as worldly circumstances permit – all the injunctions laid down so explicitly in the Qur-an. Hard and fast rules under one set of conditions may be fairly easy to obey, *e.g.*, Eastern conditions many centuries ago – but they may be extremely difficult to follow up in the West at the present day. We may appreciate the piety and zeal of the modern Muslim but we must also consider the great hindrances there are to, say, a modern European businessman, *who is entirely in accord with Islamic teaching in the spirit and truth of our grand religion*, who finds himself unable to conform rigidly to the letter of the law of Islam.[26]

He believed:

> There are many good and sincere Muslims who hold that their belief in the Divine Unity of God, and their acceptance of the messages delivered to the world by the inspired Prophet, and their obedience to the commandments from on High, are sufficient to entitle them to be enrolled in the ranks of the Faithful. Their failure to conform to what may be called the minor conventions is not sufficient to exclude them from the great Brotherhood of Islam. The Unity of God, duty to neighbours, and belief in the Angels and Prophets of God, together with an acceptance of the Qur-an, as revealed to the Holy Prophet Muhammad, constitute the essentials of Islam: outward forms and ceremonies cannot be held – as the Christians say their baptisms are – to be generally *necessary* to salvation.

I would say that, in presenting Islam to Westerns, stress should only be laid on the vital points, and that the main injunctions of the Qur-an – which is, of course, the Gospel of Islam – should be adhered to.²⁷

Despite the international attention his conversion had garnered just a year earlier, Headley's book received few reviews. The *Near East* newspaper in London believed that Headley had 'gone far towards the removal of many false impressions and beliefs which are current in Europe regarding the teaching of Muhammad', but that he had not produced 'a single paragraph of sufficient strength to give the professing Christian "pause to think" concerning the validity of his own views'.²⁸ Writing in the *Moslem World* from India, the missionary H. U. Weitbrecht Stanton was highly critical:

> In dealing with inquirers, only the vital points of Islam are to be insisted on: outward forms and ceremonies are not necessary. Presumably one may belong to the Woking flock without Arabic prayers or purification or fasting [. . .]. It will be interesting to see the form of Islam that will develop on the foundations of faith without the pillars of duty. [. . .] The character of Mohammed is defended, and the character of Christ belittled, on lines familiar to the newer school of Moslem apologists. [. . .] This ignorance as to facts and crudity of presentation disfigure the whole book.²⁹

Many Muslims in India also read *A Western Awakening to Islam* with interest. Notably, in 1915 the Salafi leader and scholar Vakkom Moulavi (1873–1932) proposed to translate the book into his native language, Malayalam. Moulavi also encouraged the Indian nationalist writer, K. Ramakrishna Pillai (1878–1916), to produce a translation. Unfortunately, Pillai died in 1916 and Moulavi did not complete the task before his death in 1932.³⁰ More than a decade after its publication in Britain, parts of Headley's book were, however, translated into Ottoman Turkish by a publisher in Istanbul.³¹

Practising Islam

Headley continued to reflect on the 'Westernization' of Islam as he tentatively practised his new religion, and he frequently returned to the subject. In late spring 1914, he wrote an article called 'Self-control' for *Islamic Review and Muslim India*:

> It seems to me that the man who commits many sins and indiscretions, is in a finer and nobler position than the hermit, provided of course that he is genuinely sorry for his transgressions, and never fails to ask for God's guidance back to

the straight path. [. . .] The harder the struggle the greater the victory, and the choicest rewards can hardly fail to come to those who conquer evil inclinations and attain to the blessing of self-control.[32]

He continued to advise other converts that 'I must strongly recommend a policy of advancing the *essentials* of our religion before touching on minor matters of detail'.[33] This was easier said than done and, almost fifteen years later, Headley similarly argued:

> [I]t is hard to conceive how our blessed Faith can make satisfactory advance in, say, England, without certain insignificant modifications of forms or ceremonies to suit the new environment. In other words, it must be recognized that different conditions and temperaments require special handling.[34]

Headley was not afraid to share and discuss his own experience of practising the five 'pillars' of Islam and negotiating Islamic prohibitions. Having proclaimed the *shahada* (the first pillar) in 1913, Headley initially adhered to the second pillar, *salat* or worship/ritual prayer, by joining other Muslims for *salat al-jum'a* at Caxton Hall. In the absence of a mosque in London, the WMM hired Lindsay Hall (known as the 'London Muslim Prayer House') in Notting Hill Gate in early 1914, which Headley also visited regularly for *salat al-jum'a*, and where he recited *du'a* (prayer of supplication) in English.[35] Kamal-ud-Din and other WMM missionaries encouraged Muslims to pray five times daily and produced numerous guidebooks to help them.[36] However, as Headley argued at Woking at the end of 1914,

> It is quite impossible for the busy city man to pray Muslim fashion five times a day at the appointed times: the opportunities for prostration and conventional devotion cannot be found, but the man himself may be none the less a true follower of the Holy Prophet.[37]

Headley, instead, advised that a Muslim who 'sends up a silent prayer that the Holy Spirit of Allah may *in all things direct and rule his heart* [will] surely [. . .] be accepted Above, even though he has not had the opportunity of humbly placing his forehead on the ground'. After all, 'There are many things in this world which are highly *desirable* but not *essential*'.[38] A year later he argued in *Islamic Review and Muslim India* that 'Whether lying down, standing up, sitting down, kneeling, or prostrating, with our foreheads touching the ground, we are equally acceptable to God, if our hearts are beating with a true love for Him.'[39] However, he now also recommended that public worship in a mosque should be 'supplemented by household or family prayers, where the household can be readily assembled, say, twice a day. Private prayer and praise should never really cease, but should come from the heart quite naturally, and without effort of the will being called into action.'⁴⁰

Early on, Headley recognized the vital religious, social and symbolic function of the mosque, and he therefore spearheaded a new campaign to construct a purpose-built mosque in London. In early 1916, he approached the British government through the India Office to build a mosque in memory of Muslim soldiers who had 'died fighting for the Empire', to serve London's expanding Muslim population.⁴¹ On reading Headley's proposal, Sir Arthur Hirtzel (1870–1937), secretary of the Political Department in the India Office, declared privately that 'I am <u>dead</u> against it – on grounds both of policy and religion'.⁴² While Hirtzel thought it acceptable to build a mosque in India if it was approved by the government of that country, 'that a Christian Gov[ernmen]t s[houl]d be a party to erecting one in a Christian country is to me unthinkable'. He concluded that 'Lord Headley is presumably not a person of any consequence.'⁴³ Headley complained directly to Hirtzel's boss, the secretary of state for India, Austen Chamberlain (1863–1937), that he had been informed by the India Office that 'such a course would be unprecedented and cause dissatisfaction to other religionists' in India.⁴⁴ However, he explained,

> As a Muslim myself I am well acquainted with these people and understand their warm hearted and affectionate natures and I therefore realize fully how <u>intensely</u> such a mark of goodwill and gratitude on our part w[oul]d be appreciated by them. [. . .] His Majesty's Muslim subjects outnumber those in any other denomination <u>and yet they have no suitable place of worship in London</u>.⁴⁵

The India Office stood by its decision and, consequently, Headley's campaign stalled during the First World War.

Headley did not publicly discuss the third pillar of Islam, *zakat* or almsgiving, nor was it properly addressed in *The Islamic Review* during his lifetime.⁴⁶ He was also reticent about discussing the fourth pillar, *sawm* or fasting/abstinence during Ramadan, the month in which the Qur'an was revealed, but was reported to have observed the fast on several occasions in the 1920s. Headley was a stalwart at the Muslim festivals of '*Id al-Fitr* (the feast that marks the end of Ramadan) and '*Id al-Adha*, which were always celebrated at Woking. By the 1920s, more than 600 Muslims regularly travelled to Woking for the '*Id*s (Muslim religious festivals). Few, however, could afford the money or time to undertake the Hajj, the fifth and final pillar of Islam.⁴⁷ When Kamal-ud-Din decided to make the Hajj on his way back to India in autumn 1914, Headley proposed to join him.

Preparations were made and berths booked on a steamship from London to Arabia. However, as Headley later explained, following the outbreak of war in August 1914, 'I abandoned my intended journey, as I did not feel justified in leaving a family of four young children at such a critical period.'[48]

With regards to Headley's immediate family, it was noted in the previous chapter that Kamal-ud-Din was concerned in October 1913 that Headley intended to bring his children and other relatives into Islam. After he converted, Headley realized that this might not be practical. He wrote in early 1914:

> I have four sons, all of whom will follow me in the faith; but supposing, for the sake of argument, that one of them so far forgot himself as to change his religion, should I wish him ill? No, I should be deeply aggrieved, but should not alter in my fatherly affection one iota. I should argue with him, and do my very best to show him the folly of deserting Islam, but if my arguments failed I should deal just as kindly with him as before.[49]

In fact, like most contemporary British Muslim converts living outside of established immigrant Muslim communities, Headley's children were not raised as Muslims, nor did any of them later convert to Islam.[50] In 1926, Headley admitted:

> It was not till my own sons began to grow up that I realized fully the unwisdom of trying to force young people into any form of religious belief against their will. They should *from the very earliest* date be taught the Commandments, certain prayers of a non-sectarian character, such as the Muslims' Fatiah [al-Fatiha, the first *sura* or chapter of the Qur'an which is recited during daily prayers] and Christian Lord's Prayer, and they should be strongly imbued with the *necessity of doing to others as they would wish others to do to them*. Nothing else is needed for their salvation, and I always say I shall love my children just the same whatever faith they embrace *provided they are quite honest in their conviction that it is the best*.[51]

Besides the 'pillars' of Islam, Headley discussed and wrote about many Islamic prohibitions and cultural issues, from alcohol to polygamy and the position of women in Islam. Dusé Mohamed Ali's account discussed earlier suggested that Headley was partial to whisky and, as is related later, he continued to drink alcohol after his conversion to Islam. This was not untypical of Headley's British Muslim convert contemporaries. While many were staunchly teetotal, others were partial to a glass of wine or drank alcohol without compunction.[52] The issue of alcohol highlights the diversity of belief and practice among the WMM convert community as its members negotiated being Muslim in a non-Muslim Western country. Headley was, however, conscious of his personal shortcomings. Though he drank alcohol, he said in 1914 that 'most of the crime and trouble in civilised countries of the world can be traced directly or indirectly to the abuse of alcoholic stimulants, [and] we should indeed welcome the advent of a creed which enjoins temperance and abstinence from intoxicants'. He was, however, anxious that potential new converts should not be dissuaded from Islam as a consequence: 'Drinking in moderation is the custom of the country, and it is too much to expect any sudden change.'[53] We do not know what other British Muslims, including converts, thought about Headley's advice in these years because, as was noted in the introduction to this book, their views and opinions were seldom recorded in *The Islamic Review* or elsewhere. However, as is related in Chapter 8, Headley faced criticism from Muslims overseas in the mid-1920s and then from Muslims *within* Britain as British Islam was affected primarily by disputes about the Ahmadiyya.

The British press was fascinated with the topic of polygamy and Islam, but also the wider issue of the position of women in Islam and Muslim societies. Headley, like Kamal-ud-Din and many others connected with the WMM, regularly addressed these issues in both the *Islamic Review* and mainstream publications. In 1914, Headley wrote an article that aimed to counter the many 'misrepresentations' prevalent in British society about Muslim women 'as degraded in this world, and hopeless as far as the next world is concerned'.[54] He rather naively stated:

> I have lived a long time in the East, and number among my friends many Mahomedans for whom I have a great affection and respect, and never heard of a Mahomedan ill-treating his wife. There may be such cases amongst the very low classes, but I have never come across them myself. The true Muslim regards his women folk as sacred, and he spares no pains to make them happy and comfortable.[55]

He then argued again that 'Wherever women are alluded to in the Koran the greatest respect and reverence is enjoined', and he supported his claim with quotations from an English translation of the Qur'an.[56] Later that year, he described polygamy as the 'one Eastern custom which has often been pushed to the front and used as a sort of bugbear to frighten women'.[57] While noting that Muhammad *placed restrictions on existing polygamy by limiting the number of wives a man might have*', Headley sidestepped the situation in some Muslim-majority countries and regions, and, instead, reassured his compatriots:

> As a matter of fact, very few Mahomedans have more than one wife, and no one in this country need be in the least alarmed lest the introduction of Islam

as a recognised religion should alter the laws of a Western nation. It is not my intention to go into the question of whether polygamy might or might not be beneficial in certain instances, though it would be easy enough to show that its establishment might give rise to an enormous amount of extra trouble and annoyance in this country.⁵⁸

Headley's position on Islam and women, and women in Muslim societies, changed little over the next twenty years.

The Woking Muslim Mission and British Muslim Society

It was not by any means easy for Headley or other Muslim converts to practise Islam in early-twentieth-century Britain. In a broadly Christian Western nation, Muslim religious, social and political groups and networks were crucial to affirm and nurture Muslim identities as well as to sustain the practice of Islam. With its close proximity to London, a mosque, missionaries and financial support from the Ahmadiyyat, the WMM soon became *the* centre of Islam for many Muslims in Britain, and, in particular, converts. From its inception, the WMM was also closely aligned with the well-established Central Islamic Society, which drew Muslims from across the globe to its lively meetings in London. The CIS and WMM co-hosted events and there was much mingling between its respective members, many of whom were affiliated to both groups. To give just one of scores of examples, Headley gave a lecture about 'Sister Religions' for the CIS at a London restaurant in autumn 1916. The lecture was chaired by Kamal-ud-Din, who was visiting England from India. The *Islamic Review* reported that the venue was 'overcrowded', with the audience comprising Muslims from across Britain, as well as Europe, Asia and Africa. They included stalwarts of Islam in Britain such as Abbas Ali Baig and Dusé Mohamed Ali, the Indian lawyer and former joint secretary of the Pan-Islamic Society, Shaykh Mushir Hussain Kidwai (1878–1937) and the influential Indian barrister and scholar Abdullah Yusuf Ali (1872–1953); Muslims temporarily in London like Prince Abdul Karim of the Indian princely state of Sachin, Khaja Ismail of the Indian princely state of Hyderabad and Syed Ehsan El Bakry of Egypt; the prominent Turcophile writer Marmaduke Pickthall, who converted to Islam in 1917; and British Muslim converts such as Quilliam/Léon.⁵⁹

Kamal-ud-Din had left England in spring 1914 to make the annual Hajj, before returning to India. He put Woking in the capable hands of Maulana Sadr-ud-Din (1881–1981), who became imam and co-editor (with Kamal-ud-Din) of the *Islamic*

Review until he too went back to India in 1917, and was replaced by a succession of equally competent imams including Kamal-ud-Din's elder son Khwaja Nazir Ahmad (1897–1970) and Maulana Abdul Majid (1896–1977).[60] Plagued by illhealth, Kamal-ud-Din only occasionally returned to England, but remained at the helm of the *Islamic Review* and was very closely involved in the day-to-day activities of the WMM. Consequently, the WMM continued to grow, attracting born Muslims and many new converts to prayer meetings and *'Id*s in Woking and London.

Although there were peaks and troughs in terms of the annual number of new converts between the formation of the WMM in 1913/14 and its demise in the 1950s, a total of some 2,000 predominantly white Britons converted over that 40-year period.[61] In 1914, Khalid Sheldrake of the CIS and WMM wrote excitedly in *Islamic Review and Muslim India* that, thanks to Kamal-ud-Din, 'Now we [Muslims] have a permanent programme and address; we can look forward to the future with full confidence.' Sheldrake added that, when he had converted to Islam a decade earlier, 'I was alone – isolated; but you can now mix with brethren and realize the perfect harmony that reigns in Islam.'[62]

The community that Sheldrake heralded was sufficiently strong by the summer of 1914, so Kamal-ud-Din and Headley decided to establish a British Muslim Society (BMS). The BMS initially comprised around thirty members, including Quilliam/Léon. Headley was elected BMS president, a role he retained for life; Parkinson was honorary vice-president and Sheldrake the honorary secretary. The BMS gained new members rapidly, primarily Britons who converted through the WMM, but also Muslims from all over the world who temporarily or permanently lived in, mainly, England. As Headley explained in 1914, the Society's principal aims were 'to show all those we come in contact with that our religion is not exactly antagonistic or hostile to what is now called Christianity', and 'to give most careful attention to the very difficult and delicate task of showing that a universal adoption of the Faith by Western nations is *possible* without seriously interfering with the manners and customs of the West or the spirit of the teachings we find in the Quran'.[63] He again reminded Muslims to focus on the 'essentials' of their faith and concluded that 'There is so much adaptability in Islam that we may hope to surmount any difficulties which may arise.'[64]

Muslim loyalty and politics during the First World War

The foundation of the BMS was an important event in the history of Islam in Britain, but its formation and early years were overshadowed by the First World War and its impact on the *umma*. Under Headley's leadership, the BMS would constantly grapple with questions of Muslim identity and politics as well as the theology and practice of Islam in the West. But, as Europe edged towards war in the summer of 1914, Headley's immediate concern, shared by Kamal-ud-Din, was to reassure the country and government that Muslims within Britain and across its vast Empire were loyal to the Crown. Writing in early July, after the assassination of Archduke Franz Ferdinand (1863-1914), which precipitated the First World War, Headley said:

> We need the whole-hearted support of all loyal subjects, of whatever creed or nationality, and we can safely look upon our Mahomedan fellow-subjects as ranged on the side of Law and Order. As a religious body they are by far the largest in the British Empire. The Quran expressly forbids all sedition and rebellion and insists that there shall be no violence or compulsion in religion.[65]

A month later, on 4 August 1914, Britain declared war on Germany. Headley convened a BMS meeting at Woking, which carried a motion to

> offer our whole-hearted congratulations to our Eastern brethren going to the front, and to express our delight to find that our co-religionists in Islam are fighting on the side of honour, truth, and justice, and are thus carrying into effect the principles of Islam as inculcated by the Holy Prophet Mohammed.[66]

The motion was widely reported in the British press and a copy sent to the Foreign Office, which was duly acknowledged and forwarded to British embassies in Cairo and Constantinople (Istanbul).[67]

Speaking at Woking less than a week after war was declared, Kamal-ud-Din solemnly predicted that 'The mad dogs of war are unchained, and the world unfortunately is going to see the most disastrous havoc ever wrought upon humanity since its creation.'[68] There was much debate in the pages of *Islamic Review and Muslim India* and *The Islamic Review* about the ethics of Britain's declaration of war, with contributors including Kamal-ud-Din and John Yehya-en-Nasr Parkinson concluding that it was justified in terms of self-defence and self-preservation.[69] Headley, however, had no qualms at all about war with Germany:

> The Germans might be of any religion or no religion, it mattered not what they were; [by invading Belgium] they were breaking a solemn and binding written promise, and placing a deep and never-to-be-forgotten insult on the British Empire by asking us to be a party to a great international crime.[70]

He wrote:

> We are now putting together a glorious page of history, which countless generations of our descendants will read with honest and grateful pride. To feel

that one actually belongs to a grand Empire, whose sons are freely pouring out their life blood in defence of honour and for the love of truth and justice, and to think that one is permitted to live and see heroism and devotion on such a magnificent scale, thrills the soul to its very innermost recesses.[71]

As is related later, Headley's position hardened and was publicly expressed through a national anti-German campaign. As early as October 1914, he warned Muslims:

There are, unfortunately, a few misguided and unpatriotic persons, calling themselves British, who would willingly hand over our glorious Empire to the modern Huns; but they are only traitors, and their seditious utterances are drowned in universal acclamations coming from [. . .] the Empire.[72]

Parkinson may well have been referring to Headley when, in the November 1914 issue of *Islamic Review*, he wrote:

I personally, as a friend put it in a letter to me a few days ago, have no desire to tear the heart out of the [German] Kaiser or to dip him in boiling oil. I have very little appreciation of him as a man, and I detest the system of militarism of which he is the head. [. . .] I refuse to condemn the good men of a country or race on account of the bad; to do so would be to condemn the whole of humanity.[73]

The loyalties of many British Muslims were tested when Ottoman Turkey entered the war on the side of Germany at the end of October 1914. In early November, the German and Ottoman governments publicly issued a series of *fatwa*s (juridical opinions) by the Shaykh al-Islam, the highest religious authority of the Ottoman Empire, which called for jihad (a struggle in the path of God that could include arms) against the Allied Powers, including Britain. British Muslims rightly feared for the future of not only the Ottoman Empire but also the Ottoman Turks as leaders of the *umma*. Quilliam/Léon, for example, had long argued that Sunni Muslims were duty-bound to pledge their allegiance to the Caliph, who was also the Sultan of the Ottoman Empire. Quilliam was personally devoted to the former Sultan, Abd al-Hamid II, regularly visited his court in Turkey and, in the 1890s, claimed that the Sultan had personally given him the honorary title Shaykh al-Islam of the British Isles. After the Sultan was deposed by the Young Turks in 1909, Quilliam found the centre of his allegiance evaporate and, thereafter as 'Henri Léon', he took a more relaxed position, but one that still argued for the validity of Sublime Porte (the Ottoman government) in Constantinople as the seat of the Caliph.[74]

Marmaduke Pickthall disagreed with Quilliam/Léon about the merits of the deposed Sultan-Caliph and what he called the latter's 'military despotism', but he welcomed the Young Turks as reformers of the *umma*.[75] Indeed, though they argued about who should lead it, most British Muslims in 1914 considered Turkey to be at the spiritual and political centre of contemporary Islam, and they also recognized that this view was shared by many millions of Muslims in India and elsewhere. For Parkinson, writing at the end of 1914, 'the people of Turkey are allied to the Muslims of the [British] Empire by a common bond and a common creed'.[76] Although he urged Muslims to support Britain and its Empire, he expressed 'regret' that his country was at war with Ottoman Turkey and 'a people with whom I sympathise on many national ideals and to whom I was bound by the aforesaid bonds'.[77]

Headley had some sympathy with Parkinson's sentiments, but not with either Quilliam/Léon or Pickthall's politics. He was also less concerned about war with Turkey, which he made clear in his inaugural BMS presidential address at Woking in December 1914. For Headley,

> It is a most lamentable fact that Turkey has been for a long time past giving a too willing ear to the advice of an unscrupulous so-called Christian country. We now see how greatly this is likely to damage Turkey as a Power in Europe, and Asia too: and we feel deeply for our Muslim brethren who are under the rule of his Majesty the Sultan, but have no sympathy whatever with the ill-judged Young Turk movement, or with German machinations. [. . .] It is deeply to be regretted that Muslims should have to be opposed to Muslims, but it cannot be helped.[78]

When, the next month, a newspaper suggested that Headley 'might find his adherence to Mohammedanism clash with his duty as a patriot during the war', he replied firmly that 'the Sultan of Turkey has no power whatever over Moslems outside the Turkish dominions, and [. . .] all over the world Moslems owe allegiance to their own particular sovereigns'.[79]

Headley also explicitly warned BMS members in December 1914 that 'we must not enter into the field of politics, for if we do so we shall be certain to come to grief, either through internal dissentions or through collision with some outside authority'.[80] He cautioned that 'to succeed we must not allow any political considerations to in any way interfere with the propagation of Islam'.[81] As an example, he spoke about an approach he had received in 1913 to become a vice-president of the Anglo-Ottoman Society (AOS). The AOS was one of two pro-Ottoman organizations established in Britain in 1913. Headley said that he had also been asked to become a member of the other organization, which was called The Ottoman Society:

> Now, whatever my sympathies may have been at that time, I felt strongly that by joining either of those societies I should have identified myself irrevocably with one particular country which might not always be in complete harmony with other countries of the same religion.[82]

He felt vindicated in declining membership of both societies: 'I am now perfectly free – had I joined my position would have now become very anomalous, for I should have been a member of two Turkish societies whilst Turkey is at war with my country.'[83] Notably, just a few weeks before Headley's speech, Quilliam/Léon had resigned his position as a vice-president of the AOS to demonstrate his loyalty to Britain and opposition to the Young Turks.[84]

However, Quilliam/Léon could not resist joining Pickthall, Sheldrake, Mushir Hussain Kidwai and other Muslims to publicly defend the integrity of Ottoman Empire and the Caliphate during the war. By contrast, Headley did not sign the many resolutions calling upon the British government to guarantee the preservation of the Ottoman Empire and, later, Turkish independence, and he was remarkably absent from the scores of public meetings and demonstrations organized by the AOS, CIS and other pro-Turkish and pan-Islamic groups.[85] While Headley shared pan-Islamic concerns about the deterioration of the *umma* and of the Ottoman Empire in particular, and he admired pan-Islamic ideals of internationalism and religious solidarity, he was not comfortable with being part of a united Islamic front against European domination, especially as it undermined British rule in India and elsewhere.

Towards the end of the war, Pickthall and others also lobbied the government to abandon proposals for the establishment of a Jewish state in Palestine.[86] A letter of protest was sent to the Foreign Secretary in 1918, signed by Kamal-ud-Din for the WMM, Kidwai for the CIS and Mirza Hashim Ispahani for the All-India Muslim League. Headley did not sign the letter in his own right or for the BMS.[87]

With so many 'Woking' Muslims and associates connected to the pro-Turkish campaign, the mosque and WMM were put under police surveillance during the First World War. Kidwai and Pickthall were singled out by the authorities as 'agitators' of the 'Woking mosque gang'.[88] Headley, by contrast, was not mentioned in any of the surveillance reports. With many contacts in government departments – not least the Foreign, India and Colonial Offices – Headley perhaps knew about or suspected the surveillance and he kept his distance from the overtly political activities of other Muslims. Instead, he aligned himself with what he considered to be a truly patriotic campaign group.

The Anti-German Union

In February 1915, Headley chose 'Toleration' as the theme for an address to Muslims at Woking mosque, and he expanded on this for an essay published in *Islamic Review and Muslim India* a couple of months later. He emphasized that 'Charity and toleration are very nearly akin to one another; indeed, a charitable person in the fullest sense must be able to tolerate those who hold different views, say, in the matter of religion, and should not condemn them because they see things from a different standpoint.'[89]

There was a certain irony that Headley did not extend his call for tolerance beyond religion during the war years. Headley not only shared the anti-German views of many Britons at this time but, soon after the war began, he also called publicly for the internment of the approximately 65,000 Germans living in Britain as a precaution against spying, and he pleaded to the British government to terminate its employment contracts with 'persons of German descent, and those who are married to German wives'.[90] He made no distinction between those Germans who retained their nationality and those who were naturalized subjects. Headley also wrote in the national press about the 'uneasy' feeling across the country that the Austrian-born Prince Louis of Battenberg (1854–1921) was British First Sea Lord at the outbreak of war. In a letter published in *The Globe* on 28 October 1914, the very day that Prince Louis resigned his position, Headley argued that 'it is impossible for the man in the street to believe that [Prince Louis] has not some feelings of sympathy with his Vaterland.'[91]

Headley was one of the founding vice-presidents of a new national movement, the Anti-German Union (AGU, which was renamed the British Empire Union, BEU, in 1916). The AGU was launched in spring 1915 with a high-profile press campaign and a xenophobic and inflammatory slogan: 'Britain for the British'.[92] The AGU aimed to 'unite British-born men and women, without respect to party, class, or creed':

(1) To foster national ideals and to keep alive the patriotic spirit of the people.
(2) To defend British freedom, rights and privileges from German invasion.
(3) To defend British industry and British labour against German competition.

(4) To fight against German influences in our social, financial and industrial and political life.⁹³

Panikos Panayi has shown that the AGU/BEU secured 'a substantial national membership' (approximately 10,000 by the end of the war) and argues that it was not a fringe group because it had many establishment figures among its senior members.⁹⁴ It was certainly not, however, beyond reproach: for example, writing in 1915/16, the prominent British pacifist (and later Labour MP), E. D. Morel (1873–1924), claimed that the AGU and its parallel organization, the Anti-German League, 'take advantage of the mental dislocation which war brings and, coldly, with calculation, trade upon hate and fear, orienting these elements towards ends frankly material. They are the exploiters of hate, analogous to the ghouls of the battlefield.'⁹⁵ Headley was singled out in the press as 'the most uncompromising of Anti-Germans'.⁹⁶ It was widely reported that, in the first year of the war, he devoted himself to 'amateur detective work in hunting down German spies and dangerous aliens, spending night after night disguised as a labouring man in the worst districts of London and Liverpool'.⁹⁷

In October 1915, German Zeppelin raids on London killed more than seventy civilians. Headley spoke at public meetings across England and wrote letters to the press calling on the British government to adopt 'the hostage system, started and used by the Germans themselves'.⁹⁸ He suggested that 2,000 prominent Germans should be held, and advocated 'the putting to death of ten for every English woman killed by a bomb from a Zeppelin airship'.⁹⁹ He also demanded that the British government step up its internment of all 'enemy aliens'.¹⁰⁰ In a sign of his rising public profile, at the end of 1915 Headley was selected by Douglas B. W. Sladen (1856–1947), editor of the annual *Who's Who* directory, to appear in a new edition intended to be 'far more exacting as to the importance of the persons whom it will include'.¹⁰¹ Headley was thrilled to be selected, and asked Sladen to add to his biography that 'I advocated the employment of the Hostage System as far back as 19 Oct. 1914 but [. . .] our Ministers were too polite to think of such a measure.'¹⁰²

In November 1915, Headley introduced his anti-German views to the pages of *Islamic Review and Muslim India*. He denounced the Zeppelin raids and the recent 'revolting cold-blooded' execution of the British nurse Edith Cavell (1865–1915) by a German firing squad in Brussels.¹⁰³ Headley attempted to defend his views, specifically the taking of German hostages, from a Muslim perspective:

> When we contrast the chivalry and delicacy of feeling shown on all occasions by the Holy Prophet of Islam with the coarse brutality and fiendish cruelty of

certain modern Christians and the pretended followers of the great Martin Luther, how our heart-strings contract and how our cheeks burn with shame! We of the West who are, alas! so nearly connected by blood ties with this race of Huns, this race of unspeakable savages which is struggling to gain for the devil the mastery of the world! Ah! Muhammad, most noble exemplar of truth and love, herald of the sacred will of Allah, how we now long for you as our champion of all that is good and just.[104]

Headley took the stage at anti-German rallies organized by the AGU/BEU in Hyde Park in 1915. There he found an unlikely ally in the leading Suffragette, Christabel Pankhurst (1880–1958), who strongly supported the war against Germany and also advocated the internment of 'enemy aliens'. Headley subsequently wrote for Pankhurst's newspaper *The Suffragette* and its successor, *Britannia*, the official organ of the Women's Social and Political Union. He fulminated against cotton exports from the British Empire to Germany and again castigated the British government for, in his view, its lax internment policy.[105] He repeated this at AGU/BEU meetings across England in 1916, and also attacked pacifists, socialists and trade unions as threats to the war effort.[106] For Headley, 'The only place for people who, with deliberate intent to diminish the country's turnout of munitions, spread poisonous doctrines amongst the workmen, is prison, and after the war trial for treason or treason felony'.[107] At Warwick in July 1916, Headley was introduced to an audience of mainly AGU/BEU members by their honorary secretary, Sir Spencer Pocklington Maryon-Wilson (1859–1944), who was the brother-in-law of Headley's sister, Stephanie. Headley stoked fears prevalent in the country that an

> 'unseen hand' had been at work for a long time, and had made the difficulty of approaching the alien a very great one. There was no comparison between the spy and the traitor. One had a sort of admiration for a spy, because he was working for his country and was risking his life. With the traitor it was different. He was against his country, and a more despicable creature could not be imagined.[108]

Fall from grace

Headley was riding high on the attention that he received for his anti-German activity when he suffered another sudden fall from grace. Ignoring his own advice to fellow Muslims of practising 'self-control', he was arrested on a charge of drunk and disorderly behaviour outside London Waterloo railway station on the evening of 31 October 1916. The incident was, to Headley's embarrassment, reported widely in the press and seems to have not only abruptly ended his association with the BEU but also triggered a bout of depression and probable breakdown in the winter of 1916/17.[109]

Full details about the incident came out when Headley appeared in court in December 1916. The police constable who had arrested the defendant recalled that Headley 'was under the influence of drink' and had 'placed his arm around the neck of a woman' who was standing nearby on the street. Headley was cautioned by the policeman but 'replied abusively' and was alleged to have bragged that 'I am a very powerful man. I am Lord Headley'.[110] He was taken to the local police station, 'resisting violently'.[111] The *Times* reported that 'in the witness-box the defendant declined to take the oath [on the Bible], stating that he would swear "on his honour and as a peer of the realm"'.[112] Headley explained that, when he reached Waterloo station,

> he was excessively sleepy, as he had been at work all the previous night on intricate calculations. He recollected saying his prayers at the police station in accordance with the Mussulman practice. He had a dim recollection of telling the inspector, when he pushed him and tried to awaken him, to 'Go to hell', or something of that sort, or perhaps even stronger. [. . .] He denied that he put his arm round the neck of a woman. He might have so far forgotten himself as to try and kiss a pretty young woman – he had done it before – but not an old frump.[113]

Headley insisted:

> He could swear on his honour as a gentleman, an Englishman, and a peer of the realm that he had drunk no more than two bottles of stout and a cup of coffee afterwards. He had been brought up on stout and should continue to drink it, but his religion forbade excess.[114]

Amid public ridicule (the evangelical *The East and the West* journal felt 'aggrieved' that Headley had 'fallen below the standard of his adopted religion'),[115] Headley appealed against his conviction. He told the judge that he could not have been drunk because, as a Muslim, he was forbidden wine:

> Whether it was due to sleepiness, which was mistaken for drunkenness, I cannot say, but I do say this, that if I had not another moment to live I had nothing on that day except that stout. If I drank in one day the whole of my week's consumption of drink I should not be drunk.[116]

He added that he was 'rather a breezy person' and called a doctor, a nurse and other witnesses 'to testify to his breezy temperament, and it was stated that he was of a pronounced Celtic disposition – an Irishman'.[117] The court rejected

Headley's appeal and he settled a fine of ten shillings. He later suggested that he might have been targeted by the police: 'possibly my position as an English Muslim offered irresistible attractions for assault from below.'[118]

Although he remained defiant, the public humiliation of the court case (Headley was, after all, a magistrate in Ireland) and failed appeal increased Headley's anxieties and he sank into a deep depression. As he emerged from illness in spring 1917, Headley submitted to *Islamic Review and Muslim India* a short prayer and poem with the candid title 'On Recovery from Severe Mental and Physical Illness'. Echoing verses published in *Thoughts for the Future* in 1913 (see Chapter 3), Headley's new prayer concluded thus:

> I have been as one in the mire of sorrow, but my soul has been maintained throughout by Thy loving support and has never been lost in the oblivion of evil. Preserve me from future errors and sickness, and so direct my footsteps that they wander not from the path Thou hast chosen for me.[119]

The same issue of *Islamic Review* included a sobering message from Professor Nathan/Nur-ud-Din Stephen (1846–1928) of Liverpool – a close friend of Quilliam/Léon who had frequently lectured at the LMI, contributed to *The Crescent* newspaper, and was described by John Yehya-en-Nasr Parkinson in 1917 as 'the grand old man of the Muslims in the West'.[120] Stephen emphasized that 'the use of intoxicants is forbidden',

> but I have known some professing Muslims who are not above reproach in this matter. This is not the fault of the faith, but of the fact that they set themselves and their own desires above the teachings of Al-Quran, placing self and self-indulgence before even fidelity to their faith.[121]

Headley continued to write for *Islamic Review and Muslim India*, but never again with the same frequency as he had done up to 1917. In November of that year, he wrote an article called 'Warnings', a rambling and difficult read as he struggled to understand and explain his conviction for drunkenness, suggesting at one point that he had inherited certain 'weaknesses' from his ancestors.[122] He proposed that his experience over the past few months 'will, however, afford some gratification to my Muslim brethren as well as to myself, for we can surely feel that after all the trials, anxieties, and losses suffered there is now presented so good an opportunity for explanations which may be of service to others'.[123] On reflection, he felt that 'Strong drink is not by any means a *necessity*, and when one thinks of the awful consequences which may result from one indiscretion, any slight inconvenience arising from abstinence sinks into insignificance.'[124] He concluded,

> even the moderate use of alcohol in certain conditions and on certain temperaments may easily lead to disaster, and I have therefore given up the use of all stimulants – even my favourite beer – in the hope of setting a good example and avoiding giving offence to anyone.[125]

Headley followed up 'Warnings' with another wayward article entitled 'Good and Bad Impulses' in which he tried to understand 'the question of "mind poisons" and the extremely insidious character of their assaults and their far-reaching ultimate effects'.[126] The latter article was cited as evidence of Headley's 'eccentricity' (a common epithet for Western converts to Islam, past and present)[127] in his short profile for the *Oxford Dictionary of National Biography*, published in 2004.[128] The content of Headley's article is, indeed, eccentric, but it is not by any means representative of his literary efforts and was written at a time when he was clearly not of sound mind. Headley was, in fact, grappling to understand the causes of the depression that affected him throughout his life. He strangely suggested that 'it would be of interest to ascertain the effect of alcohol on the "conscientious objectors," for it seems that, administered medicinally of course, it might have the effect of stimulating the patriotic feelings which appear to be dormant for the time being.'[129] He had also been 'credibly informed' that 'the excessive drinking of strong tea, which has been allowed to stew on the hob day after day, has a most deleterious effect, and that in certain parts of the United Kingdom a great deal of the insanity amongst women is directly attributable to such tea drinking'.[130] More concretely, he declared that he was not only 'in favour of total abstinence' but that he had 'forbidden the use of all alcoholic drinks in my house'.[131] Alas, again there was no editorial comment about Headley's article or any response from other Muslims published in subsequent issues of *Islamic Review and Muslim India*.

6

Muslim peer of the realm
The first decade, II: 1918–23

Continuing the story of Headley's first decade as a Muslim, this chapter begins by examining two aspects of his personal life: his second marriage in 1921 and bankruptcy in 1922. It then considers the complicated politics of the post-war peace negotiations as they affected the future of the Ottoman Empire, Turkey and the Caliphate. It outlines Headley's tentative involvement in post-war politics on behalf of British Muslims up to the peace settlement with Turkey in 1923, which was followed by the abolition of the historic Ottoman Caliphate.

Barbara Baynton

As Headley recovered from the humiliation of prosecution and illness in 1917/18, his personal life took an unexpected turn. Early in the First World War he had met the Australian writer Barbara Baynton (1857–1929) and their relationship developed as the conflict drew to a close. Baynton had made her name as the author of *Bush Stories* (1902), a collection of tales based on her experience of the harsh and haunting but beautiful Australian outback, where her Irish parents had emigrated in the 1840s. After the death of her second husband in 1904, Baynton invested wisely in stocks and spent much time in England, where she successfully established herself in London society.[1]

During the First World War, Baynton famously opened her London and Essex houses to servicemen, especially Australians. Fearful of German infiltration in Britain, she joined British Empire Union rallies in Hyde Park and found herself on the speakers' platform with Headley. Just two years apart in age, Headley and Baynton had much in common, including their Irish heritage, London society friends and conservative politics. Convinced that women were unsuited to wield authority, Baynton actively campaigned against women's suffrage.[2] She would also have empathized with Headley's precarious mental health, having herself been hospitalized with 'exhaustion' on at least one occasion.[3]

It is unclear what Baynton thought about Headley's conversion to Islam, but she was not alarmed by it. Baynton's biographer, Penne Hackforth-Jones, has noted that she was interested in 'Arab and Muslim cultures' and that she had 'an instinctive love of splendor and pageantry, all things mystic and powerful. The might of religious experience expressed in cultures other than her own impressed her: it matched her own depth of feeling.'[4] Baynton did not convert to Islam or any other religion but, profoundly shaken by the war, she explored other faiths, primarily Hinduism, 'to find some answer to the spectre of death that seemed to ride with her'.[5] Hackforth-Jones concludes that Baynton's 'search into other religions never replaced the early disillusionment of her days in the small chapels of outback Australia. She believed in prayer but seemed to turn to it only in a crisis, and she used religion as a prop to her existence, to inspire or dramatize, not as a substructure.'[6]

By the time Headley met Baynton, she was a successful businesswoman who, according to a contemporary, had acquired 'the taste for high life'.[7] She was also a formidable character who, after the war, adopted 'a perceptively higher tone of querulous disapproval with the world around her'.[8] Headley evidently welcomed the challenge of this forthright woman. He was also attracted by her wealth at a time when he was struggling to maintain his family (including four growing sons and two dependent sisters) and estates in England and Ireland; and Baynton, in turn, was seduced by his aristocratic background and had romantic ideas about joining the Anglo-Irish landed gentry.[9]

After their first meeting, Headley took Baynton to tea with his sons, and he continued to visit her when she was in London. The details of their relationship derive largely from Baynton's account, often filtered through the reminiscences of her direct descendants and friends. However, it is clear that the friendship soon became a courtship – even though, as far as the public was concerned, Headley was happily married to Teresa. (Notably, when Headley's religious conversion was announced in 1913, several newspapers published an old portrait photograph of Headley with Teresa.)[10] It was surely no coincidence that, in summer 1919, Headley publicly advocated reform of the restrictive English and Welsh divorce laws, which made divorce expensive and extremely difficult to obtain, especially for women.[11]

The campaign for divorce law reform continued throughout the interwar years, with new legislation that made divorce easier to access introduced in

1923 and 1937. Headley, however, had long since stepped back from the public campaign, perhaps because, in October 1919, his personal circumstances changed suddenly when Teresa died in Dublin.[12]

Baynton visited her daughter and new grandchild in Australia for most of 1920, while Headley was busy working as a director of a transport company and revising his first book, *Boxing* (1889), for an expanded edition.[13] When Baynton returned to London at the end of 1920, she was engaged to Headley. The engagement was kept short and secret from all but close family. The press did not receive news of the engagement for a couple of months. On hearing about Headley's engagement, a provincial newspaper noted 'how completely of late the Peerage has flung aside conventionality in the matter of wooing. It used to be considered absolutely essential for the marriage of a Peer to be solemnly discussed for months by the whole family until every shred of romance was worn off the "happy event".'[14] Headley, however, obtained a special licence to marry Baynton at Marylebone registry office on the morning of Friday, 11 February 1921.

The wedding was so hastily arranged that Baynton's family were not present and, according to the press, she 'surprised a few friends by asking them whether they would like to come along and see her married'.[15] Headley walked to the registry office with his elder son and best man, Paddy. Baynton, bejewelled with a huge black opal and carrying a bunch of mimosa ('a memento of her association with the Australian troops'), arrived in a closed carriage with a female companion.[16] After a private ceremony, the couple posed outside the registry office for society photographers (Figure 8), and then went to Claridge's hotel for lunch.

With the wedding reception over, Headley and his bride left London for Birmingham, where he was scheduled to give a speech in his capacity as the recently elected president of the Society of Engineers for 1921. Rather ominously, the new Lady Headley told the press that 'the rest of the honeymoon would be spent in that unromantic centre'.[17] Headley too spoke to local reporters as soon as he arrived at Birmingham. The *Birmingham Daily Gazette* noted that 'He finds no difficulty in reconciling a registry office wedding to the tenets of Islam. The principles of Mohammedanism in their relation to marriage were, he said, quite simple, and did not affect the validity of any marriage even if the bride was not of the same faith.'[18] Headley used his Birmingham speech to promote an ambitious money-making scheme. He had recently become spokesperson for a consortium of businessmen that planned to tunnel under Goodwin Sands, a huge sandbank on the south coast of England which had created thousands of shipwrecks over

Figure 8 The wedding of Lord Headley and Barbara Baynton, London, February 1921. Second left to right: Headley's elder son, the Honourable Rowland 'Paddy' Allanson-Winn; Barbara, Lady Headley; Lord Headley; Headley's sister, the Honourable Helen Allanson-Winn.

Source: Courtesy of Janet Webb / The Estate of Fifth Lord Headley.

many centuries. Headley expected to find buried treasure and 'undreamt of wealth' hidden in its stricken ships.[19] He continued to promote the scheme into 1922 but it seems to have fizzled out thereafter.[20]

The wedding made the front pages of many newspapers in Britain and Baynton's native Australia, with reporters quick to hint at the convenience of the marriage for Headley in particular. Headlines included 'Irish Peer Marries Wealthy Widow' and 'Peer's Hyde Park Romance. Marries Rich Bride'.[21] Indeed, the marriage seemed set to stabilize Headley's precarious finances. According to Headley, Barbara promised to provide him with an annual allowance of £1,000. He retained Ivy Lodge in St Margarets, but moved into his wife's impressive house at Connaught Square, just north of Hyde Park. Headley also expected Barbara to fund the Glenbeigh estate, which was heavily mortgaged and in need of extensive and costly repairs. He was, however, very quickly disappointed as circumstances beyond his control put a strain on his marriage.

Between 1919 and 1921, British forces sought to repel a guerrilla war waged by Republicans in Ireland. County Kerry experienced some of the bloodiest and most protracted conflicts during what became known as the Irish War of Independence.[22] In summer 1921, Headley's Aghadoe House and grounds (which had not sold in 1913) were 'damaged by wandering bandits' and 'Winn's Folly', Glenbeigh Towers and Castle, were looted and later destroyed by fire.[23] Barbara's dream of life in a country house in rural Ireland was shattered, as were her husband's finances. Furious, she left Headley in London and returned to Australia in 1921. She told a reporter in Perth that Glenbeigh "'supplied the family rent-roll'" and that, as a consequence of the fire, "'Lord Headley is now land poor, and his two unmarried sisters have lost almost everything'".[24] In her view, all was not well in post-war Britain:

> 'The motto, England, Home and Beauty, which has endured for centuries, looks as if it will have to be replaced,' remarked Lady Headley. 'England has a war legacy, a new rich and a new poor, and the new rich have everything. Indeed, a man by the name of Mr. Smith seems to own all England. The new poor are mainly England's aristocrats. They pride themselves on their self-denial. They have cut down their staffs 50 per cent, and their stately homes are beginning to show the neglect. In many cases these stately homes have been sold to the new rich, as well as most of the heirlooms. Mr. Smith cannot buy the family traditions, but the grass grows just as well and the places in his hands have all the pre-war upkeep.'[25]

Her third husband was clearly not a 'Mr Smith' and, as Barbara's biographer has noted, Lord and Lady Headley soon 'found it difficult to meet on any terms'.[26]

It is unclear whether or not Headley immediately returned to Ivy Lodge but, as early as August 1921, Headley apparently confided to friends that his marriage was a failure.[27] Barbara returned to England a few months later and there seems to have been some kind of reconciliation, if only for appearances' sake, as Lord and Lady Headley hosted a formal reception for the visiting Premier of Western Australia at Connaught Square in May 1922.[28]

Remarkably, the drama of Headley's relationship was fictionalized by the writer Martin à Beckett Boyd (or Martin Boyd, 1893–1972) in his novel *Brangane: A Memoir*, which was published under the pseudonym Martin Mills in 1926.[29] A fellow Australian, Boyd had lived with Barbara at her London home during the war, and he returned to live there at the time of her marriage to Headley in 1921. The central character of Boyd's novel, the wealthy 'Brangane Winter', was a thinly disguised Barbara Baynton; the impoverished Catholic aristocrat 'Lord

Pulborough' was Lord Headley; and Pulborough's country estate, 'Walton Park', was Aghadoe House or Glenbeigh Towers.

Mills' Brangane and Pulborough meet at a dinner party. Finding themselves alone together at the end of the evening, Brangane and Pulborough chat and, within twenty minutes, the latter makes a proposal of marriage. An inveterate social climber, Brangane looks up Pulborough in a guide to the British aristocracy and ponders the social advantages of his proposal:

> 'A countess', thought Brangane, as, clad in sables, she walked through Lansdowne Passage. 'Only a grade below Angela, above Dorothea and Daphne. Born a Winter, married to an earl, surely there will be some solidity in that – if I get him.'[30]

Just like Headley and Barbara, Pulborough and Brangane are quickly married, dispense with a proper honeymoon and settle in Brangane's elegant townhouse. However, 'The strain of living for nearly a month with a comparative stranger, and the effort of being continuously even-tempered were beginning to tell on Brangane'.[31] She finds Pulborough untidy and is irritated by his pipe-smoking:

> She was sitting over the drawing-room fire when her husband entered. The very sight of him irritated her. Brangane liked people with vigour, people like Daphne with whom one could exchange hearty blows. Pulborough gave her no sense of resistance. He had something of the quality of a mouse. Even his hair and his eyebrows and his eyes were mouse-coloured. He was like a very tall mouse.
>
> 'Do you mind if I smoke?' he asked.
>
> 'Yes I do,' said Brangane sharply.
>
> He gave a slight bow and sat down.
>
> 'The servants complain that you are untidy,' she said, opening the attack.
>
> 'Are you accustomed to accepting the judgement of your servants?' he asked quietly.
>
> 'I am not accustomed to an untidy house.'
>
> 'Naturally.' He spoke with no trace of feeling.
>
> Brangane's annoyance increased. Why couldn't the man answer back instead of sitting there, so indifferent and self-possessed?
>
> 'By the way, I'd be glad if you would use the other bathroom,' she added, hoping to sting him to retort.
>
> 'Certainly', said Lord Pulborough, and opened an evening paper.
>
> Brangane sat staring at the back of his paper. She was hot with anger, and then the obsession of 'reality' attacked her. Was it because he was real that he could retain his dignity, even after having been bought by a woman for his title? She could bear his presence no longer and left the room.[32]

Bankruptcy

Boyd unashamedly borrowed heavily from fact in his account of the breakdown of Lord and Lady Pulborough's marriage. In real-life 1922, Headley was declared bankrupt. He told his creditors that his wife had paid him only a quarter of the annual allowance she had promised when they married, and that he 'had reason to fear that the lady's views of her financial position were exaggerated'.[33] Mills describes Pulborough as having 'imagined and calculated' that, as Brangane's husband, he would 'once more become a peer of some importance':

> By the marriage contract Brangane was to allow him two thousand a year, or a fifth of her income should it fall below eight thousand pounds. In return he settled on her Walton Park. [. . .] Brangane, however, discovering that Walton was in bad repair and heavily mortgaged refused to pay him a penny. Lord Pulborough's sole advantage from the marriage was release from maintaining his bed-sitting-room in Jermyn Street, and even this was not lasting.[34]
>
> Lord Pulborough stood up and blew his nose.
>   'It is time, perhaps, that I put my case,' he said mildly. 'It is a little crude, but necessary, to point out that persons of our age who marry are not actuated entirely by romantic motives, but largely by the hope of some advantage. You have repudiated the marriage settlement which was to bring me the advantage I had contemplated. Your house is comfortable, if slightly bizarre, but you appear to resent my presence here. I think, perhaps, it was a mistake, your marrying into the middle class.'
>   'Middle class? What do you mean?' Brangane asked contemptuously.[35]

Pulborough leaves Brangane and returns to his bed-sit in Jermyn Street. Headley left Barbara and returned to Ivy Lodge in 1922.

While Headley scorned his wife for failing to pay him the allowance he desperately needed, he attributed the dire state of his affairs primarily to the policies of the British government and, specifically, the ruling coalition led by David Lloyd George (1863–1945). Headley claimed that his assets were valued at no lower than £22,000, and his liabilities were approximately £6,500; he was, therefore, 'abundantly solvent' but, since the government was unable to administer Ireland, its laws had 'become inoperative' and he was unable to realize his property and claim rent arrears from his tenants in County Kerry.[36] Headley argued in a series of public statements and letters to the press that he was 'not responsible in any way for his present position' and that 'We loyalists have, for the sake of the lives of those dependent upon us, forsaken our homes, suffered destruction of property, and in many other ways become impoverished'.[37] There was, he continued, 'something Gilbertian in a solvent man being forced into bankruptcy through the inability of the Courts to protect him'; it was 'an intolerable and disgraceful state of affairs'.[38]

Headley also filed claims against the British government for damage to his Irish property and, when Aghadoe House was again looted and destroyed by fire in October 1922 (just two months before the formal establishment of the Irish Free State), he made a claim against the Provisional Government of Ireland.[39] The legal wrangling for compensation dragged on in the courts for several years, but Headley's personal campaign against his bankruptcy was successful and, at the end of 1922, the judge reviewing the case gave him an unconditional discharge on the basis that Headley 'had honestly believed his bad position was only temporary' and because 'it was not proved that he was guilty of any of the wrongs within the meaning of the [Bankruptcy] Act as reported by the Official Receiver'.[40] Headley eventually received modest compensation from the Irish Free State government, and Aghadoe House was rebuilt to its original plan.[41] However, he could not afford to restore Glenbeigh Towers and Castle, which are today a picturesque ruin.

Post-war politics and the end of the Ottoman Empire

As was highlighted in the previous chapter, Headley largely steered clear of the pro-Turkish movement during the First World War, and, instead, devoted himself to the anti-German campaign until he was side-tracked by his arrest for being drunk, which was followed by a period of poor health. Once the war was over, however, Headley found himself sucked into the politics of the Caliphate, the Ottoman Empire and the wider Middle East.[42] This was somewhat inevitable as the capitulation of the Ottoman Turks in 1918 signalled the end of the war in the Middle East and the end of the Ottoman Empire. Few in Britain had much sympathy for the 'treacherous Turks', not least the prime minister, Lloyd George, who early on in the war had declared: 'I am glad that the Turk is to be called to a final account for his long record of infamy against humanity.'[43] The British government and its Allies had drawn up secret agreements in preparation for the dismemberment of what remained of the Ottoman Empire. Worryingly for many British Muslims after the Armistice, some politicians and senior civil servants in Britain had come to believe that the Arabs had a better claim to speak for Islam than the Turks, and it followed that the Caliphate should relocate to the Arabian Peninsula.⁴⁴ The future of Turkey and the position of the Turkish Caliphate was hotly debated in the British press, with many editors arguing that the millions of Muslims in the British Empire – especially India – were not duty-bound to pledge their allegiance to the Ottoman Caliphate.⁴⁵

Consequently, in 1918, the wartime campaign led by Mushir Hussain Kidwai, Marmaduke Pickthall and others to defend and secure the Ottoman Empire swiftly refocused with the aim of achieving a just peace settlement for Turkey and maintaining the historic Sunni Caliphate in that country. The situation became more desperate when, in May 1919, Greece launched a campaign to secure territorial gains at the expense of the defeated Ottoman Empire. The subsequent Greco-Turkish War dragged on until autumn 1922.

Any doubts Headley might have had about participating in the pro-Turkish movement were to some extent assuaged by the close involvement of, in Headley's eyes, the most respectable of Muslims such as Syed Ameer Ali and the Aga Khan (Sir Sultan Mahomed Shah, 1877–1957). It was a sign of the importance of the issue for Muslims regardless of background that these Muslim leaders and many other Muslims and non-Muslims stood together in defence of Turkey and the Caliphate in that country: Ameer Ali was Shi'i, the Aga Khan was leader of the Isma'ili Shi'a,⁴⁶ and Headley was a Sunni closely connected to the Lahori Ahmadiyya. They defended Turkey through an assortment of organizations including the Central Islamic Society, Woking Muslim Mission, Anglo-Ottoman Society, as well as a new and more radical group led by Kidwai, Pickthall and Mirza Hashim Ispahani initially called the Islamic Defence League but later renamed the Islamic Information Bureau.⁴⁷ The destruction of Turkey was not, they all argued, compatible with British imperial interests or conducive to the peaceful development of Asia and especially India, whose Muslims were, contrary to press speculation, loyal to the Caliphate in Turkey and had sacrificed so much for the Allied war effort.⁴⁸

These Muslims sent countless petitions and protest letters to the British government as the Allies debated the future of Turkey in 1919/20, some of which Headley signed. For example, in July 1919, Headley was signatory to an important 'memorial' sent to the prime minister, which expressed 'regret and disappointment at the reply by the Peace Conference to the Turkish delegate's plea for equitable treatment'.⁴⁹ Headley and his co-signatories argued that the Allies were blinkered by their many grievances against Turkey, and consequently did not consider the factors which were truly responsible for holding that country back from the path of development and progress: namely, persistent Russian encroachment on Turkish territories, Austrian ambitions and rising nationalism in the Balkans, and foreign intervention that thwarted internal reform. In short, Headley appeared to agree with other British Muslims that Turkey was the victim of the intrigues of its Christian neighbours.[50]

In September 1919, an All-India Muslim Conference held at Lucknow declared 17 October a 'Day of Prayer for the Sultan-Caliph'. The day was marked by a special meeting at the WMM's 'Muslim Prayer House' in Notting Hill Gate chaired by Pickthall, who had been temporary imam for the WMM during most of 1919.[51] Despite his earlier misgivings about the conduct of Abd al-Hamid II, Pickthall defended the incumbent Sultan-Caliph as 'our Khalifah and Imam, the revered successor of Thy final Prophet'. Pickthall decried 'an attempt upon the part of Christian Powers to introduce into Islam the irreligious, anti-human error of aggressive nationalism – that poison which has wrecked the life of half the world – an evil which Islam abolished for all true believers'.[52] He also condemned 'attempts by Christians to persuade us Muslims that the Khilafat should be hereditary in the Prophet's family, and [the claim] that, because our holy Prophet was an Arab, his successor always ought to be an Arab too'.[53]

Headley, however, remained quiet on the issue of the future of the Caliphate. His prime concern in 1919 was that the removal of the Caliphate from Turkey would provoke widespread unrest in India. Headley believed in and defended the British Empire, especially in India, as a benign act of civilization, offering law and education, good government and protection for minorities such as Muslims from the Hindu majority. The political situation in India was already unstable in the context of Mahatma Gandhi's (1869–1948) civil disobedience campaign and then the Amritsar massacre (or Jallianwalah Bagh) occurred when, in April 1919, British Indian Army troops fired at a peaceful gathering. The massacre was condemned internationally and ushered in the Non-Cooperation Movement (1920–22) against British rule in India. At the end of 1919, a new Government of India Act expanded the participation of Indians in government and provided dual administration in the major provinces. Headley did not want what throughout his life had been called the Eastern Question to undermine Muslim loyalty to the British Empire or further upset the fragile balance of power in India. Many Muslims in Britain shared this view and it was publicly echoed by leaders such as Ameer Ali and the Aga Khan. However, politicians and the press were less sympathetic. For example, the London *Times* wrote in December 1919 that the Turkish settlement depended on 'larger considerations than the sentimental and rather modern interest [of Indian Muslims] in the rulers of Turkey'.[54]

Headley was, however, instinctively cautious when a delegation of the Indian Khilafat Movement (1919–24) visited England in March 1920 to make its case for restoring the Ottoman Caliphate.⁵⁵ The delegation was led by one of the founders of the Khilafat Movement, Mohamed Ali (also known as Muhammad Ali Jauhar).⁵⁶ Ali and his colleagues accepted an invitation to visit Woking mosque at the end of March 1920 and the occasion was caught on movie camera by British Pathé. The newsreel shows Ali and his associates leaving the mosque accompanied by, amongst others, Abdullah Quilliam/Léon.⁵⁷ Headley does not feature in the Pathé film because he did not attend the meeting. In the absence of the BMS president, Quilliam/Léon led the special open-air meeting at the mosque, during which Ali delivered an impassioned speech. His words caused a minor sensation when they were reported in the newspapers the following day. According to the *Daily Herald*, Ali

> said he had got to say new and startling things with regard to the situation in Turkey. Let the power which attempted to crush Islam beware, for it would be crushed itself to-morrow – and by the truth. The Moslems demanded the truth, and would not be crushed by Mr. Lloyd George or any show of arms. [. . .] If England fought the Turk the Moslems would fight for the Turk.⁵⁸

Mohamed Ali's Woking speech was the subject of a question in the House of Commons and some parliamentarians demanded that the government take action against him.⁵⁹ However, the British government did not pursue the matter and Ali and other members of the delegation returned to Woking in June and August 1920 to celebrate *'Id al-Fitr* and *'Id al-Adha*, respectively. Again, Headley was conspicuous by his absence from both events, likely because he simply did not want to be associated with the controversial Khilafat Movement. Notably, moderate Muslims such as Ameer Ali and the Aga Khan, who initially supported the Khilafat Movement, quickly distanced themselves from it as its leaders became more radical.⁶⁰

The fate of Turkey was sealed by the Treaty of Sèvres in August 1920, when it was formally decided that the Ottoman Empire should be partitioned. After the Treaty was signed, Kamal-ud-Din said that he had (like Headley) avoided politics in recent years but that disquiet amongst Muslims in India about the Treaty, and its impact on the Caliphate and the integrity of Turkey impelled him to intervene: 'in what way the weakening of Turkish rule can be expected to contribute to the solidarity of the British Empire is a mystery. [. . .] You cannot rule India quietly without making friends with the Turk.'⁶¹ Kamal-ud-Din's position seems to have given Headley the impetus to selectively re-engage with the issue. In March 1921, with the Greco-Turkish War in full swing, he formally received at Woking a Turkish Nationalist delegation which was in England to discuss the claims of Turkey in relation to the Treaty of Sèvres.[62] A year later, at a BMS meeting, Headley stated:

> It is our earnest prayer that, in the light of [. . .] the difficulties that to-day are harassing Islam and the Khilafat may be speedily dispersed, in the only manner acceptable to Muslims of every race; and that the integrity of the Turkish Empire, with the authority of H.I.M. the Sultan as Khalif and Guardian of the Holy Places, may be fully re-established and maintained. We pray that it may not yet be too late to undo much of the mischief that has been wrought by the blunders of the past few years, and are one with, as we honestly believe, the vast majority of our countrymen, in resenting the misguided action of Great Britain (in whose Empire Muslims outnumber Christians) in lending support – moral or otherwise – to Greece against Islam, when bare justice – apart from policy – forbids it.[63]

It soon became apparent that the British government and its Allies had come around to the idea of an independent Turkey. In September 1922, Headley presided at a BMS meeting in London which passed a resolution protesting against the Greco-Turkish War, and requested that the British government 'renew friendly relations with the Muslim [sic] Empire and leave the Khilafat affairs solely in the hands of the Muslims'.[64]

Headley's rather selective involvement in the politics of Turkey was further evidenced in relation to reports about the massacre, or what has been widely recognized in recent years as a genocide, of Armenians by the Ottoman government during and immediately after the First World War. Like Pickthall and other Turcophiles, Headley defended the Turks when allegations of the systematic deportation and extermination of its Armenian Christian subjects in the eastern provinces of the Ottoman Empire resurfaced in the 1920s.[65] For Headley, the reports of massacres were evidence of biased reporting in the Christian West. When, in England, the Archbishop of Canterbury publicly expressed his anxiety about the safety of Christians in Turkey, Headley responded:

> One point I think we sometimes lose sight of is that whatever a man's religion may be, he should abide by the laws of the country in which he is domiciled.
>
> Some of the laws in many Eastern countries for the putting down of theft and other minor offences strike one as Draconian in their severity. Most of these laws would be unsuitable for England, but an Englishman should hold himself bound by them if he takes up his abode in such a country – whether he be a Christian, a Jew, or a Moslem. We now hear a great deal about the Turks and their cruelty to Christians in a particular portion of Asia Minor, but I cannot remember any similar outcry when religion was thrown to the winds in Russia.[66]

Headley conceded that 'it is probable that there have been outrages in Armenia', but he was 'perfectly satisfied that the number and extent of those outrages have been enormously exaggerated'. After all, 'Misrepresentations have been so frequent that an air of scepticism surrounds the whole matter. [. . .] My own experience is that the average Christian missionary is guided more by zeal to spread his views than by a strict regard to truth.'[67] As far as is known, Headley did not comment further on the issue.

When the Turkish Nationalists led by Mustafa Kemal (1881–1938; known as Atatürk from 1935 onwards) defeated Greece in autumn 1922, Britain and its Allies abandoned the Treaty of Sèvres and indicated their intention to negotiate a new treaty with the Turkish Nationalists. The victorious Turkish Nationalists had to urgently address the question of the Sultanate and Caliphate, which was a fundamental problem for their new nation. Asserting people's sovereignty, the Grand National Assembly of Turkey abolished the Sultanate on 1 November 1922. Muslims in Britain and across the world were divided on how the Caliphate could and should survive after its detachment from the Sultanate.[68] As a Sunni Muslim, Headley was keen for the preservation of the Caliphate, ideally in Turkey. By the time the Allies reached a settlement with Turkey at the Conference of Lausanne in 1923, he was philosophical about the destiny of the Caliphate and, unlike most of his British Muslim contemporaries, was open to the idea that it could be reinstated in Arabia (see Chapter 7). It came as little surprise to Headley and other British Muslims when, in 1924, the Grand National Assembly formally abolished the Caliphate.

Ten years as a Muslim

Headley's first decade as a Muslim began in 1913 with the euphoria of religious conversion, and was followed by his assumption of a leadership role in the British Muslim community and life in the public eye. It was, however, also punctuated with a series of low points, not least his conviction for drunk and disorderly behaviour and subsequent problems with his mental health and well-being, and a failed second marriage. The Ottoman–German alliance in 1914 made life difficult for British Muslims during the First World War and afterwards, as the fate of the Ottoman Empire and the Caliphate was decided. Headley remained a committed British Muslim leader throughout those years but personally distanced himself from the pro-Turkish politics of Pickthall, Quilliam/Léon and many other Muslims for fear that it would compromise his loyalty to Britain and the British Empire.

Headley's religious faith and confidence in Islam do not appear to have wavered and, despite the personal setbacks, he grew in stature as a Muslim leader during the decade after his conversion to Islam. In 1923, he marked the tenth anniversary of his religious conversion with the publication of a second collection of polemical essays entitled *The Three Great Prophets of the World: Moses, Jesus and Muhammad*.[69] In the slim book of six chapters, which went almost unnoticed by reviewers, Headley documented the 'improvement and reform' Muhammad had achieved in seventh-century Arabia.[70] He did not seek to address the subsequent schisms in Islam or the many problems in the contemporary world, especially the Middle East, that would deeply affect him and many other British Muslims in the later 1920s and 1930s.

Arabia, the birthplace of Muhammad and Islam, was on Headley's mind when his new book was published by the WMM in 1923. Exactly ten years after he had originally planned to visit Arabia, Headley proposed to Kamal-ud-Din that they make the Hajj together in the summer of 1923.

7

Pilgrimage to Mecca, 1923

As the fifth 'pillar' of Islam, the Hajj, or pilgrimage to Mecca, is a religious duty for Muslims who are in good health and can afford to travel to western Arabia. Very few Britons had legitimately made the Hajj before Headley visited Mecca as a guest of the King of the Hijaz, Hussein ibn Ali al-Hashimi (1853–1931), in 1923. This chapter therefore examines in detail Headley's Hajj. It narrates the sequence of Headley's Hajj and considers not only its spiritual impact on Headley as a Muslim but also its political significance, especially from the perspective of the British authorities because the 1923 Hajj coincided with the Conference of Lausanne, which decided Ottoman Turkey's post-war fate. It shows that while Headley attempted to refute the notion that there was any political significance to his making the Hajj, he became captivated by the personality of Hussein and, after leaving Arabia, publicly championed him as the potential successor of the Ottoman Caliph.

The lure of Mecca

A decade after he had first proposed to make the Hajj, Headley finally left London for Arabia on 22 June 1923. His destination, the city of Mecca, is located inland of the Red Sea, to the far west of what is now Saudi Arabia. Today, Saudi Arabia is known as an oil-rich state governed by an absolute monarchy, the House of Sa'ud. In 1923, Arabia had just gained independence from the Ottoman Empire, but was divided into four dominions and had not yet discovered oil. Mecca was in the geographical centre of the Kingdom of the Hijaz, which stretched down the Red Sea coast, from what today is Jordan in the north towards Yemen in the south. It is a city that has long fascinated Westerners as it was – and remains – closed to non-Muslims. Mecca is, after all, the most holy city in Islam. It is the birthplace of Muhammad, the direction towards which all Muslims pray, and therefore the metaphysical heart of Islam.

Few Britons had been to Mecca before Headley arrived there in 1923. The first to do so, in the seventeenth and eighteenth centuries, were British captives of Barbary pirates like Joseph Pitts (c.1663–1739), who had been forcibly converted to Islam and made the Hajj with his Algerian master in about 1680.[1] By the nineteenth century, a handful of travellers and explorers, most famously Sir Richard Francis Burton (1821–90) in 1853, masqueraded as Muslims to penetrate the mysterious, exotic Holy City. Burton went to great lengths to pass as a Muslim: he was apparently circumcised, had shaved his head, grown a beard with twirled mustachios, donned a muslin turban and successfully entered Mecca as 'Abdullah', a Pathan wanderer.[2]

At least three British Muslim converts also made the Hajj between the 1870s and early 1900s, probably using aliases or some form of disguise, and none of them published first-hand accounts of their experiences.[3] Some of the most prominent British Muslim converts of the period, including Lord Stanley of Alderley, Abdullah Quilliam/Léon and Marmaduke Pickthall, said that they hoped to make the Hajj but did not manage to do so. Stanley of Alderley came closest, visiting the port town of Jidda, the gateway to the Holy Cities, shortly after his conversion to Islam in 1859. Consequently, Headley was one of the first Britons, and possibly *the* first, to publicly make the Hajj without compulsion or subterfuge.

Headley planned to write a book about his Hajj, but this never appeared.[4] Instead, the core surviving record of his journey is a twelve-page transcript of a lecture entitled 'Pilgrimage to Mecca' that he delivered as a newly elected member of the Central Asian Society in London in October 1923. Headley's written account is unique, but little known today. It was soon afterwards eclipsed by lengthy travelogues written by British Muslim contemporaries such as Eldon Rutter (1894–c.1956) in 1928, Lady Evelyn Cobbold (1867–1963) in 1934 and her host in Jidda, Harry St John Bridger Philby (1885–1960) in 1943, as well as other European Muslim converts, notably the Austro-Hungarian-born Islamic scholar Muhammad Asad (1900–92) in 1954.[5]

Preparations

The political situation in the Hijaz was, as a consequence of the First World War, unstable when Headley prepared to leave London for Arabia in summer 1923. Hussein ibn Ali al-Hashimi had been the Amir (governor)[6] of Mecca since 1908. Backed by Britain and its Allies, Hussein famously declared the 'Arab Revolt' against the Turks and proclaimed unilateral independence from Ottoman sovereignty in June 1916. Soon afterwards, Hussein announced himself to be 'King of the Arab lands', but the Allies, anxious about the reaction of other Arab leaders, recognized him as 'King of the Hijaz'. By 1923, Hussein was struggling to control the warring tribes within his kingdom, some of whom looked to his bitter rival Ibn Sa'ud (1875–1953), the Sultan (ruler) of the Najd (the central region of Arabia), and he was furious about what he considered to be a betrayal by the British and French over their post-war carve-up of the Ottoman Empire, especially in Syria and Palestine. Hussein had always been cantankerous, but was now belligerent in his dealings with the British authorities.[7]

Headley needed Hussein's permission to enter Mecca, but he was not particularly concerned that the political wrangling between the King of the Hijaz and the British government would affect the decision. Indeed, in May 1923, Headley boldly wrote to the British consul in Jidda informing him that he intended to make the Hajj that summer.[8] Headley was confident of a warm welcome from the King of the Hijaz, not least because he said he was 'well acquainted' with Hussein's second son, Abdullah (1882–1951), the Amir of Transjordan. In fact, they had probably met only once, when Abdullah visited Woking mosque with Harry Philby during a trip to England in November 1922 (Figure 9).[9]

The British consul in Jidda, on the other hand, 'anticipated difficulties' in getting Hussein's permission 'owing to the extreme susceptibility of King Hussein to criticism (which is not lacking) of his alleged subservience to British influence'. The consul explained to Headley in June 1923: 'Than such subservience nothing could, in fact, be further from the truth, but His Majesty's unwillingness to give colour to the rumour that Mecca is now in British servitude has hitherto debarred English pilgrims from the Haj.'[10]

Headley was permitted to make the Hajj thanks to Kamal-ud-Din, who acted as intermediary and liaised directly with the Hashimite administration during the spring of 1923. Finally, Hussein sanctioned the pilgrimage on the condition that Headley be accompanied by Kamal-ud-Din, who had previously made the Hajj. Headley would have to act 'as if he is an Indian pilgrim' and, like Kamal-ud-Din, 'should dress himself in the Indian fashion'.[11] Shaykh Fu'ad al-Khatib, secretary of state for Foreign Affairs in Mecca, assured Kamal-ud-Din that the Hashimites did not question Headley's sincerity as a Muslim, nor did they object to his returning from the Hajj 'showing his nationality, if he likes', but he felt that 'the present political circumstances' necessitated caution. Al-Khatib stressed that the conditions set by Hussein were essential 'because you will see many newspapers saying that we sold the country to the English people and that the

Figure 9 Group photograph outside Woking mosque, November 1922. Formally seated, left to right: Abdullah Quilliam/Henri Léon (wearing a fez); Lord Headley; Khwaja Kamal-ud-Din; Abdullah, the Amir of Transjordan; unknown; James William/ Habeeb-Ullah Lovegrove. Headley's granddaughter, Vivienne, is standing in the centre of the back row.
Source: Courtesy of Janet Webb / The Estate of Fifth Lord Headley.

two sanctuaries [of Mecca and the holy city of Medina] became a colony and here are the English going there and coming back'.[12] The majority of the 100,000 Muslims who made the Hajj annually in the early 1920s were Indians,[13] and so Headley was expected to blend into the crowd.

Headley's real concern before leaving England for Arabia was that he might be accused by his own government, the press and others, of undertaking the Hajj for political reasons. He therefore went to great lengths before, during and after his Hajj to emphasize that, as a Muslim, his motivation was solely religious. Addressing the Central Asian Society in October 1923, Headley stated:

> I wish to emphasise the fact that before starting for the East I was careful to point out that there was nothing of a political nature in the undertaking. It was purely a religious move. I said at the time: 'My reverence and admiration for the Prophet is very great, and I am doing this in honour of his memory, and for that alone. There is no political significance whatsoever.'[14]

An anxious Headley nonetheless made an appointment to see Lancelot Oliphant, assistant secretary at the Foreign Office in London, before leaving England. Oliphant reported that Headley 'most earnestly hoped that his journey would in no way cause any embarrassment to His Majesty's Government'.[15]

Headley genuinely wanted to make the Hajj: he had been a Muslim for a decade and it was probably his last chance to make the physically arduous journey, one that was all the more demanding in 1923 because the Hajj occurred in the swelteringly hot month of July. Shaykh Fu'ad al-Khatib advised Kamal-ud-Din that 'it is with regret that it is quite hot this year. The best way to withstand it is to keep patient in it. For the Hajj comes in the hottest time.' He added that, due to the movement of the lunar Islamic calendar, the Hajj 'will come in a better climate only after about three years'.[16] Headley had turned sixty-eight in January 1923 and was not prepared to wait three more years. As he said in July, he 'did not suppose that he had many more years to live'.[17] Headley's doctor also made 'a few rather discouraging remarks' about his age and the likely impact of the Arabian heat on his health.[18] Headley admitted to Oliphant that, besides the climate, he was rather afraid of Bedouin raids on pilgrims in the Hijaz. Oliphant concluded: 'Though I had never seen Lord Headley before I had often heard of him and I own to having been very agreeably surprised by his apparently sensible outlook about his journey.'[19]

London to Port Said

Headley and Kamal-ud-Din were accompanied on the journey by Shaykh Abdul Mohye, who was sometime *mufti* (legal scholar) at Woking. As they left London Liverpool Street railway station on 22 June 1923, the pilgrims were given 'a hearty send-off' by 'a huge concourse of friends'.[20] They boarded the P&O steamer, SS *Macedonia*, in east London. The ship was bound for Port Said, and the pilgrims planned to visit Cairo and Alexandria before reaching Arabia. The journey to Egypt was uneventful, and they arrived at Port Said on 4 July. Yet, even before stepping on Egyptian soil, Headley was being watched and his every movement documented by British intelligence officers and consular officials. This was hardly surprising: besides the declining relationship between Britain and Hussein, the post-war fate of Turkey was being concluded at the Conference of Lausanne in the summer of 1923, and the political stability of Egypt, a former province of the Ottoman Empire, was fragile. After an Egyptian revolution in 1919, Britain had given Egypt limited independence and its new constitution was not promulgated until April 1923.

By the time Headley arrived at Port Said, Britain had recognized Egypt as a sovereign state, but still retained significant control of its communications and defence.[21] British officials therefore noted with some alarm that Headley, described in an intelligence report as 'the well-known English pervert to Islam', and Kamal-ud-Din as 'a particularly active Islamic propagandist', were to receive 'an official welcome' in Egypt from the influential nationalist Wafd (or 'Delegation') Party.[22] Copies of the classified surveillance report were sent from Cairo to the Secret Intelligence Service in London, as well as British consular offices in Turkey, Switzerland, Italy and Arabia. The British authorities were right to be anxious: Muslim leaders and politicians in Egypt did seek to capitalize on the arrival of the Woking pilgrims. Viscount Allenby (1861–1936), who had been Commander of the Egyptian Expeditionary Force during the Arab Revolt, was High Commissioner for Egypt and the Sudan in 1923. Allenby reported to the Foreign Secretary, Lord Curzon (1859–1925):

> Considerable publicity was given to [Headley's] visit to Egypt before his arrival here and both the Watanist and the Zaghlalist [sic; Wafd[23]] parties showed themselves anxious to act as his host during his stay in Egypt, hoping doubtless thereby to gain some local political advantage. Reception Committees were formed in Port Said, Alexandria and Cairo, and in each of these towns Lord Headley was the object of most marked attention, while the meetings held in his honour were remarkable for their enthusiasm.[24]

Another British surveillance report concluded that the reception committees were of 'an indeterminate political character, with Zaghlolist [sic] leanings. The programme is designed to evade [British] restrictions against political meetings as much as to welcome the visitors.'[25]

Headley was rather naïve if he truly believed before setting out for Arabia that his well-publicized trip would not cause a stir. The *Islamic Review* thought 'It was but natural that everywhere the news should have roused special interest'.[26] According to the *New York Times*, 'doubtless' Headley's 'social position also gives his hajj a semi-political complexion at a time when British prestige in the Mohammedan world is somewhat impaired.'[27] Before leaving England, Headley had been told to expect formal welcome committees of Muslims in Port Said, Cairo and Alexandria. As the pilgrims passed through the Strait of Messina in the Mediterranean, Headley received a 'long wireless message from Port Said', asking him 'to accept the hospitality of Egypt' and, 'a little farther on, another message reached the ship offering me the loan of a very fine yacht during my stay, so I was not altogether unprepared for what followed.' When the anchor was dropped off Port Said, 'we were boarded by about fifty of the delegates appointed by the three reception committees, and three addresses were read and replied to.'[28] The *Islamic Review* reported:

> Mr. Najib Bey Barada, Barrister-at-Law, in an eloquent speech, welcomed the guests to Egyptian shores, in the course of which he made reference to the Quranic verse: 'Behold the Sun and his light; and the Moon when she borrows light from him.' Khwaja Kamal-ud-Din, he observed, was the spiritual sun that had dawned on the horizon of the West. Lord Headley, having, like the moon, absorbed his light, was shedding his lustre amongst his countrymen.[29]

Headley, Kamal-ud-Din and Mohye climbed down from the SS *Macedonia* to board the first of 'over twenty gondolas', which formed an elegant convoy to the international port town.[30] The *Westminster Gazette* said that Headley was accorded 'a reception unprecedented in the case of a Britisher'.[31] Headley explained that he was given a tour of Port Said, 'in a long procession of carriages; beautiful bouquets of flowers were presented, and altogether one felt almost like a royal personage instead of an ordinary pilgrim'.[32] The party moved on to the Khalili mosque for late-afternoon prayers. Kamal-ud-Din accepted an invitation to give the sermon and Headley addressed the congregation. The long day ended with an evening party in honour of the guests which was 'attended by the cream of the society'.[33]

Cairo and Alexandria

Headley and his companions did not linger in Port Said. Within a day of arriving, they boarded a train to Cairo. The *Islamic Review* reported that they travelled in a saloon carriage organized and paid for by the Port Said reception committee, and were accompanied by their Cairo and Alexandria hosts:

> From Port Said right up to Cairo, the train passed no station, great or small, but found a large gathering already on the platform to show their affection for the guests. Everywhere people would shake hands with Lord Headley and reverentially kiss the Khwaja's hands. Young and old joined together in lusty cheers of 'Long live Lord Headley!' and 'Long live Khwaja Kamal-ud-Din!' At such of the stations where stoppage was not less than three or four minutes the guests would speak a few words, which Mr. Najib Bey interpreted into Arabic.[34]

At midday the train reached Cairo station, which was 'crowded to the last inch'.[35] Headley wrote that they were not only met by 'a large crowd inside the station on the arrival platform', but also 'a much larger one outside the big square; more bouquets were presented, and there was a beautiful motor-car waiting, lent by one of the leading ladies in Cairo for my use during our stay in the city'.[36] The pilgrims lodged not at one of the city's many luxurious hotels, but in a large house belonging to Syed Ihsan Bekri, a Sufi Shaykh who had lived in England and was very interested in the activities of the Woking Muslim Mission. Headley received at least one local journalist at Bekri's house, whose report appeared in Muhammad Rashid Rida's *al-Manar* magazine in July 1923:

> His Lordship received me with his great polite and nice manners. On his head he wore the Egyptian *tarbush* [*tarboosh*, a fez] put on his grey hair that reflected the redness [of the *tarboosh*] in a beautiful rosy colour because of his white face and moving blue eyes.[37]

Headley did not meet Rida in Egypt, but the latter wrote that 'anybody reading this report with a heart should feel that it was said out of truth and sincerity'.[38]

Headley did, however, meet many other Cairo notables, including the Grand Mufti of Egypt (the highest religious legal authority), and a representative of the King of the Hijaz. He also found time for some sightseeing. Headley visited al-Azhar mosque (dedicated in 972), and its university. Al-Azhar was firmly on the tourist trail by the 1920s; Baedeker's *Handbook* for Egypt, which Headley would have carried, warned that visitors 'should carefully abstain from any manifestation of amusement or contempt'.[39] Headley thought al-Azhar 'a most splendid institution': 'they take in and feed numbers of poor people who cannot afford to pay for their education; board, lodging, and instruction are given free of all cost.'[40]

The *Islamic Review* noted that an extravagant dinner for the Woking pilgrims was arranged by an uncle of Syed Ihsan Bekri: 'Five hundred people, representative of all stages and grades of society, assembled in the courtyard of a palatial building presented an impressive scene. The whole arrangement was a display of highly refined taste.' Before tea, the Cairo reception committee formally welcomed the pilgrims, and 'poems in praise of the Khwaja and Lord Headley were read'.[41] After tea, Headley and, then, Kamal-ud-Din addressed the audience in English, with simultaneous translations in Arabic made by members of the audience. Headley talked about the spread of Islam in Britain. As usual, he compared the 'brotherhood', 'reason' and 'simplicity' of Islam with the 'sectarianism' and 'dogma' of modern Christianity. His speech was reported in some detail in the Egyptian press. The *Egyptian Gazette* recorded that, for Headley, Islam was really pure Christianity as taught by the Prophet Jesus – he taught his beautiful lesson and then went away, all too early. The teachings of Moses, Christ and Mohammed were all in essence the same, varied a little according to the locality in which the prophets delivered their messages. They all taught our duty to God and our neighbour.[42]

Headley made similar speeches elsewhere in Cairo; *The Light* of Lahore reported that, at the mosque of al-Husayn, 'the throng' to hear Headley speak 'was so great that special police were summoned to control the congregation'.[43] The *Islamic Review* explained that 'So far as expression of thankfulness was concerned, as well as the spread of the Islamic Movement in England, Lord Headley did the part, and did it exceedingly well. Lectures on Islamic topics fell to the Khwaja to deliver.'[44]

After three days in Cairo, the pilgrims moved on to historic Alexandria. They stayed in 'a beautiful suite of rooms' at the grand Savoy Palace Hotel on the rue de la Porte-Rosette. Shortly after arriving, a reception was held for them in the great hall of the hotel, chaired by Prince Omar Toussoun (or Tusun, 1872–1944), who was 'a bright gem of the Egyptian Royalty' in the opinion of *The Islamic Review*.[45] Headley noted that 'A great many speeches were made, and the recitation of poetry elicited hearty applause from the large audience. The Prince speaks excellent English, and we chatted on various matters connected with the Muslim world.'[46] The pilgrims attended another large banquet in their honour, visited the local mosques to pray, saw the main sights of Alexandria, and attempted to meet the new King of Egypt and Sudan, Fuad I (1868–1936), but discovered that he was out of town.

Headley and Kamal-ud-Din met Viscount Allenby at the British Residency in Alexandria. The *Islamic Review* noted that the High Commissioner 'received them with all pleasure and courtesy and invited them to dinner, which they were unable to accept for pressure of engagements'.[47] Instead, they had, in the words of Headley, 'a very pleasant interview'.[48] Allenby's anxiety that Headley's presence in Egypt would increase pan-Islamic feeling seems to have been allayed. He reported to the Foreign Secretary in London that 'Lord Headley showed himself as an ardent Moslem and the speeches which he made revealed great devotion to the Mohammedan faith'.[49] He added that Headley

> was at pains to impress upon me that he was visiting me in my capacity as His Majesty's Representative in this country, and he repeated this statement to me in the presence of Khoja Kamel ad Din [*sic*] and two Egyptian members of the Alexandria Reception Committee, and added that he wished to assure me as

High Commissioner here that his visit had nothing to do with politics and was undertaken solely for religious purposes. He made similar remarks on more than one occasion in public at the various receptions which were held for him.[50]

Allenby conceded that Headley's 'utterances on more than one occasion caused considerable resentment' among local Christians, 'particularly the Syrian Catholic community'. However, he reported that Headley's visit 'passed off without incident'.[51] The pilgrims returned to Cairo on 10 July and, as Headley noted, 'busied ourselves with serious preparations for the pilgrimage to the Holy City'. Indeed, they 'made no long delay' in Cairo, and 'pushed on' to Suez.[52] On 11 July, they boarded the Khedivial Mail liner *Mansurah*, which would take them to the Arabian city of Jidda, the seaport of Mecca.

Jidda

Headley had a pleasant voyage through the Gulf of Suez and down the Red Sea. He was surprised to wake each day to a cool breeze wafting through the ship. It was not until he reached Jidda on 16 July that 'the wind fell, and we felt the heat considerably'. In a scene curiously reminiscent of his first voyage to India thirty years earlier (see Chapter 2), Headley witnessed 'a sad accident' outside the port:

> There were two ships close together, and the second engineer in one of them was handing something across to a man on the other ship when he slipped and fell, striking his head against a projection of the ship. Being stunned, he could not see the ropes which were immediately thrown to him, and just then, whilst he was completely insensible, the ships came together and he was smashed to pieces between them. His body was at once eaten up by the sharks, which are very plentiful in that neighbourhood.[53]

The Woking pilgrims' arrival was eagerly awaited in Jidda. On 5 July, the Hashimite newspaper *al-Qibla* (or *al-Kibla*) had reported that Kamal-ud-Din was expected to arrive within days 'with his distinguished pupil Headley'.[54] As soon as they landed in Jidda, Headley, Kamal-ud-Din and Mohye were formally received by Hussein's representative and invited to another formal banquet. They had little time to look around the town, described as 'enchanting' by Headley's friend Lady Evelyn Cobbold when she visited in 1933. Jidda was, she wrote, 'A white and brown town giving the idea of a fortress, as it is enclosed on three sides by a high wall, its minarets stand out against the sky, its quaint carved wooden windows bulge over the streets'.[55] Headley took several photographs of the traditional townhouses adorned with the timber façades and ornate latticework, heavy shutters and mock balconies and balustrades that the intelligence officer and writer T. E. Lawrence (1888–1935) described as 'gimcrack Elizabethan exaggerated'. When Lawrence first visited the town during the Arab Revolt in 1916, he was surprised that 'The tone of public opinion in Jiddah is rollicking good-humour towards foreigners'.[56]

Headley also found Jidda and its townsfolk to be hospitable. He thoroughly enjoyed the banquet, which was attended by Jidda's many foreign consuls. Headley described in some detail the after-dinner entertainment, which included a traditional Arab sword dance performed by a hundred men:

> The dancers formed a very large circle, and we could look down on them from the balcony of the big room in which we had dined. The scene was a weird one – the active, lithe figures, the firelight causing the shadows to dance upon the high white walls of the courtyard, reminded me of a scene in some opera.[57]

The dancers 'stood in the circle with a curious clapping of the hands and rhythmic swaying movement of the body, accompanied by a monotonous singing'. Headley found the singing rather 'tedious', but the dancing 'energetic to the verge of *frenzy*' because

> every now and then two or three of the dancers would detach themselves from the ring and whirl towards the centre of the circle, twisting and turning with incredible speed. They twisted like tops, brandishing their swords in every direction, so that it seemed nothing short of a miracle that half the people present were not decapitated.[58]

Headley met the new British consul, Reader Bullard (1885–1976), at the banquet. Bullard had arrived in Jidda to take up his position the previous month. In his private correspondence, Bullard initially described Headley as 'a dear old gentleman', but he quickly turned against him:

> He knows no more about Islam than I do about Chinese metaphysics, but he believes that the rather vague notions about being good and brotherly which he holds are the essence of Islam, so he calls himself a Moslem, and as the Moslems of England (most of them Indians or Egyptians) don't catch a peer of the realm every day of the week they make much of him. This flatters his innocent vanity.[59]

Bullard believed that Headley was 'very much under the thumb' of the 'sinister-looking' Kamal-ud-Din and the 'rather nice old man', Mohye. Bullard claimed to be unsure of Mohye's name because 'Headley, who has mixed with Moslems for many years without learning how to pronounce even their most common names, called him all sorts of unintelligible things.'[60]

Arrival in Mecca

The morning after the Jidda banquet, Headley, Kamal-ud-Din and Mohye set off for Mecca. Bullard, who was very wary – and weary – of the 'cunning childish' Hussein, reported that 'the King decided to make a fuss' over Headley, who was set to make 'a pilgrimage *de luxe*'.[61] The Hashimite authorities had, indeed, made special arrangements for the Woking pilgrims: a motorcar was prepared to take them from Jidda to Mecca, onwards to Arafat, and back. The London *Times* reported that the car was driven by the King's private doctor, 'doubtless as a double precaution – first, against accidents; and, secondly, if misfortune should be encountered, to ensure that medical aid should be immediately at hand.'[62] Shaykh Fu'ad al-Khatib noted that it was 'a special car as it is difficult to go by motor there because motors disturb the camels which will be filling the roads and the deserts'.[63] Settled in the car, Headley was relieved not to be taking the traditional mode of transport to the Holy City: 'to ride in on camel-back [. . .] takes a day and a half instead of two or three hours, which is the time taken by the car.' Moreover, 'the route is indicated by the bleached bones of dead camels which have been engaged in the pilgrimage'.[64]

The ride to Mecca was not entirely smooth. Headley reported that the car got caught in a sand-drift, causing its wheels to sink so deep in the sand that 'we had to get the assistance of some natives at a place called Hadda to pull us out'.[65] Ever the engineer, Headley noted that 'a very good road might be made between Jiddah and Mecca, as there are no stiff gradients, no rivers, no tunnels to construct. It is almost dead level, and there is an abundance of excellent metal, fragments of the igneous rocks of which the steep little mountains are composed.' He supposed that the lack of a road (or railway line) was not in the interest of the owners and drivers of the camels, donkeys and mules, 'and there would be the usual outcry which invariably attends the march of useful devices for the benefit of mankind'.[66] Headley could not, in the summer of 1923, have foreseen the immense changes that would be brought about by the Saudi annexation of the Hijaz soon after his visit. The multi-lane Highway 40 today links Jidda and Mecca in modern Saudi Arabia in an hour but, like the original dusty road, is jammed with buses of pilgrims during the Hajj season.

Before entering the city, Headley donned the obligatory *ihram* – two pieces of white cotton cloth worn by male pilgrims, 'one for round the loins and the other for the shoulders' (Figure 10).[67] He considered the symbolic equality and humility of the *ihram* to be 'very beautiful': 'We brought nothing into the world, and we give up worldly thoughts and approach our Maker in deepest humility,

Figure 10 The 'Woking' pilgrims at Mecca, July 1923. Left to right: Khwaja Kamal-ud-Din, Lord Headley and Shaykh Abdul Mohye.
Source: Courtesy of Ahmadiyya Anjuman Isha'at Islam Lahore (UK).

asking His blessing and direction in the right path.'[68] Nevertheless, Headley, who was used to wearing a tweed suit and was a physically large man, found that the *ihram* cloths 'are not always easy to manage or to wear gracefully. They are cool, but one always feels anxious about them, because they are apt to slip off at all sorts of times.' Indeed, he recalled later that, during a meeting with Hussein, 'when I wanted to look very dignified, [. . .] one of these sheets slipped and as nearly as possible came off altogether. I grabbed it only just in time and saved the situation.'[69] Eldon Rutter, a British Muslim convert who made the Hajj disguised as a Syrian merchant in June and July 1925, also complained that the *ihram* was, for Europeans, 'the most comfortless form of dress conceivable, and its use, continued for a period of days, almost amounts to torture'.[70]

Bullard wrote privately from the British consulate: 'It would have been asking for death for an Englishman of sixty to go seven times round the Kaaba [the cube-shaped structure at Mecca] in the Hejaz sun.'[71] But he still found it

> rather amusing to see this pink-and-white old gentleman decked out in the costume which pilgrims to Mecca have to wear. [. . .] I confess that it gave me secret pleasure to see the old man fumbling round his middle for a stubby lead

pencil or for his pipe, in obvious anxiety the whole time lest his costume should disintegrate altogether.[72]

Bullard bragged to Whitehall that 'Lord Headley conformed to the pilgrimage rules to the extent of wearing the towel-like pilgrim robe [. . .], but refused either to grow a beard or to go bareheaded, offences for each of which it is understood he proposes to slay an additional sheep at Mecca.'[73] Headley was always clean-shaven except for a carefully clipped moustache, and was not prepared to stop shaving during the Hajj. Echoing Bullard, though, he did justify wearing a turban:

> With the ihram dress, you are supposed to wear nothing on the head and only sandals on the feet, leaving the instep bare. I had to point out that it would be impossible for me to go in the sun with my bald head, and that if it was expected that I should do so it would be just as well to dig my grave at once. I was allowed to wear a white turban and slippers.[74]

Headley's insistence paid off: the turban and slippers protected him from the debilitating sunstroke that affected many pilgrims in 1923.[75]

Suitably attired, Headley and his companions were met in Mecca by Hussein's eldest son, Prince Ali. They then met King Hussein for the first time. Headley later said that he would 'never forget the brotherly affection' of the King's greeting.[76] As in Egypt, Headley was struck by the fraternity of the Muslims he encountered, Hussein included: 'I was no stranger, and I did not feel like one. I was his brother from the West, inspired with exactly the same love of Islam, imbued with the same reverence for our Holy Prophet, and anxious to ever worship the same Almighty Allah.'[77]

The pilgrims inspected Hussein's troops at the Hashimite barracks just outside the city, had dinner with the King and visited the ancient cemetery of Jannat al-Mu'alla. Headley paid his respects at the 'various shrines commemorative to those who were dearest to the Blessed Prophet', including Muhammad's first wife, Khadija. Headley was probably the last Westerner to see the cemetery intact. Eldon Rutter noted that the tombs had been 'crowned by small but handsome domes', but he arrived in the Hijaz in 1925, not long after its occupation by Ibn Sa'ud's army, and found all the monuments, 'without exception [. . .] demolished, together with most of the tombstones'.[78] The clearing of Jannat al-Mu'alla, as well as Jannat al-Baqi' cemetery in Medina, which contains the graves of many more of Muhammad's relatives, was ordered by Ibn Sa'ud in line with Wahhabi[79] strictures (reputedly inspired by Muhammad himself) that prohibit the building of monuments on graves. Cobbold found Jannat al-Mu'alla in 1933 to be 'now a stretch of empty desert'. She wrote that the Wahhabis under Ibn Sa'ud 'wish to cleanse Islam of all the superstitious growth of centuries and restore it to the simple faith taught by the Koran, and are no doubt in the right, but one cannot but regret the disappearance of so much beauty'.[80]

At Mecca, Headley and his companions lodged in a 'beautiful house' near the Sacred Mosque, 'where from the upper windows we had a perfect view of the Kaaba'.[81] The Ka'ba is the cube-shaped structure at the heart of the Sacred Mosque complex, and long predates Islam. According to the Qur'an, Abraham declared the Ka'ba to be a Sanctuary and place of pilgrimage for the worship of the one Creator God.[82] Muhammad, in the seventh century of the Common Era (or AD), was deeply troubled by the paganism that had been associated with his hometown and its Sanctuary for perhaps a thousand years.[83] As the final Prophet, Muhammad began publicly preaching the essential teachings of monotheism that constitutes Islam in c.610. Twenty years later, Muhammad and his followers cleansed the Ka'ba by destroying the pagan idols, and reconstituted the Sanctuary to God. It was not until 632, the year of his death, that Muhammad made his first and only Hajj, the 'Farewell Pilgrimage', which set the pattern of Hajj that Headley followed and pilgrims know today. It is a series of ritual re-enactments of faith-testing events from the life of Abraham who, according to tradition, was ordered by God to leave his wife Hajar and their infant firstborn, Ishmael, in the desert valley of the Sanctuary. The second *sura* of the Qur'an exhorts Muslims to 'Make the pilgrimage and visit the Sacred House for His sake'.[84]

Setting foot in the Sacred Mosque thirteen hundred years after Muhammad, Headley caught sight of the Ka'ba. It was, he recalled, 'standing in all its grand and solemn simplicity in the midst of the great courtyard'.[85] He wrote very little else about the Ka'ba or Sacred Mosque (or the other sites of the Hajj), but they are well described by British Muslims who visited later. Rutter, for example, proclaimed the Ka'ba to be 'the most important object in Mekka'; it is, he added, 'a stone building which measures, roughly, forty-five feet in each direction. It is not a perfect cube'.[86] For Cobbold, a decade after Headley, 'I am in the Mosque of Mecca, and for a few seconds I am lost to my surroundings in the wonder of it.' Like Headley before her, Cobbold walked on the white marble through 'a great vault whose ceiling is full fifty feet above us', and entered 'pillared cloisters holding the arched roof and surrounding an immense quadrangle. The vast magnitude of the Mosque appals me. I had never imagined anything so stupendous.' In the centre of the gravelled quadrangle, Cobbold viewed the Ka'ba, 'the Holy of Holies, the house of Allah, the great black cube rising in simple majesty'.[87]

The Hajj

Headley began the Hajj proper by returning to the Sacred Mosque on 21 July, almost a month after leaving London. Guided by Kamal-ud-Din, he performed *tawaf* by circling the Kaʻba counter-clockwise seven times and, as was just about possible in the years before pilgrim numbers exploded to the annual two million today, kissing the black stone on the eastern corner of the structure to symbolically discharge his sins. *Tawaf* demonstrates the unity of Muslims as they circumambulate the Kaʻba in unison, and Headley revelled in the communal worship and devotion of his co-religionists.

Reflecting on his first day of Hajj, Headley wrote: 'The first thing that struck me on arriving here [. . .] was the complete elevation of the mind above earthly matters. All the tens of thousands of pilgrims, and indeed all the people in the place, are so much bent on serving God that they have no room in their minds for other considerations.' For Headley, 'The most impressive sight of all is the service at the big courtyard surrounding the Kaaba. At the appointed times, five times a day, the *Muezzin* calls to prayer, and the whole huge area is filled with earnest worshippers. In *unison* they bow and prostrate.'[88] Cobbold was deeply affected by the experience of *tawaf*. Undoubtedly a more reflective writer than Headley, she concluded:

> It would require a master pen to describe that scene, poignant in its intensity of that great concourse of humanity of which I was one small unit, completely lost to their surroundings in a fervour of religious enthusiasm. Many of the pilgrims had tears streaming down their cheeks; others raised their faces to the starlit sky that had witnessed this drama so often in the past centuries. The shining eyes, the passionate appeals, the pitiful hands outstretched in prayer moved me in a way that nothing had ever done before, and I felt caught up in a strong wave of spiritual exaltation. I was one with the rest of the pilgrims in a sublime act of complete surrender to the Supreme Will which is Islam.[89]

After *tawaf*, Headley performed *saʻi* by walking and running seven times between the two small hills of Safa and Marwah (then located just outside the Sacred Mosque, but today enclosed within its complex), 'in memory of Hagar's [sic] search for water when she and her son Ishmael were perishing of thirst in the desert'.[90] Headley returned to the Sacred Mosque, prayed and drank from the Zamzam Well, the spring that miraculously appeared and saved Hajar and Ishmael from certain death.

At four o'clock the next morning, Headley and his companions left Mecca for Mina and Arafat, 'both well within ten miles of the city'.[91] Headley explained that their motorcar joined the King's 'imposing' cavalcade:

> First came the Camel Corps of Bedouins, all armed to the teeth with scimitars, rifles, pistols, and javelins. Then we followed in a carriage drawn by four splendid mules, the quietest and best-behaved animals of their kind I ever came across. Immediately after us came the beautiful Arab stallions of the King's stable. These pure-bred animals were led in long procession, one after the other, by their grooms, and at short interval came the King, rising upon a magnificent white Arab stallion and surrounded by his guards and standard-bearers.[92]

Progress to Arafat was slow. The procession stopped at Mina, where 'the guns boomed out in salute, the echoes of which seemed never to die out amongst the endless ranges of mountains'.[93] The pilgrims prayed, and slept outside, under the stars. Arising very early again, they reached Arafat on 23 July. In his published account, Headley wrote little about this crucial part of the pilgrimage, known as the 'Day of Hajj', when pilgrims return to the site of Muhammad's final sermon. Having climbed Mount Arafat, Cobbold felt that she was 'on sacred ground'.[94] Headley noted more objectively that he 'duly attended the service and listened to the sermon' in memory of Muhammad, 'from time to time calling out the well-known cry [...] "I am here, Lord; I am here"'.[95]

After sunset, when the heat of the day lifted, Headley re-joined the King's cavalcade as it made the return journey to Mecca, breaking at Muzdalifah, where they once more 'slept out in the open in the gentle breezes and in sight of the thousands of twinkling lights which illuminated the vast plain and made it look almost like an inverted star-spangled vault of heaven'. Headley claimed that, to his great surprise, it was only after the journey that he was told that the camp-bed he had slept on belonged to Hussein, and that the King had slept on the ground so that the Englishman could sleep comfortably. Headley said that he 'felt covered with confusion and remorse – it was another instance of the King's thoughtfulness and kindness'.[96]

Back in Mecca, Headley joined Hussein in repeating *tawaf* and *sa'i*. He then 'lost no time' in returning to Mina, to join fellow pilgrims in the symbolic 'stoning of the devil', which involves throwing small stones at pillars, each representing the different places where Abraham was tempted by Satan to disobey God's order to sacrifice Ishmael: 'Each time a stone hits the pillar we invoke God's protection and defence against the wiles of Satan.'[97]

Mina is also the site for the ritual slaughtering of animals that commemorates the sheep that God accepted from Abraham in lieu of Ishmael. To some extent,

Headley used his lectures back in England in the autumn to address and correct Western misconceptions about the Hajj. He was particularly vexed by the 'good deal of nonsense talked about the cruelty of the sacrifices by people who should know better'. Headley told the Central Asian Society: 'There is no more cruelty than there is when your butcher kills a sheep which provides you with a mutton chop for lunch.' He emphasized that 'All the slaughtered animals' at Mina 'are eaten by the poor pilgrims, and the skins are turned into leather for the use of the people.'[98] Headley also said that, having participated in the pilgrimage of between 70,000 and 100,000 Muslims,[99] he now 'most thoroughly' understood what 'the wondrous brotherhood of Islam' really meant.[100] At Mina, he had stayed in a house from which 'there was a fine view of the never-ending and wonderful procession of pilgrims returning from Arafat':

> Almost every nationality one can think of passed by, and the scene, with the gorgeous colouring of the East, produced a succession of kaleidoscopic views entrancing to behold. [. . .] Thoughts of the Brotherhood of Islam came into my mind very often when watching this ever-changing spectacle; all these people of widely differing temperament, different manners and customs, unable to speak each other's language, yet irresistibly drawn together by the great tie of earnest belief in the One and Only God and the Brotherhood of Man.[101]

Having 'performed all the duties and rites connected with the pilgrimage', Headley happily 'received congratulations from many friends in the market-place of Mina'.[102] His return to Mecca brought the Hajj to a conclusion. Headley watched preparations for the pilgrim caravan to Medina, the location of Muhammad's tomb, but chose not to join it. The journey to Medina is not part of the Hajj and Headley was keen to get back to Mecca because, in 1923, 'trouble [was] anticipated from the Bedouin tribes, some of which are turbulent and lawless and give cause for anxiety'.[103] Above all, perhaps, the 68-year-old pilgrim was spiritually lifted but physically exhausted, and Medina is more than two hundred miles north of Mecca. The heat was also relentless. While much 'impressed' by Mecca as a 'fairly well-cared-for city', Headley concluded that it was too 'hot and dusty, and most undesirable as a place of permanent residence'.[104]

Farewell Arabia

Headley stayed in Mecca for several days after the Hajj, resting and reflecting on his experience. He returned to the Sacred Mosque for communal prayer. Before leaving, he witnessed the removal of the black and gold *kiswah*, or pall, that covers the Ka'ba during the month in which the Hajj occurs ('a fresh one is placed round the Kaaba each year'). He took numerous photographs of the holy sites and the town itself, having been given permission by the Hashimite authorities to photograph 'the Grand Mosque, the minarets, and, indeed, anything that I wished to be reminded of when away from the city'. From the upper windows of his temporary home in Mecca, he 'obtained a splendid view of the Seven Minarets, the Zam Zam Well, the Ali Gate, and the Way of the Saiee. Of course, I took advantage of this, and succeeded in getting quite a nice lot of snaps, which came out very sharp and clear.'[105] He used these images to illustrate subsequent talks and lectures. Several of the photographs also formed an exclusive feature for the London *Sphere* in September 1923, and accompanied a chapter on Arabia in the popular *Countries of the World* series published in the 1920s and reprinted in the 1930s.[106]

Headley's time in the Sacred City was drawing to a close. He paid his respects to Hussein, who gave Headley several gifts. These included a 'gold-embroidered robe' and two sections of the *kiswah* which, following its removal from the Ka'ba, is traditionally cut into small pieces and given away. Headley told reporters that the larger of the two pieces was destined for Woking mosque, and the other for his drawing room at Ivy Lodge.[107] On behalf of the King, Prince Ali bestowed on Headley the Order of the Nahda (Renaissance) First Class, which Headley proudly said was 'the highest order that can be given in Arabia'.[108] The ornate silver medal was first given by Hussein to British subjects (including Allenby) in 1918 for their services during the Arab Revolt.

In mid-August, Headley returned to Jidda. He called on Bullard, joining him and 'an Indian doctor' for lunch. Bullard wrote that 'On the whole I like the Indian better than Headley. He's got brains, anyhow, whereas Headley is one of those bird-like gossips who know nothing and understand nothing.'[109] Bullard was clearly exasperated by Headley. When, in November, Bullard heard (incorrectly) that Headley had remarked during his Central Asian Society lecture that he had been welcomed by the Jidda consul, he reported to London that: 'If, as the report implies, Lord Headley means that the British consul went to meet him, he is saying that which is not true; if he simply means that the British consul was pleased to see him he is clearly mistaken.'[110]

Headley seems to have been unaware of Bullard's hostility, which ran deep: in May 1924, Hussein debarred an English Muslim, a Mr J. H. Bamber, from making the Hajj on the grounds that he was a British spy; Bullard wrote in his monthly report to the Foreign Office that Headley had been permitted to enter Mecca the previous year because he had already been received in Egypt 'as a Mahometan', but 'everyone else here believes that he was allowed to go to Mecca because the King had information that he was not only devastatingly stupid, but also completely under the control of the Imam of the Woking Mosque'.[111] In July 1924, Bullard read 'an article, written by a Moslem, in which the "hardships" which Headley went through in making the pilgrimage are described in order to exalt the noble peer for his devotion'. Bullard wrote privately that 'Compared with those of the real pilgrim they seem about as terrible as the experience of the *nouveau riche* family in *Punch* who at a picnic had to drink their champagne out of tumblers.'[112]

British *Hajji*

Having completed the Hajj, Lord Headley was legitimately able to prefix his name with '*Hajji*', the title given to male Muslims who complete the pilgrimage to Mecca. This further distinguished him in the British Muslim community and, given the rarity of Western pilgrims in this period, greatly enhanced his status among Muslims throughout the world.

The Woking *hajjis* left Jidda on the same steamer that had brought them to Arabia the previous month. After three days of quarantine 'tedium' in Suez, they returned to Cairo. They made a quick trip to see Prince Omar Toussoun in Alexandria, where they also finally met King Fuad I. The Woking group broke up at Cairo: Mohye stayed in Egypt, Kamal-ud-Din went to India and Headley returned to England.

Headley gave interviews about his Hajj to several journalists before leaving Cairo and as soon as he arrived in London at the end of August 1923. The Cairo correspondent of the London *Times* highlighted the significance of Headley's Hajj: 'Lord Headley is not only the first British peer to perform the pilgrimage, but, so far as is known, the first Englishman who has made the journey to Mecca under his own name and as an Englishman.'[113] Headley was briefly as newsworthy as he had been when he converted to Islam in 1913. Reporters and a press photographer went to meet Headley at his home in St Margarets, and the BBC asked him to give a twenty-minute talk about his 'recent experiences at Mecca' for its early radio station, 2LO London.[114] Headley also spoke about his Hajj at several events, including the British Muslim Society annual general meeting, as well as for the Evolution Society and the Central Asian Society in London. The gossip columnist for the *Pall Mall Gazette* attended the latter lecture and sarcastically reported:

> Everybody knows the type of traveller whose account of his wanderings reveals very little of strange lands but a great deal of himself.
>
> Lord Headley answers to this description. When he lectured [...] last night he might just as well have been describing a visit to a Turkish bath as a pilgrimage to Mecca, apart from his photographs of that forbidden city.
>
> What with his habit of leaving sentences unfinished, his trick of getting tied up with the lantern illustrations, and his inability to lay his hand on the fragment of holy carpet when he wanted to do so, Lord Headley made us all smile good-humouredly.[115]

A friend suggested to Headley that he wear the robe and turban given to him by Hussein for public engagements. Headley thought 'it is better to remain a Western in appearance, the tarbush, the turban, and the Arab head-dress all being somewhat out of place in this climate, besides which I have no wish to be accused of "showing off"'.[116] But this was false modesty: he happily posed in Arab dress, complete with the Order of the Nahda medal on his lapel, for the press photographer who visited him in St Margarets. The image was circulated and reprinted in newspapers and magazines worldwide (Figure 11).[117]

The press was especially surprised and intrigued by Headley's tale of modernity in the mysterious Hijaz. Headlines in both national and the most obscure of provincial newspapers included: 'Forbidden City is like Modern American Town'; 'In Holy Mecca: The March of Progress'; 'Finds Luxuries of West in the Forbidden City; Briton Sees Autos, Airplanes and Even Wireless Towers in Ancient Mecca'.[118] The *Franklin Times* of North Carolina reported that

> newsboys now cry in the sacred city the latest editions of the local newspaper, which has a very good foreign news service and an alert local staff. Pilgrims wishing to inquire about relatives or friends who are still on the way may go into telephone call offices and talk to the neighbouring towns of Jeddah, Taif and Medina. If Mohammet's coffin is not to be seen suspended between heaven and earth, its place is taken by the airplanes of the King of Hedjaz and the more up-to-date pilgrims now use automobiles to visit the holy place.[119]

Headley was, however, 'somewhat annoyed' to find that in England 'certain mischievous persons have put about a report [. . . endeavouring] to show that there was a political meaning' attached to his journey.[120] He continued to emphasize that the Hajj was 'purely religious', but that he was 'glad to find since my return that in the opinion of many influential Muslims and Christians a

Figure 11 Lord Headley at home in St Margarets after completing the Hajj, August 1923. Headley is wearing the gold-embroidered robe, turban and Order of the Nahda medal, and standing next to a section of the *kiswah* (lower left), given to him by Hussein ibn Ali al-Hashimi, King of the Hijaz.

Source: Courtesy of Janet Webb / The Estate of Fifth Lord Headley.

good effect has been produced. Many letters have reached me to this effect, and especially pointing out that it has tended to cement the feelings of kindness and brotherhood existing between Muslims of various nationalities.'[121] He concluded his Central Asian Society lecture with a quasi-political message:

> Let us try to see if we cannot regard ourselves as all equally loyal British subjects, bound together by ties of brotherly love, instead of looking down on others because they happen to be born on another part of the globe and are not quite like ourselves in some respects. I know that my brothers in the East love me and I love them. I don't say that I don't love you of the West also – I do, for I am one

of you; but I love my Muslim brothers all over the world quite as much as I love anybody.¹²²

Indeed, Headley's position was rather contradictory. Astute reporters realized that his description of the modern Hijaz was an implicit endorsement of King Hussein and his fragile government. But Headley was also, on occasion, explicit in his support for Hussein. The London *Times*, for example, reported in August 1923 that 'Of King Hussein and his hospitality, Lord Headley is loud in his praise', and it added: 'All that was observed of the local administration went to show that King Hussein's Government is a progressive one.'¹²³ Most press reports were based on an interview Headley gave to a Reuters representative as soon as he returned to England. The reporter noted that Headley 'found the King to be broad-minded and liberal, and wedded to the spirit of his religion'.¹²⁴

At the end of his Central Asian Society lecture, Headley was challenged about Hussein's leadership and the merits of Ibn Sa'ud, Sultan of the Najd. Headley argued that, while he had never openly endorsed Hussein as 'the head of all Arabia', he thought that 'it would be a very good thing if he were. He is a man of very great character and very sound. He is about seventy years of age, but always on the *qui vive* to do whatever is good and useful for his country.'¹²⁵

Headley's comments and actions irritated the British authorities. In September 1923, Headley wrote rather pompously to the Foreign Office to tell them that he had received the Order of the Nahda and to ask for official permission to wear the medal in recognition of the 'valuable service' he had given Hussein.¹²⁶ The Foreign Office noted that 'As Lord Headley himself states, his pilgrimage to Mecca was undertaken merely to show reverence to the memory of the Prophet and had no political significance whatsoever.'¹²⁷ A furious Headley replied that 'King Hussain [*sic*] is under the impression that I have rendered very valuable service to the cause he has so much at heart and said so over and over again.' He also played the India card: 'All the Muslims in India who know me well look upon this honour as equivalent to an honour bestowed upon them – and the same may be said of the English Muslims.' Headley now claimed that, by marking his 'deep respect for the Prophet' in Mecca, he had promoted 'a better feeling between the Christians and the Muslims and thus rendering good government easier'. Evidence of this was, he said, to be found in a recent letter he had received from a government official 'in the East' who wrote that the Hajj had 'helped greatly to bind anew the bonds between East and West'.¹²⁸ Headley argued:

> I am well known all over the Muslim world and this expression of opinion is from a Christian Gentleman who knows me and is in the service of our country.

The small recognition by King Hussain is also well known of by every Indian and African Muslim and if it became known that the leave to wear the decoration had been refused by the King of England, who rules over more Muslims than Christians, there would be unpleasant remarks made, for the chief British Muslim and the only British Hadji would seem to have been slighted and, through him, thousands of other loyal subjects of our King.[129]

Foreign Office officials were in no mood to negotiate with Headley. A civil servant advised colleagues:

> At the risk of losing India and of mortifying the 'only British Hadji', express regret that the S[ecretary]. of S[tate]. is unable to modify the views already expressed. [. . .] Lord Headley implies [. . .] that he has promoted a better feeling between Christians and Moslems. It is not apparent on what ground this renegade Peer is able to act for the Christians.[130]

Writing to her father from Bagdad in December 1923, the traveller and diplomat Gertrude Bell (1868–1926) noted that Headley's account of 'that old rogue' Hussein and his government 'is of as much value as that of a farm labourer, who has spent a drunken day at a fair, on the observance by the manager of the show of the Children's Employment Act 1903'.[131] Yet, Headley was so enamoured with Hussein that, when the Turkish Nationalists abolished the Caliphate in March 1924, he was uncharacteristically vocal about the potential reinstatement of the Caliphate in Arabia under Hussein:

> It has always been thought possible that he might be chosen Caliph – certainly it would be impossible to find a more genuine man or one more loyal to his country's welfare. He is an Arab of the Arabs. He is in direct male descent from the Caliph Ali (656–661), and you feel when with him that you are in the presence of one who is both great and good.[132]

Headley was, however, out of step with both British diplomatic thinking and the situation on the ground in Arabia: within a year of his Central Asian Society lecture, Ibn Sa'ud began an assault on the Hijaz. Ignoring protests from its Muslim subjects in India and elsewhere, the British government sought to form an alliance with Ibn Sa'ud. The Saudis took Mecca in 1925, abruptly ending seven centuries of Hashimite rule. Hussein was forced into exile, and died in Transjordan in 1931. In January 1926, Ibn Sa'ud became King of the Hijaz and he united the dominions of Najd and Hijaz as the Kingdom of Saudi Arabia in 1932.

8

Ambassador for British Islam, 1923–29

Headley's public profile and his status within the British Muslim community and across the *umma* increased after he completed the Hajj. Alongside the Aga Khan, Headley was arguably the most recognizable Muslim figure in Britain between the two world wars and he was well connected with Muslims abroad, especially within the British Empire. Headley was increasingly in demand from the national and international press to speak for and about Muslims in Britain and he became an unofficial ambassador for British Islam or, more accurately, Muslims associated with the Woking Muslim Mission and British Muslim Society, on trips overseas. However, this chapter highlights that the 1920s was a difficult period for Headley as a Muslim. Disputes among Muslims in Britain and elsewhere about the Ahmadiyya and the institutionalization of the Qadiani Ahmadi movement in England brought to the fore theological and practical questions about the nature of Islamic 'brotherhood' and 'unity' for Headley. It forced Headley to more explicitly express his views about Islam to his co-religionists and compatriots through both his writings and speeches as well as in his efforts to create a major new Muslim institution in London.

Domestic religious and social networks

The core London-centric Islamic network to which Headley belonged between the wars comprised mainly middle-class Muslims and allies from a variety of ethnic backgrounds. Headley was especially fond of Indian Muslims like Abdullah Yusuf Ali, who also lived in west London, and Syed Ameer Ali. A close mutual friend and non-Muslim ally was Charles Cochrane-Baillie, the second Lord Lamington (1860–1940), a former Conservative MP and governor of Bombay. Lamington was a Turcophile and dedicated his retirement to improving what he called 'West–East' relations. During the 1920s and 1930s, Headley joined

Lamington and others at scores of London events organized by groups such as the Central Islamic Society, Central Asian Society, East India Association, Near and Middle East Association and the British Red Crescent Society. This network also kept Headley loosely in touch with the traveller and sometime chief British representative in Transjordan, Harry Philby, whom he had probably first met in 1922 (see Chapter 7). After leaving the British diplomatic service in the mid-1920s, Philby began a trading company in Jidda. He sought advice and financial backing from several people in Britain, including Headley. Headley was not, however, very encouraging; replying to Philby in 1926, he cautioned that 'when I went to Mecca in 1923 I was not much impressed with the possibilities of doing anything in the way of trading with that very parched and barren land with its jagged ranges of low hills and bands of lawless robbers'.[1]

Headley's defence of Islam and Muslims invariably led to some awkward discussions and arguments with Christian clergymen in particular. However, Headley also attempted to build bridges with non-Muslims through speaking engagements and attending a wide variety of ecumenical and non-religious group events. For example, in the mid-1920s he was a guest at meetings of Lady Townshend's United Family League, which was intended 'to take in members of all creeds and classes at a subscription of a penny a head and obviate class warfare by getting them all to meet at tea'.[2] At the first meeting, in north London, Headley was joined by 'the Rabbi of Hampstead, a Catholic Bishop from Ontario, a Dominican Prior from Highgate, and a Salvation Army Captain [... and] a random selection of Hampstead people, including a party of roadmen'.[3] The following year, Headley gave a lecture at the East London Seamen's Mission, which was run by Methodists. Afterwards, the general organizing secretary, Reverend Charles H. Lodge, admitted to Headley: 'I shall in future hold in greater respect the Muslims who visit this Mission from time to time. I have always admired them for the wonderful sincerity and reverence they displayed. There is a saying down here, "that a good Muslim is better than a bad Christian"'.[4] Headley subsequently made a private donation to support the work of the Seamen's Mission.

Headley also personally introduced several Christian friends to Islam. Some of them converted, notably two aristocrats who became high-profile Muslim figures between the two world wars: Sir Abdullah Archibald (Watkin) Hamilton (1876-1939) and Sir Omar Hubert Rankin (1899-1988). Hamilton was, like Headley, staunchly conservative. He was a former military man who lost faith in Christianity during the First World War, when one of his sons was killed.[5] Rankin's politics shifted from right to extreme left, but he had also been in the army until he was invalided out in 1922. Shortly after leaving the army, Rankin met Headley and they discussed faith and Islam.⁶ Headley showed Hamilton and Rankin around Woking mosque, where they met other Muslims. Hamilton converted to Islam in 1923 and Rankin converted in 1927.

Headley remained particularly friendly with Quilliam/Léon. Masquerading as Professor Henri Léon in the 1920s, Quilliam was a less vocal British Muslim than he had been in Liverpool. Indeed, he quietly abandoned the title of Shaykh al-Islam and pursued an eclectic range of intellectual subjects in London. Quilliam/Léon founded two organizations, both of which Headley joined: the Société Internationale de Philologie, Sciences et Beaux-Arts, which reflected Quilliam/Léon's long-standing interest in the study of languages, and the London College of Physiology, 'founded for the special study of Physiology and the kindred sciences'.⁷ Headley became a vice-president of the Société, whose members also included Dusé Mohamed Ali and the Sufi teacher Inayat Khan (1882–1927), and Muslim converts such as Khalid Sheldrake, Marmaduke Pickthall, Professor Nathan/Nur-ud-Din Stephen, Lady Evelyn Cobbold and Dr Ameen Neville J. Whymant (c.1895–1970), an academic and linguist who converted to Islam during the First World War.⁸ Many of those Muslims also joined the London College of Physiology, of which Headley was sometime chairman and where he served as honorary lecturer. The College gave Muslims and peoples of other faiths the opportunity to explore and debate the relationship between religion, spirituality and modern science.⁹ Headley was keen to engage in these discussions, particularly when they touched on Spiritualism, the belief that the spirits of the dead exist and can communicate with the living. Headley admitted that he had 'experienced the very greatest relief and satisfaction from visitants from the other side' and concluded from a Muslim point of view that

> so far as I can see, Spiritualism need not interfere radically with any man's religion. Jews, Christians and Muslims need be no worse off by a belief in a nearer connection with the spirit world: I will go further and say that anything which induces reverence for sacred things and belief in a future state, can hardly fail to do good, and may save certain people from giving way to despair.¹⁰

Transnational connections and disconnections

While Headley was closest to Muslims in Britain, his relationship with the WMM and BMS ensured that he was also part of broader transcultural networks. Often informal, these networks connected him with Muslims across the globe, primarily in the British Empire and especially in West and South Africa, India and Ceylon (Sri Lanka). The networks meant that Muslims separated by great distances could share information and collaborate quite effectively. For example, in 1923, the Reverend W. H. Shaw, an Anglican missionary in the British Colony and Protectorate of Kenya, publicly defamed the Prophet Muhammad in a letter published in the popular *East African Standard* newspaper. It is a sign of Headley's standing within the British Empire by the 1920s that Muslims in Mombasa and nearby Zanzibar cabled news of the defamation to him in London. Headley assured them that he would do his best to raise the issue at the highest level. Indeed, he alerted other prominent Muslims in England, including Ameer Ali, and wrote to Victor Cavendish, Duke of Devonshire (1868–1938), who was secretary of state for the colonies. Headley highlighted 'the highly injudicious and inflammatory language now being used by a clergyman of the Church of England respecting the Muslim faith' and surmised that the Duke of Devonshire would,

> I feel sure, agree with me that insulting language and vilification of a sister religion – Muhammadanism and Christianity being identical in the great essentials of duty to God and one's neighbour – are in the last degree undesirable.[11]

Headley sent copies of his letter to the British press, and it was published in the *Times* and elsewhere. Transcripts of the original cables between Kenya and London were printed in *The Islamic Review*.[12] Ameer Ali also lobbied the Colonial Office to take a stand against Shaw. The Duke of Devonshire subsequently reassured the British Muslims that he condemned Shaw's comments and had relayed his feelings to the governor of Kenya. Shortly afterwards, the governor confirmed that the government and the bishop of Mombasa had publicly dissociated themselves from Shaw and published a public apology in the *East African Standard*. Shaw was impelled to write to the governor to express his 'deep regret for his action'.[13]

Comparative research on transnational connections between Western Muslims is in its infancy, but Headley appears to have had little contact with other nascent Western Muslim communities in the interwar period. The most prominent of those communities in Europe was in Germany, with a parallel Lahori Ahmadi mission centred around a mosque in Berlin led by former WMM imam and editor of *The Islamic Review*, Maulana Sadr-ud-Din. However, there was surprisingly little cooperation between Muslims in Woking and Berlin once the Berlin Mosque and Mission was established in 1923/24. Perhaps this was due to the sensitive post-war relations between Britain and Germany. Given his past anti-German activism, it is hardly surprising that Headley was not personally connected with the Berlin Mosque and Mission, nor its rival, the radical Islamische Gemeinde zu Berlin e.V. (IGB), which was established in 1922 by the Indian Marxist and pan-Islamist Abdul Jabbar Kheiri (1880–1958).[14] There is also little evidence of substantial contact with Muslims in nearby France, though Headley visited the Grand Mosque and Muslim Institute in Paris not long after it was completed in 1926.[15]

Beyond Western Europe, sizeable Muslim communities were to be found in the United States in the 1920s. Quilliam and members of his LMI had been closely associated with North American Muslims in the late-nineteenth and early-twentieth centuries, but those links faded with the closure of the LMI in 1908.[16] Dusé Mohamed Ali, who was well integrated with Muslims across Britain (see Chapter 4), left England for the United States in the 1920s, but he seemed to lose touch with British Muslims, including Headley. By the interwar period, the Qadiani Ahmadis rather than the Lahoris had the strongest institutional base in the United States under the direction of a former London Qadiani missionary, Mufti Muhammad Sadiq (1872–1957).[17] It follows, therefore, that Headley and the Lahori-connected WMM had no contact with the Qadiani Sadiq and little interaction with his several hundred Muslim converts. Patrick D. Bowen has noted in his survey of the history of conversion to Islam in the United States that, later in the 1930s, the WMM established good relations with a Sunni Muslim organization, the American Islamic Association, but since the WMM had no official representatives in the United States, its reach and influence there were limited.[18]

Surprisingly, the WMM received tentative support from some Salafis in Egypt. Umar Ryad has shown that, while Muhammad Rashid Rida's *al-Manar* and another Egyptian Salafi magazine, *al-Fath* ('The Opening'[19]) adamantly rejected Mirza Ghulam Ahmad's claims to prophecy, the editors of both publications 'appreciated the religious work of the Ahmadiyya in interwar Europe and the conversion of many Europeans to Islam', especially at Woking.[20] Ryad describes how European converts to Islam were caught up in debates among Egyptian Muslims about the Ahmadiyya and the 'authenticity' of their converts. As one of the first and most prominent Western Muslim converts associated with the Lahori Ahmadiyya in the interwar period, Headley was frequently cited in both *al-Manar* and *al-Fath*, and his motivations and actions scrutinized. This led to contradictory conclusions among Salafi writers. Rida, for example, praised Headley in *al-Manar* and disagreed with some Muslim commentators who questioned the sincerity of his religious conversion.[21] Moreover, as was highlighted in Chapter 4, *al-Manar* translated and quoted Headley's writings at length, including his *A Western Awakening to Islam*, 'in order to counter the arguments of "westernized" Muslims who criticized and distanced themselves from Islam'.[22]

King of Albania?

In the 1920s, Headley had a direct but brief association with Muslims in Albania, which had declared its independence from the Ottoman Empire in 1912. The pre-Ottoman, medieval kingdom of Albania had been a monarchy and, as the new nation state evolved, Prince Wilhelm of Wied (1876–1945) was installed as king. However, Wilhelm found his position untenable and reigned for only six months in 1914 before fleeing into exile in Germany. After the war, influential Albanians backed by British prime minister Lloyd George (who was conscious of British oil interests in Albania) seriously considered appointing a king plucked from the ranks of the British aristocracy.[23] These efforts came to nothing, not least because, in Britain, Albania was considered to be a poor and lawless country. As the *Belfast Telegraph* put it in 1924, 'There is a throne going begging in Europe, and no one seems to want it.'[24]

Islam was and remains the largest religion in Albania. In early 1925, the press reported that an Albanian Muslim delegation had visited Woking mosque and offered the throne to both Sir Abdullah Archibald Hamilton and Headley. Hamilton politely declined: 'I felt it my duty to stay in England, I am an Englishman, and I suppose "Once an Englishman always an Englishman."'[25] Headley claimed that he had been offered the throne not once but *three* times over the course of several years because the Albanians wanted 'a Britisher, a Peer, a Moslem'.[26] That he had been approached more than once seems feasible because, by all accounts, he was not yet estranged from his second wife, Barbara, when he was first offered the throne. Penne Hackforth-Jones argues that the socially ambitious Barbara was jubilant when some Albanians met her husband: 'Barbara's phoenix, having settled on a rickety branch of the English aristocracy, now took off in full flight. Thrones, processions, regalia. The sense of unreality, and a feeling of increasing transitoriness that she detested would vanish completely under the weight of a crown.'[27] Headley was, however, considerably more cautious and, to the utter dismay of his wife, he declined the initial offer.

About a year later, when Headley returned from the Hajj in autumn 1923, he submitted a petition for a decree of judicial separation from Barbara on the grounds of 'desertion'.²⁸ According to Martin Boyd, who was still lodging at Connaught Square and later wrote the novel *Brangane* (see Chapter 6), Headley tried to subpoena him 'as a witness that Barbara took drugs'. Boyd promptly left London for the Wiltshire countryside 'so L[ord] H[eadley]'s lawyers would not find me'.²⁹ When Headley's petition reached the Divorce Court in March 1924, it was announced that both parties had agreed terms with a deed of separation, and the charge of desertion was withdrawn. The case was reported in the British and Australian press: 'Mr Justice Hill said the Court was never better employed than when the parties adjusted their differences instead of calling on the Court to decide them.'³⁰

It is unlikely that Headley and Barbara met again. When asked to explain the separation, Barbara purportedly replied that her husband was a 'dis*gust*ing old man'.³¹ In October 1925, Headley petitioned for a divorce.³² However, Barbara had left England for Australia. Although she occasionally returned to London, Barbara severed all connection with her husband. In 1927 she announced to the press that she intended to stay permanently in Australia 'because England has altogether lost its refinement'.³³ Barbara died in Australia in May 1929. Bedridden with a broken hip, she spent her last days writing a series of contradictory wills. Her final wish was, however, emphatic: she wanted to be buried alongside her *second* husband, Dr Thomas Baynton, in Sydney, and an inscription to be added to his tombstone: 'and his wife Barbara'.³⁴

In 1924, in the midst of the legal battle with his wife, Headley was again offered the Albanian throne. He now told the Albanians that he would consider their offer if they could guarantee him an initial payment of £100,000 and an annual salary of £10,000. The Albanian delegation would not agree to Headley's terms, and he therefore went public. Headley said that he could not accept the throne because 'There is no salary attached to it. The only thing that goes with it is trouble, and the almost certainty of assassination.'³⁵ Hedging his bets the following year, Headley unabashedly restated his position:

> The dignity of a Kingship cuts no ice so far as I am concerned. I look upon it as a business deal. I am willing to risk my neck for the sum stated, and I do not think the price is too heavy, knowing the country as I do. [...] I am not a rich man, and so I make no bones about the business aspect. The money, if it were paid, would have to be British currency, so that there could be no quibbling afterwards.³⁶

Headley's demands were evidently not taken seriously. The throne was eventually restored in 1928 when an Albanian Muslim, Ahmet Muhtar Zogolli, or Zog I (1895–1961), became king.

Ahmadi disputes and rivalries

After the Ahmadiyya split into two groups in 1914 (see Chapter 4) and despite his connection with the Lahori Ahmadis, Kamal-ud-Din continued to present the Islam that he and his missionaries propagated from Woking as mainstream and avowedly 'non-sectarian'. It was a position that strongly appealed to Headley, who was very critical of what he called 'sectarian bigotry' within Western Christianity. Confident of Kamal-ud-Din's message and, no doubt, with the idealism of a new convert, Headley had announced in his article 'The Religion of the Future' for *Muslim India* in 1913 that 'Bigotry and fanaticism have wrought havoc in the contending Christian Churches, but this cannot be said of Mohamedism, which is a united church, save only for some minor disputes as to the descendants of Mahomet'.[37]

Like the majority of 'Woking' converts, Headley was not and never claimed to be an Ahmadi. In fact, he indicated later in life that he was a Sunni Muslim, but he was not afraid to show his respect and admiration for the Lahori Ahmadis. He had stood shoulder to shoulder with Kamal-ud-Din, quoted Mirza Ghulam Ahmad in his early writings about Islam and, in 1914, described Ahmad's *The Teachings of Islam* as 'a remarkable work'.[38] During the First World War, Headley contributed the foreword to a popular booklet written by one of the founders of the Lahori Ahmadiyyat, Maulana Muhammad Ali, and he regularly wrote for the Lahori Indian journal *The Light*, in the 1920s.[39]

In the first few years after the Ahmadi split, Headley – along with friends like Abdullah Quilliam/Léon and Khalid Sheldrake – demonstrated his inclusive approach to Islam by attending lectures in London presented by the Qadiani Ahmadi and former WMM missionary, Chaudhry Fateh Muhammad Sayal (see Chapter 4).[40] In March 1920, the Qadiani's Urdu-language newspaper, *Al-Fazl*, claimed that Headley had benefited from 'the table of the Ahmadiyya' (shorthand for the Qadianis), but had not joined the Qadiani *jama'at*.[41]

Tensions between the Ahmadis in Woking and London simmered during and after the First World War, but did not cause significant problems until the mid-1920s. Though he was based mainly in India, Kamal-ud-Din contained the issue within the WMM and at Woking, and so did Headley as president of the BMS. There was very little discussion of the issue or about the differences between Muslims of other schools of thought or 'sects' in the pages of *The Islamic Review* before the 1920s. As was evident at WMM and Central Islamic Society prayer meetings, 'Ids and events, Ahmadis, Sunnis, Shi'is and Isma'ilis mixed freely; they socialized and prayed together, presumably by adopting Sunni modes of prayer. Despite differences of opinion about the Ottoman Empire, Turkey and the Caliphate outlined in the previous chapters, relations between Muslims in and around Woking and London remained fairly cordial. As far as can be ascertained, the exception to this was the young, outspoken and ambitious Khalid Sheldrake, who had converted to Islam at the beginning of the twentieth century (Chapter 4). As early as 1914, Sheldrake wrote to the British government on official WMM notepaper as 'Sheikh of the British Muslims'.[42] Whether or not Headley was resentful of Sheldrake's self-aggrandizing is unclear, but some Woking Muslims definitely were, and Sheldrake was ejected from the WMM in 1915.[43] Sheldrake was shortly afterwards readmitted but, as is related later, he became a problematic figure for both Kamal-ud-Din and Headley.

In 1920, a reporter for the *Rangoon Mail* pressed Kamal-ud-Din on the issue of 'Muslim sectarianism' in the modern world. Kamal-ud-Din's response was published in *The Islamic Review*:

> Islam on its doctrinal side does not admit of any sub-section and sub-division. Difference of opinion in matters not cardinal should not be mistaken for differences of doctrines. All the so-called sects of Islam do converge on their fundamental doctrines. The only difference in them is in things of no importance from [a] religious point of view. Islam allows differences of opinion and respects personal judgement.[44]

He insisted:

> Islam is a religion without sect, in the real signification of the word 'sect'. I do not believe in preaching sectional differences in propagation of Islam in non-Muslim countries. They don't carry any weight in Islam. My preaching has been, and will remain always, free from sectarian principles.[45]

The problem for Kamal-ud-Din was that not all Muslims in Britain or elsewhere shared his liberal interpretation of Islam. Divisions between Sunnis and Shi'is were evident throughout the *umma*; Wahhabism was triumphing in Arabia; and the Ahmadis were bitterly divided in India. Differences of opinion and rivalries between the Qadianis and Lahoris in India began to be felt in England, and specifically at Woking. The *Islamic Review* reported in 1924 that some 'childish' and 'malevolent' (Qadiani) Muslims in India had spread the word that Kamal-ud-Din and Headley had undertaken the Hajj as agents of the British government, and that the WMM was backed by the government. Pickthall, who had left England for India in 1920 to become editor of the *Bombay Chronicle*, defended Kamal-ud-Din and the WMM in his newspaper.[46] The *Islamic Review* stated that allegations that Headley was 'a secret emissary of the Government of Great Britain' would be 'merely laughable were it not for the mischief at the back of it'.⁴⁷

However, the main challenge for Kamal-ud-Din, Headley and the WMM came from within Britain. Sayal and others had not only commenced a Qadiani mission in London but also planned to build a Qadiani mosque in Southfields, Putney. In autumn 1924, the Qadiani *khalifa* (spiritual leader) Mirza Bashir-ud-Din Mahmud Ahmad (1889–1965) visited London, and took the opportunity to lay a foundation stone for the new mosque. He also appointed his private secretary, Abdur Rahim Dard (1894–1955), to lead the Qadiani *jama'at* in Britain. While the *khalifa* was in England, a rumour spread that Britain's most high-profile Muslim convert, Headley, was also 'an Ahmadi', and implied that he was a Qadiani. Headley denied the allegations in the press. He said that he respected Mirza Ghulam Ahmad as 'a most saintly man', but did not accept that Ahmad's son, Mirza Bashir-ud-Din Mahmud Ahmad, was the *khalifa*:

> Lord Headley surmises that this extension may lead to the setting up of a certain form of Apostolic succession similar to the Papal succession in the Roman Catholic Church. [. . .] [I]t seems to him that such innovations may not be in the best interests of the broad and tolerant Islamic faith. There are quite enough complications already.⁴⁸

Kamal-ud-Din returned briefly to Woking in autumn 1925. While there, he finished a short tract about Muhammad called *The Ideal Prophet*, for which Headley wrote the foreword. Headley took the opportunity to rebuke recent criticism of the WMM by Qadianis and other Muslims in India and Britain: 'attempts have been made to show that we Muslims are endeavouring to paint the Prophet in quite a different colour and set up a New Islam with the view of furthering our Faith by these means.' Echoing his previous statements, Headley emphasized that 'Our critics forget one thing: the historical facts connected with Muhammad stand out too prominently and are too well established to allow of any innovations.'⁴⁹

Trust for the Encouragement and Circulation of Muslim Religious Literature

In the wake of criticism from Indian and British Muslims, and with a view to more effectively promoting Islam in the West, Kamal-ud-Din and Headley established a Trust for the Encouragement and Circulation of Muslim Religious

Literature. Headley was appointed a trustee alongside a long-time supporter of the WMM, Abbas Ali Baig and Kamal-ud-Din's son and former Woking imam, Khwaja Nazir Ahmad. Headley said that the Trust planned to publish a new English-language edition of the Qur'an to be sold 'at a nominal price' or distributed for free, and to produce other books and pamphlets about Islam that would 'remove doubts, which exist, as to what the Muslim Faith really is'.[50] The trustees proposed to raise funds from Muslims across the British Empire and, to that end, in late 1925 Headley and Kamal-ud-Din prepared to visit the Union of South Africa (present-day Republic of South Africa).

Although Islam was a minority religion in South Africa, in the early-twentieth century there were significant Muslim communities in major cities such as Cape Town, Johannesburg and Durban. Many South African Muslims had been or were descended from indentured labourers from the Malay Peninsula and the Indian subcontinent.[51] Kamal-ud-Din had good connections with those Indian Muslim communities, and, indeed, they extended a warm welcome to him and Headley when they landed at Cape Town in February 1926. As in Egypt less than three years earlier, Headley and Kamal-ud-Din were greeted by large parties of Muslims wherever they went, and they spoke at a number of receptions organized by local Muslim groups.[52] At Cape Town, Headley said:

> In accepting the hospitality of our brethren in South Africa, we are reminded of the fact that, though many thousands of miles lie between Woking and Cape Town, our hearts are united in Islam just as though we all lived in the same house.[53]

Headley made similar comments about the 'unity' and 'brotherhood' of Islam at subsequent events in Johannesburg, Durban and Maritzburg.[54]

Unlike their 1923 tour of Egypt, Headley and Kamal-ud-Din were consistently criticized by the local press and some Muslims in South Africa. It was again alleged that the Woking Muslims had a political agenda, though quite what that agenda was remained unclear. Headley nevertheless spent much time during the tour writing letters to local newspapers to deny the allegation.[55] According to the *Indian Opinion* of Johannesburg (established by Gandhi when he was living in that city):

> Lord Headley has said that the visit to South Africa has no political significance; but his first address of a series to be given in the Union was largely an exposition or arguments for 'propaganda with the object of encouraging Westerners to go over to Islam', the 'beauty and simplicity' of which was dealt upon.[56]

Headley said that he was also criticized for wearing Western attire:

> [T]here were certain Indian Muslims and others who thought that I could not be a genuine or *pucca* Muslim if I did not wear the 'fez' or 'tarboosh' and I had to explain that, according to my lights, the true Muslim heart could beat just as freely beneath the British waistcoat made in London as beneath the flowing and far more picturesque robes turned out in Cairo or Calcutta. My brain was just as strongly working for Islam under the shade of my sensible 'Trilby' as it could have beneath the brimless and sunstroke-encouraging 'Fez'.[57]

The two-month tour of South Africa undoubtedly strengthened relations between Muslims in that country and the WMM. It is not clear how successful the trip was in terms of fundraising for the Trust for the Encouragement and Circulation of Muslim Religious Literature. Headley's *The Affinity between the Original Church of Jesus Christ and Islam*, published by the Trust in 1927, was dedicated 'with affectionate regard and esteem to my dear Muslim brethren in South Africa', and may well have been wholly or partly funded by their donations.[58]

The London Mosque Mission and Western Islamic Association

Kamal-ud-Din went back to India after the South Africa tour, and Headley returned to England. Soon afterwards, Headley found himself caught in the crossfire of a dispute involving his friend James William/Habeeb-Ullah Lovegrove (1867–1940), who had succeeded Sheldrake as BMS secretary, and the London Qadianis. Lovegrove had shared a platform with some 'Indian Ahmadia people', by which he meant Qadianis, during a public debate. According to Lovegrove, the Qadianis had refused to take a cup of tea from or shake hands with the organizing party's female president. Lovegrove fulminated in the Lahori's *The Light* newspaper: 'Idiots! The Muslims are in the position they are now through the retardation of the so-called priestly class. Christianity was the same and all religions have suffered. Islam is a manly religion, simple and supreme. Be Muslims at heart and ignore the bigots!'[59] Headley agreed with Lovegrove and wrote a letter to 'a Muslim brother of a different school of thought' – probably Abdur Rahim Dard of the Qadiani London *jama'at* – which was also published in *The Light*:

> That there should be a scintilla of friction between us equally true Muslims and influenced by the same love of Islam and the teachings of our Holy Prophet, is

indeed a source of deep regret to me. [...] I have seen fights between the Sunnies and Shiahs and I firmly believe that there are certain fanatical Wahabis who would cheerfully decapitate the Khwaja [Kamal-ud-Din] and me, and also you my Brother, because we are not sufficiently orthodox to satisfy their own ideas of 'Holiness' – they would cut off our heads to save our souls! And I believe there are people in the most orthodox Christian sects who would not hesitate to take the same drastic measures.[60]

In October 1926, Abdur Rahim Dard oversaw the formal opening of the Qadiani London Mosque, also known as the Fazl Mosque, in Southfields. The mosque consolidated the Qadiani *jama'at* and mission in Britain. Yet, despite having the first purpose-built mosque in London, the Qadianis were much less successful in securing converts compared with the WMM.[61] Headley maintained cordial relations with Dard, who became the first imam of the London Mosque, but he kept away from its official opening ceremony. Notably, both Quilliam/Léon and Sheldrake accepted Dard's invitation to attend. Quilliam/Léon was one of the only Woking Muslims to comfortably and confidently associate himself with both the WMM/BMS and the rival Qadiani London Mosque Mission. The same cannot be said of Sheldrake: for reasons unknown, at the time of the London Mosque opening, Sheldrake and four other converts left the WMM and BMS. They established the Western Islamic Association (WIA), which was 'non-sectarian' and aimed to become an 'International Islamic Organisation' with affiliated branches across the world.[62] Headley and other Muslims at Woking continued to associate with Sheldrake in the months after he left the WMM. Sheldrake also contributed articles to *The Islamic Review* for another year and he attended 'Ids at Woking in 1927. This suggests that, initially, Sheldrake's breaking away from Woking might not have been considered too problematic for the WMM or BMS. Headley's good friend the Aga Khan backed the WIA when it was founded, and became a patron.[63] The WIA secured some international affiliates and the American Islamic Association mentioned earlier was originally conceived as the North American branch of the WIA.[64] Unlike Headley and others at the WMM, Sheldrake also reached out to the historic Arab Muslim community in South Shields in the early 1930s, but the WIA fizzled out shortly afterwards.[65]

Back in London, in January 1927, Headley and Dard of the London Mosque attended a discussion led by the Indian-Afghan writer, Sirdar Ikbal Ali Shah (1894–1969), on the theme of 'Ferments in the World of Islam' at the Central Asian Society. Unfortunately, only the official edited account of the discussion as published in the Society's *Journal* survives, but that alone indicates Headley's impatience with differences of opinion among Muslims, especially in Britain, by the late 1920s.⁶⁶ Headley admitted publicly for the first time that, while working in India in the 1890s, he had, in fact, witnessed 'certain sanguinary conflicts which took place between the Sunnis and the Shiahs', and he regretted that now 'we have the Wahabis [. . . who] are rather strict and intolerant people':

> They are great sticklers as to the letter, but do not seem to care so much about the spirit, it seems to me, though I may be doing them an injustice. There is another sect of excellent people I have been with. I am very fond of them, but they have an idea that Mirza Ghulam Ahmad, whose book I have here, was the Promised Messiah, and they make very stringent rules which seem to me to be rather unfair and derogatory. For instance, a man who is an Ahmadi [i.e. a Qadiani] is not allowed to attend a funeral and say prayers over the dead body of a man who does not happen to be an Ahmadi, although he may be a good Moslem; nor is a man allowed to say his prayers under the leadership of another Moslem unless that Moslem happens to be an Ahmadi.⁶⁷

Headley concluded that 'With regard to the ferments, I think a good many of them are likely to be caused by the Wahabi influence and Ahmadi influence, and I think it is a great pity.'⁶⁸

Dard, who was sitting close by, naturally responded to Headley's comments. He argued that the Qadiani movement 'stands for the moral and spiritual regeneration of Islam. I think Lord Headley has been either misinformed or has consciously misrepresented our teachings.'⁶⁹ Dard went further:

> I am sure Lord Headley, if he belongs to any sect, though I do not think he does, will have to admit that it is one of the beliefs of the orthodox Moslems that those who do not believe in the Holy Prophet Mohammed are eternally damned. He may disassociate himself from this and create his own Islam as it were, as he sometimes tries to do, but that will not do.⁷⁰

It would have been out of character if Headley had not, in turn, replied to Dard, not least to the allegation that he sought to 'create his own Islam'. However, any further discussion between the two men is not recorded in the published transcript of the meeting. Dard apparently ended by claiming:

> It is a grievous and painful thing to have to refer to such things. I wish [Headley] had kept silent; but I remember, some time ago, it was he who suggested that drinking was forbidden by Islam only for hot countries. It does not apply to this country. He went so far as to suggest that Moslem prayers required some modification to suit the Western people. I can show him British people who kneel with me, behind me, like all Moslems, and do not want any modification at all.⁷¹

After the meeting, an incensed Headley submitted a note to the Central Asian Society, which was published in its *Journal* as an addendum to the edited transcript of the discussion. Headley again affirmed that he held Mirza Ghulam Ahmad 'in the highest esteem and veneration' and, while admitting that he had 'given offence to Mr. Dard', felt that, given the theme of the discussion, 'I think I was well within my rights in calling attention to the attitude and aspirations of certain Islamic sects which have been undeniably productive of no little commotion and ferment.'[72] He argued that 'To my simple and, I hope, unbiased mind', the Qadianis' declarations 'are far too dictatorial and can hardly fail to promote dissension, since they must prove distasteful to a large proportion of the great Moslem community':

> Not very long ago I informed Mr. Dard that I could not myself subscribe to them as they savoured too much of Christian intolerance, and might almost be inspired by the spirit of the Athanasian Creed which most of us unite in condemning. [. . .] The high-handed line now being taken by the Ahmadis is hardly in accord with the true spirit of Islam which places toleration very high amongst the virtues to be encouraged.[73]

Undoubtedly prompted by his experiences in South Africa and the public disagreement with Dard, Headley wrote a long article called 'The Strength of Islam' for *The Islamic Review*.[74] It is one of Headley's better *Islamic Review* articles. He began by addressing Dard's criticism of his call for the 'modification' or 'Westernization' of Islam in Britain:

> It is much to be regretted that puritanical teachings have contributed so much towards the retardation of our efforts to spread the details of true Islam in the Western world.
>
> The precepts to be found in Leviticus might have been desirable or necessary amongst a lot of savages thousands of years ago, but these teachings are quite out of place and ridiculous in the twentieth century.
>
> In this age of reason it is intolerable to be asked to believe that certain forms and ceremonies are necessary to salvation. What I mean is this: that religion which insists that non-observance of forms or ceremonies is to be visited with the same punishment as the commission of sin, cannot be expected to find any favour with the mass of intelligent people.[75]

Headley used a familiar analogy to make his case:

> If you insist on the Yorkshire, or indeed any British farmer, giving up his dish of bacon and eggs or his glass of beer – a diet which has been found very wholesome for many generations – and tell him that its continuance is going to

jeopardize his chances of salvation, you will fail to convince him of the breadth and sincerity of Islam.

If you make it a *sine qua non* that the busy city man is to say his prayers openly, and with the usual prostrations, five times a day, you will not make any converts. What is very easy for the Arab, with his loose and inexpensive garments and ample sandy desert surroundings, will be impossible for the busy city man clad in expensive clothes. The idea of kneeling down and prostrating in wet and muddy streets is an absurd one. Such a man will have to consider his tailor's bill, and will not think this sort of thing can be necessary for his salvation – the surroundings are unsuitable, and the acquisition of eternal happiness should not depend upon whether a man is born in Mecca or Old Broad Street.[76]

For Headley,

> A religion which is hide-bound and bigoted can never become world-wide, as we wish Islam to be. There must be great elasticity, so as to bring all the nations of the earth under that one beneficent canopy which I cannot help regarding as the protecting wings of the Almighty.[77]

Headley ended his article by explicitly referring to the Qadianis. He echoed the points already made in his note for the *Journal of the Central Asian Society*, and added that Qadiani strictures

> strike a blow at the solidarity of Islam which is greatly to be deplored. One cannot find fault with the Ahmadis (*Qadianis*) for thinking anything they like (it is a free country), but one may reasonably object to being excluded from the ranks of the Faithful at the behest of a small number of zealous adherents of a certain idea.[78]

He concluded:

> I do not myself think that Islam has anything to fear from outside attacks, or even from the unworthy misrepresentations of which I have so frequently complained, for these will fade away as the Truth becomes evident. What may cause obstruction and delay is the attempt to establish fresh sects *within* the great fraternity of Islam.[79]

Responses from British Muslims were not published in *The Islamic Review* and there is no evidence to suggest that Headley's proposals for the 'Westernization' of Islam were *formally* adopted by Muslims at Woking or elsewhere (but this is not to suggest that they were not noted or accepted by some Muslims). However, in a sign of the global reach of *The Islamic Review*, Headley said that he received letters about his 'The Strength of Islam' article from Muslims overseas. One of the letters, from a Muslim in Ceylon, was published in *The Islamic Review*. While welcoming Headley's arguments about the Westernization of Islam, the correspondent added that 'It is being insinuated here in Ceylon that your Lordship, in conjunction with your brother Al-Hajj Khwaja Kamal-ud-Din, has permitted the British Muslims to freely partake of *bacon and beer*.'[80] Headley brushed the allegation away as 'a silly misrepresentation – possibly due to ignorance', and advised fellow Muslims that 'Scandalmongers and mischief-makers will always be, and I am sure you will agree with me that except for a flat denial of their false allegations we should pity and ignore them.'[81]

India and the London Mosque Campaign, 1927–28

In summer 1927, Headley announced that he planned to tour India and then Ceylon, the apparent source of recent misrepresentations about him and the WMM. The primary aim of the trip was to raise funds for a London mosque. Headley had revived the scheme he had abandoned during the First World War (Chapter 5). He was encouraged by the opening of the Grand Mosque in Paris as well as the Qadiani London Mosque in Southfields. In summer 1926, Headley had moved from St Margarets to an apartment in Kensington Hall Gardens, West Kensington. He spotted a potential site for the mosque nearby, but was unable to make any progress without significant funding. It is not clear why Headley did not simply join forces with the pre-existing London Mosque Fund (discussed in Chapter 4), which, in the 1920s, was still being championed by friends such as the Aga Khan, Ameer Ali and Lord Lamington. Instead, Headley resumed his own campaign by reiterating the symbolic and practical importance of a London mosque at BMS, WMM and other meetings and events while Kamal-ud-Din was in England in 1927.

With donations not forthcoming from British Muslims or the British government, it was agreed that Headley would accompany Kamal-ud-Din on his return to India. A six-month fundraising tour of India would commence with two official engagements that underlined Headley's ambassadorial role for British Islam.[82] He was to preside at an All-India Tabligh (Preaching) Conference in Delhi, and then go directly to Lahore to preside at the first session of the Ahmadiyya Anjuman Isha'at-e-Islam annual meeting. The latter engagement also publicly confirmed Headley's close association with the Lahori Ahmadis.

Headley and Kamal-ud-Din left England for India on 25 November 1927. India was socially and politically unstable in the late 1920s, with clashes between

Hindus and Muslims and fierce debate regarding the country's future governance and status. Peaceful calls for national liberation and dominion status for India were lambasted by violent revolutionaries who demanded complete sovereignty and an end to British rule.

Shortly before he left England, Headley found himself caught up in the politics of a notorious legal case involving Indian Hindus and Muslims known as the Rangila Rasul case. In response to a pamphlet written by a Muslim that depicted the Hindu goddess Sita as a prostitute, an anonymous polemicist from the Arya Samaji (Hindu reform movement) had published a tract entitled *Rangila Rasul* ('The Merry Sage'), which denigrated the image of the Prophet Muhammad and mocked his marriages and sex life. Indian Muslim activists successfully generated international condemnation of the pamphlet and its publisher, who was arrested but could not be prosecuted because there was no law against insulting a religion in British India.[83] Headley received cables from exasperated Muslims in India who wanted the tract banned and its publisher prosecuted. He raised the case at the India Office and wrote about it in both *The Islamic Review* and *The Light*. Headley concluded that 'the Government of the Punjab can deal effectively with such a case as this and if the law, as it stands, is not sufficient to put a stop to such incentives to breaches of the peace fresh laws will immediately be passed enabling the authorities to deal effectively with such cases as may arise in the future.'[84]

In the weeks before he left England, Headley also reiterated his support for the British Raj and its protection of Muslims:

> [T]he administration has been conducive to peace and commercial prosperity. Most of the Indian Muslims with whom I am acquainted realise that *without* such a rule there would speedily ensue a condition of internal strife and disorder. [. . .] Mistakes there may have been, but where, in the whole of this world of inequalities and enigmas, can we point to a condition of affairs which is independent of, or above, human error? Let us by all means go for Government to that power which seems swayed by reason and justice. We may aim at perfection, but we can only achieve improvement.[85]

Kamal-ud-Din, however, warned that Headley would not be returning to the India he fondly remembered from the 1890s:

> It may well be that Lord Headley will not feel at home with the present India, infested as it is with petty jealousies and party strife [. . .]. Lord Headley has no light task before him, more especially when we consider how present-day India is riddled with schism of every kind, possible and impossible; but knowing him

as we do, we are confident that he will steer the ship of debate clear of all the reefs and shoals that imperil the fortunes of many a conference.[86]

Symbolically, Kamal-ud-Din considered 'the journey of Lord Headley's, seven thousand miles away from his native country, as one more link forged in the chain of brotherhood which unites the Muslims of the East and West'.[87]

When he landed at Bombay (Mumbai) after three weeks at sea, Headley was quizzed by the local press about the ongoing conflict between Hindus and Muslims. However, once he was in India, Headley refused to be drawn into political issues: 'I have got my own views of what is right and what is wrong, but I am not going to be dragged into any political discussions.'[88]

Headley and Kamal-ud-Din attended a lavish dinner held in honour of the King of Afghanistan who was also visiting Bombay, and then went on to Delhi, where they were received by a jubilant reception committee headed by a local Muslim, Khan Bahadur Pirzada Muhammad Husain. Headley was, Husain remarked, 'one whose name is well known in the Islamic world'. He added that 'Letters received from some places in India tend to show that His Lordship's brethren-in-faith are very desirous of seeing him. If his Lordship can see his way to visit some places in India, the cause of Tabligh is sure to receive another impetus.'[89]

Headley opened the All-India Tabligh Conference with a long and rambling but sincere speech which drew heavily on the Qur'an to emphasize the importance of unity within Islam and among Muslims.[90] Headley was conscious of the many problems affecting India as well as the friction caused by disputes among Muslims around the world:

> A true religion [...] should not come to fan the fire of hatred and disaffection based upon [...] racial prepossessions; on the other hand, it should create such broadness of mind among its followers as may lead them to tolerate others' differences in the affairs of life. [...] Some Indian Nationalists hold that the elimination of [the] religious element from India is the only remedy for the present trouble. Perhaps they are right, when religion [...] becomes confined to the observance of certain rituals and rites, and to the worship of certain national heroes [...], but if religion creates in us such broad-mindedness and liberal ideas as I was speaking of, will not religion in itself be the most efficacious and effectual factor in cementing those in unity that are at daggers drawn with each other?[91]

Directly addressing the subject of the conference, Headley spoke about the challenge of propagating Islam, 'especially in the West':

> But may I put one question to my brethren-in-Islam? They should search their own house first. If they wish to show the light of the Qur-an to others, and they

are right in doing so, why are they shutting themselves far off from the same light? A sort of blight has overtaken the Islamic world. It, no doubt, is greatly owing to others' economic pressure; but we should study our own life and see how we are ignoring the Qur-anic ethics![92]

If success follows 'Tabligh' in the terms of the Qur-an, it can only be carried on successfully if the cord of Allah is unitedly in our hands and if we are not affected by internecine differences. [. . .] Do we not – Sunnis, Shias, or others – believe in one God and in the Messengership of Muhammad, whose advent sealed the door of Prophethood for ever? [. . .] I am absolutely at a loss to understand the causes of the trouble brewing in our atmosphere on sectional grounds. And let me be frank to tell you one thing: Don't entertain any hope of success in the spread of Islam, especially in the West, if you carry your religion to them in all such sectional spirit, so rife in this country.[93]

Headley proposed the WMM as a model for the propagation of Islam. He argued that the WMM 'preached to the West a "Religion without Sect," as Islam really is'.[94] Ignoring recent disputes with the Qadianis and the WMM's London-centrism, Headley nevertheless correctly pointed to the breadth of its congregations: 'Muslims of every nationality living in England resort to the [Woking] Mosque and present a unity of hearts in religion unknown to Christendom. Sunnis, Shias and others, stand shoulder to shoulder before their Lord under the leadership of one Imam.'[95] This was a convenient way to introduce the London mosque scheme to the conference audience. Headley proposed the building of a mosque in the capital city of the British Empire 'that may act as a beacon-light of Islam for the West in religious matters'.[96]

After three days at the conference, Headley and Kamal-ud-Din went directly to Lahore for the Ahmadiyya Anjuman Isha'at-e-Islam annual meeting. The *Light* reported that, on arriving in Lahore, Headley led a procession which passed through the city. Its reporter 'was vastly impressed by the obvious sincerity of the welcome accorded to an English Muslim by his Indian brothers in the Faith':

On that day Lahore appeared to be a Muslim city thronged and packed by Muslims exclusively who showered flowers and scents upon the processionists. Repeatedly did the individuals of that great crowd break through the police barriers to seize Lord Headley's hand or those of the two European soldiers in uniform who took part in the procession.[97]

Headley was introduced to Maulana Muhammad Ali, president of the Anjuman, and many other prominent Muslims, including the lawyer Sir Mian

Muhammad Shafi (1869-1932) and leading lights of what became the Pakistan Movement, Sir Muhammad Iqbal and Maulana Zafar Ali Khan.

The *Light* noted that 'Although [Headley] is now not in his youthful vigour, his energy and earnestness in the work of progressing Islam do not fail to keep pace with those of any Muslim'.[98] It considered the decision to appoint Headley as president of the annual meeting 'a remarkably wise and successful move': 'The propaganda value of the Muslim peer's visit to Lahore has been enormous and the effects of the visit are likely to be lasting'.[99] After three more days of discussion and debate, Headley was guest of honour at a tea party hosted by the Anjuman and he addressed a public meeting on New Year's Day 1928 when he again called for Muslim 'unity'.[100]

From Lahore, Headley travelled to more familiar territory in north-west India. He headed for the ancient city of Peshawar at the eastern end of the Khyber Pass, stopping for a day at Rawalpindi where he was special guest at a garden party. The colonial press noted that, at Peshawar, 'there was something unprecedented. Chiefs from Trans-Border and other Frontier Districts travelled hundreds of miles to meet and hail his Lordship with cordial greetings'.[101] Accompanied by Kamal-ud-Din's son, Khwaja Nazir Ahmad, Headley visited the Khyber Pass as the guest 'of an independent tribe' and he 'also stepped into Afghan territory where he was welcomed by the people and officials there'[102] (Figure 12). He then went south-east, to Wazirabad, and west to Sargodha: 'His Lordship everywhere preached tolerance and non-sectarianism in Islam' and he also appealed for donations towards the building of a London mosque.[103]

On 20 January, Headley returned to Lahore, where he joined *salat al-jum'a* in the mosque within the Ahmadiyya complex.[104] He bade farewell to the Lahoris and travelled far south to the British cantonment at Secunderabad in the princely state of Hyderabad. Headley was formally received by the political secretary to the Nizam (ruler) of Hyderabad, Asaf Jah VII (1886-1967), and attended the Nizam's birthday banquet in the capital, Hyderabad city.[105] Although there is no record of their meeting, it is very likely that Headley met Pickthall in Hyderabad. After leaving the *Bombay Chronicle* in 1924, Pickthall had accepted a position in the Hyderabad civil service. He was granted two years' leave in autumn 1928 to write a now celebrated English edition of the Qur'an, so was still living and working in Hyderabad when Headley visited in January of that year.[106]

Headley met the Nizam of Hyderabad several times during his stay in the princely state. Pickthall probably helped arrange the meetings, though whether or not he also joined them is unclear. Impressed by Headley and his plans for a

Figure 12 Lord Headley at the Khyber Pass, India, January 1928.
Source: Courtesy of Janet Webb / The Estate of Fifth Lord Headley.

London mosque, the Nizam pledged five lakhs – approximately £60,000 – towards its construction. The Nizam's Council stipulated that the mosque be named the 'Nizamiah Mosque' and managed by an independent Nizamiah Mosque Trust Fund, completely separate from any of the pre-existing London mosque funds and the WMM.[107] The Trust Fund was duly formed. A deed was executed and registered in India and also lodged with the Charity Commission in England. Headley was appointed chairman of the Trust Fund, and other trustees included Ameer Ali, Abbas Ali Baig, the Aga Khan and Lord Lamington co-opted from the London Mosque Fund, Kamal-ud-Din and a representative of the Nizam.[108] Delighted, Headley continued his tour of India, zigzagging across the country. He ended the trip with a final visit to Jammu and Kashmir. At Srinagar, Headley returned to the many local mosques he had first seen in the 1890s, but now he prayed inside them alongside Kamal-ud-Din and other Muslims.

In 1928, the Nizamiah Mosque was estimated to cost around £100,000 and it is unclear whether Headley secured any other significant donations towards its construction from India. However, given the Nizam's generous donation and his apparent guarantee of further funding from the great and good of Hyderabad, Headley abandoned plans to visit Ceylon and also Singapore.[109] Instead, he returned to England via Paris where he visited the new Grand Mosque and was 'much struck by the elegance of the design and the thoroughly solid and artistic work which everywhere prevails'.[110]

On the defence

The tour of India was a personal triumph for Headley: he had promoted the London mosque scheme, secured funding towards its construction, and consolidated his position as a leader of and ambassador for British Islam. Headley was not, however, beyond reproach and there were numerous fresh attempts to discredit him while he was in India and when he returned to England.

For example, shortly after Headley's visit to Hyderabad, the Cairo newspaper *Kawkab al-Sharq* published an article entitled 'Lord Headley and Islam'. The article focused not on Headley's recent travels or the proposed Nizamiah Mosque, but instead suggested that Headley had lured his friend Sir Archibald Hamilton to Islam with the revelation that Islam legalized polygamy. It alleged that Hamilton was a serial womanizer and stated that Hamilton's first wife had left him after discovering that he had had an extra-marital affair. According to *Kawkab al-Sharq*, Hamilton then 'seduced a beautiful girl of sixteen years of age with his wealth, name and fine style of living, and married her', but she had grown weary of him and 'began taking intoxicants to excess', which led to her downfall and a prison sentence. Following the death of his second wife, Hamilton had 'secretly' married his former housemaid.[111] Christian missionaries seized on the article, which was widely republished around the world, as evidence of Headley's immorality, skewed interpretation of Islam and inappropriate flaunting of his religion. Notably, writing from Cairo just before his death in May 1928, the Christian missionary William Henry Temple Gairdner (1873–1928) blamed Headley for having 'the inspiration of seizing *this* occasion to put before "his friend" the suitability of Islam as a solution to his self-caused matrimonial troubles'.[112]

In reply to a *Kawkab al-Sharq* journalist who sought to verify the original article, Headley allegedly stated that 'I feel pity for [...] Sir Archibald, and I fear that his action may draw some people to misunderstand the truth of Islam'.[113] Gairdner considered Headley's response to be 'remarkably inconclusive' but not out of character because 'this is a gentleman whom it is remarkably difficult to hold to the point. [...] We remain unenlightened about how Lord Headley proposes to justify the Hamilton case and his own advice to Sir Archibald relative to polygamy':[114]

> Frankly we fail to see that Lord Headley is a man who, either morally or intellectually, deserves to have his opinions considered. We have in our hands the newspaper report of his appearance in a London police court, where he was convicted of embracing a woman in the street when he was drunken. That was twelve years ago, and we believe and hope that Lord Headley, now over seventy, is a better and more God-fearing man. But while we have read much from his pen and other pens about his conversion to the Ahmadiyya sect of Islam, we have never learned that that conversion was accompanied by any act of confession and repentance of past shame. Until this is clearly faced we shall not feel able to place great reliance on Lord Headley's statements on religion and morals.[115]

Gairdner advised 'Mohammedans here in the east not to be too triumphant about the existence of this small group of British "Mohammedans", many of them very ill-informed and all of them falling very much short of Moslem standards as recognized by Sunnis'.[116] Gairdner continued: 'How not, when their preceptors are Ahmadiyya, whose special ideas simply cannot be reconciled with Islam at all? We fancy Lord Headley's teachers left him very much in the dark about the Ahmadiyya aspect of the matter.'[117]

Within a month of his return to England, Headley wrote what was to be his last significant article for *The Islamic Review*, initially delivered as a lecture for the BMS in July 1928 and republished in pamphlet form by the Trust for the Encouragement and Circulation of Muslim Religious Literature.[118] Entitled 'Is Our House in Order?', the article was a partial rebuttal of recent critics like Gairdner and yet another attempt to tackle the question of divisions between Muslims and within Islam. The idealism that framed much of Headley's writing during his first decade as a Muslim had clearly evaporated as he begged the question: 'Can we as Muslims claim that our Faith, as at present preached and practised, is one which is altogether free from the drawbacks which hamper other beliefs?'[119] He continued:

> I am unable to obtain any satisfactory evidence, from the Qur-an or elsewhere, that many of the outward forms and ceremonies of modern Islam were ever

laid down by the Holy Prophet of Arabia as essential to the Muslim Faith. Both [Christianity and Islam] seem to have been tampered with, and sectarianism has eaten very deeply into both the great Religions. Neither can afford to throw stones, and it is only by a full recognition of our failings that we can hope to make really satisfactory advances towards improvement.[120]

Not afraid to confront sensitive issues head-on, Headley argued that the differences between Sunnis and Shi'is over the successorship of the Caliphate 'should be relegated to the limbo of oblivion', and he reiterated that the Qadianis were 'undoubtedly Muslims, but they seem to me to have wandered somewhat far from the true path'.[121] 'There are few Muslims', he concluded, 'who will not realize that the existence of so many conflicting parties constitutes a great source of weakness to Islam.'[122] It followed that, in accordance with the wishes of the Nizam of Hyderabad, the Nizamiah Mosque in London would be 'entirely non-sectarian'.[123]

The Nizamiah Mosque

Unfortunately for Headley, his call for Muslim unity in Britain and beyond went unheeded. In fact, his 'Is Our House in Order?' lecture seems to have sparked a backlash from critics at home and overseas. Following the lecture, the press reported that Headley was seeking a suitable site for the Nizamiah Mosque and donations to guarantee its construction. In addition to the Nizam's donation of £60,000, approximately £15,000 had been pledged towards the £100,000 target. In a sign that he was no longer on good terms with Headley or others at the WMM, Sheldrake of the break-away WIA informed the London *Daily Herald* in September 1928 that 'The long-vaunted project for the construction of a Central London Mosque, which was first announced in 1906, may, with considerable luck, eventuate in the year 2,000.'[124] Sheldrake added that 'Mohammedan missionaries in England, who have been striving [...] to convert the people of this country to the faith of Islam have signally failed in their endeavour':

> Rival factions among the missionaries have so hampered the work of conversion that, despite the many thousands of pounds which have been made available for the task, a state of absolute stagnation exists.[125]

Sheldrake and, curiously, Arthur Field, who had been secretary of the Anglo-Ottoman Society and had a warm relationship with Headley as late as 1926,[126] also stirred up further trouble in India by alleging that the Nizamiah Mosque

Trust Fund was, in fact, an off-shoot of the WMM. The *Moslem Chronicle* of Calcutta (Kolkata) subsequently reported 'the undesirable arrangements' for the administration of the Fund. It stated that, with Headley as chairman, Kamal-ud-Din as executive officer and his son Khwaja Nazir Ahmad as secretary, the Trust Fund board was 'too much of a family affair':

> Lord Headley is greatly indebted to Khwaja Sahib Kamal-ud-Din for friendship and assistance of various sorts, and he is not likely to oppose the Khwaja Sahib in any matter. Thus, the London [Nizamiah] Mosque [Trust] Fund threatens to become a 'one man show' which has been the chief criticism levelled against the conduct of the Woking [Muslim] Mission.[127]

The *Moslem Chronicle* continued:

> As regards the Woking Mission, it is necessary for us to state plainly that Moslems are not entirely satisfied with the manner in which it is run. We imply no reflection on the sincerity and integrity of Khwaja Sahib Kamal-ud-Din when we point out how necessary it is that public work of the sort done by the Woking Mission and supported by funds subscribed by the public should be above all suspicion of nepotism.[128]

Headley said that the allegations of nepotism were not entirely correct and he also added that the Nizamiah Mosque in London would be non-sectarian.[129]

Even though *The Light* also published a letter from a reader who thought that 'detailed information about the actual working out of the scheme is lacking', Headley did not seek to alter the composition of the Trust Fund board.[130] Kamal-ud-Din, meanwhile, did take note of the criticism directed at the WMM and he instructed that the Mission and its related businesses, including *The Islamic Review*, were 'amalgamated and transferred to a Board constituted on non-sectarian lines'.[131] But the election of Maulana Muhammad Ali as vice-chairman to Headley, not to mention the registration of the WMM trust deeds in Lahore, did little to dispel rumours that the Mission remained an Ahmadi Lahori affair.

Undeterred by the negative publicity, Headley pressed ahead with the Nizamiah Mosque scheme. The British press reported in July 1929 that a site at Mornington Avenue, next to West Kensington railway station (and close to Headley's apartment), had been selected for the mosque. Headley said that it was 'An excellent position, it covers a little under 50,000 square feet, and cost £28,000. The next step is to invite designs. We shall be guided by a committee which will be appointed to choose the most appropriate plans and reasonable estimates.'[132] Headley proposed to return to India and finally also tour Ceylon and Singapore to raise funds. However, the timing was unfortunate as the world was gripped by the Great Depression and political unrest had spread across the Indian subcontinent. The Muslim correspondent of the *Singapore Free Press* argued that it was simply inappropriate for foreign Muslims like Headley to collect donations for their mosques when local Muslims' 'first consideration should be for the needs of local Muslim charities, or other good causes beneficial to all communities here'. The correspondent suggested that Headley should be told 'not to come here' because 'times are abnormal, business is very bad and local Muslims are finding it very difficult to collect money even to pay for the cost of building their own mosque'.[133]

Headley indeed steered clear of Singapore and elsewhere as he again put the mosque campaign on hold. Nonetheless, disapproval of the Nizamiah Mosque Trust Fund persisted. Headley complained in 1930 that there was 'a running fire of hostile criticism in the Press of India, Ceylon, South Africa, and other places abroad. The attacks are all more or less of an abusive and vulgar character, and I cannot quite make out in what way the Trustees of the London Nizamiah Mosque Fund and other institutions have offended the clique of malcontents'.[134] In October 1930, Headley was compelled to publish the accounts of the Trust Fund in *The Islamic Review* to assuage fears that the money was being used inappropriately.[135]

9

Twilight years, 1929–35

Headley was approaching his seventy-fifth year as the 1920s drew to a close. His health began to deteriorate and, after remarrying in 1929, he opted for semi-retirement in the English countryside. This chapter examines Headley's twilight years. Although Headley wrote much less for Islamic publications, he remained a dedicated Muslim leader. Having attempted to avoid politics since his religious conversion, Headley unsuccessfully devoted his final years to political causes: he tentatively dipped into the politics of the Middle East but focused, instead, on the campaign to champion Indian Muslims as a bulwark against Gandhi and the Hindu-controlled Indian National Congress as it fought for Independence. Above all, though, Headley continued to work tirelessly for the Nizamiah Mosque Trust Fund to build a 'non-sectarian' mosque in London.

Marriage and semi-retirement

Headley's estranged wife, Barbara, died in Australia in May 1929 (Chapter 8). The couple had not seen each other for several years and, in the mid-to-late-1920s, Headley met Catharine 'Kitty' Bashford (1865–1947), who became his companion. Ten years younger than Headley, Catharine was the younger daughter of Joseph Williams Lovibond (1833–1918), a brewer and inventor. Catharine had remained a spinster until, in 1919, she married Major Radcliffe James Lindsay Bashford (1881–1921). Major Bashford died less than two years later, and Catharine was a widow when she met Headley.

Like Barbara Baynton, Catharine was a successful businesswoman. Described in the press in 1929 as 'a highly capable woman', she was chair of the board of her late father's firm, founding director of a textile company with several stores in London, and 'showed a flair for real estate and took to buying property in the West End of London'.[1] Indeed, Catharine owned and leased numerous prestigious properties in central London and, when in town, lived in one of several apartments she had bought at Portland Place, south of Regent's Park.² In stark contrast to Headley's short-lived marriage to Barbara, relations between Headley and Catharine were harmonious and based on mutual affection and respect. They were married at Fulham registry office in London on the morning of 28 July 1929, exactly two months after Barbara's death. Catharine was a Protestant but, in a sign of her support for Headley's religion, the couple were also married at Woking mosque a few hours after the registry office service in London.³ Both marriage ceremonies were private affairs and the news was not released to the press until after the event.

Headley moved into his wife's Portland Place apartment. The marriage finally stabilized Headley's precarious financial position. Headley seemed to be a less troubled man in the early 1930s, partly because he was content with Catharine and no longer had financial concerns, and also perhaps because he had been reconciled with his illegitimate daughter, Ivy. Headley became especially fond of Ivy's daughter Vivienne, who, in 1930, went to live at 'The Cottage', a property on the West Kensington site that had been purchased for the Nizamiah Mosque.⁴

From the moment they were married in 1929, Lord and Lady Headley travelled almost everywhere together. Catharine did not convert to Islam but was usually by her husband's side at *'Ids* and other Islamic events. In September 1929, she hosted the annual celebration of Muhammad's birthday at a London restaurant. More than 300 Muslims and allies filled the restaurant, and Headley, Sirdar Ikbal Ali Shah, Abdullah Yusuf Ali, Abdullah Quilliam/Léon and others gave speeches.⁵

Following his marriage, Headley was also received back into the fickle world of London society, and his appearances at social events were well documented in the gossip columns. When, in October 1929, the Headleys gave an 'at-home' in their Portland Place apartment, the press highlighted that 'The invitation is from "Lord and Lady Headley." Convention demands that it should contain her name only, though there is evidently some precedent to be followed when a Mohammedan and his wife entertain. Perhaps it is a compromise in the conventions of East and West.'⁶ In December, the couple attended the annual Fairy Tale Ball at Grosvenor House, with Headley 'dressed as an Arab sheik'.⁷

As he grew older, Headley became susceptible to common but sometimes debilitating illnesses such as influenza. His doctor advised him to leave England during the cold and wet winter months, so he spent his first Christmas with Catharine in the warmer climes of Egypt (Figure 13). On their return to England in 1930, Headley decided it was time to step back a little from public life. He

Figure 13 Lord Headley and Catharine, Lady Headley, in front of the Great Sphinx of Giza, Egypt, December 1929.
Source: Courtesy of Janet Webb / The Estate of Fifth Lord Headley.

and Catharine searched for a home outside London and they settled on Ashton Gifford House in Wiltshire. It was an elegant and large Georgian-style country house of twelve bedrooms with extensive parkland that included an ornamental lake, woodland and pasture as well as various estate buildings. Thereafter, the Headleys divided their time between Wiltshire, where they enjoyed a more restful country life – hosting the local hunt and judging horticultural shows – and London, where Headley maintained his connections with the Woking Muslim Mission and Muslim community. He remained president of the British Muslim Society, which was renamed the Muslim Society of Great Britain (MSGB) in 1930, and chairman of what became known as the Woking Muslim Mission and Literary Trust as well as the separate Woking Mosque Trust and the Nizamiah Mosque Trust Fund.

Defending the *umma*: Palestine

Despite his attempt to steer clear of political issues, the turbulent politics of the *umma* in the later 1920s and early 1930s impelled Headley to selectively intervene, albeit briefly, in the affairs of Muslims in the Middle East and South

Asia. Headley had rarely written or spoken publicly about events in the Middle East during and after the First World War. It is therefore intriguing that, in July 1928, it was reported in Jerusalem and Britain that the executive committee of the Palestine Arab Congress (a collective of influential Palestinian Arabs who led opposition to British policy in Palestine) named Headley as 'being suitable for the office' of high commissioner of the British Mandate for Palestine, a geopolitical entity established under a Mandate of the League of Nations in the aftermath of the First World War. The post of high commissioner had been vacated by Lord Plumer (1857–1932), who resisted Arab demands to reverse commitments made by the British government in the Balfour Declaration (1917) to provide 'a national home for the Jewish people' in Palestine. The British government named the seasoned colonial official Sir John Robert Chancellor (1870–1952) as Lord Plumer's successor, but the Palestine Arab Congress pleaded, instead, for 'a British Moslem' to take the position.[8] Since the British authorities did not officially recognize the Palestine Arab Congress, its executive committee members were ignored. However, it is another sign of Headley's reputation among Muslims worldwide in the interwar years that he was identified and publicly named by the Palestine Arab Congress.

In October 1929, Headley wrote probably for the first time about the dire situation in Palestine and the controversial Balfour Declaration. His letter to the Colonial Office in London followed a series of violent riots in Palestine in August 1929, when almost 250 Arabs and Jews were killed. Writing on behalf of the BMS, which Headley stressed was 'a society for religious purposes only',[9] he squarely criticized the British government: 'For ten years the administration of Palestine has failed, however impartially worked, to satisfy *either* Zionist or Arab.'[10] Headley recommended 'the creation of an Arab Federated State' and warned that 'The just settlement of this Middle Eastern problem is an imperative necessity for the welfare of the British Empire, lying as the Arab world does across our Indian and Far Eastern communication'.[11] Shortly afterwards, Headley wrote again to the Colonial Office regarding 'the unsatisfactory situation in Palestine'. He stated that the BMS 'desires in no way to mix itself with political activities, but it cannot refrain from expressing sentiments of deep sympathy with its co-religionists in Palestine'.[12]

Less than six months later, in March 1930, Musa Kazim Pasha al-Husayni (1853–1934), president of the Palestine Arab Congress executive committee, led a delegation of Arab nationalists to London. The delegation unsuccessfully lobbied British politicians about the future of Palestine and protested against the Balfour Declaration. Headley met members of the delegation at Woking mosque. He posed for photographs with Mohammed Amin al-Husseini (c.1895–1974), Grand Mufti of Jerusalem (the Sunni Muslim jurist in charge of Jerusalem's Islamic holy places), and the images were circulated in the international press (Figure 14).

In May 1930, Headley hosted an 'at-home' of the MSGB (as the BMS had recently been renamed) at Caxton Hall in London in honour of the Arab delegation. The event was organized by the MSGB 'to mark their sympathy with the Arab cause as opposed to the British policy based on the inequitable "Balfour Declaration"'.[13] The *Islamic Review* reported that 'Lord Headley, in the course of his aptly chosen remarks, pointed out that the injustice which was being done to the Arab cause would never pay'.[14] The Grand Mufti of Jerusalem observed that 'the Palestinian question was not either a local or a national one. It was

Figure 14 Lord Headley with members of the Arab Palestine delegation at Woking mosque, March 1930. Left to right: Mustafa Effendi al-Husseini, nephew of the Grand Mufti of Jerusalem; Lord Headley; Mohammed Amin al-Husseini, Grand Mufti of Jerusalem; unknown; Maulana Abdul Majid, imam of Woking mosque.
Source: Courtesy of Janet Webb / The Estate of Fifth Lord Headley.

a question which involved the whole of the Muslim world'.¹⁵ Meanwhile, the Mayor of Jerusalem

> reminded his hearers of some of the broken pledges and perfidious actions of British diplomacy during the Great War. He said that if the Arabs had known how they were to be disillusioned after the war had been won they would never have espoused the cause of the Allies, and that it was their credulity for which they were paying heavily at the present time.¹⁶

The Grand Mufti and some of his colleagues returned to Woking in May 1930 to celebrate *'Id al-Adha* with Lord and Lady Headley as well as Quilliam/ Léon, Habeeb-Ullah Lovegrove, Abdullah Yusuf Ali and many other Muslims.¹⁷ Thereafter, however, and for reasons unknown, Headley was very quiet on the future of Palestine and the wider politics of the Middle East, and he was not invited to the Grand Mufti's World Islamic Congress to discuss the future of Islam in Jerusalem in 1931. Instead, Headley switched his attention to the future of India, an issue that had long preoccupied him but one that had a new sense of urgency following the election in July 1929 of a Labour government in Britain that was sympathetic to the aspirations of the Indian National Congress, popularly known as Congress.

Defending the *umma*: India

Headley was incensed that the new British prime minister James Ramsay MacDonald (1866–1937) welcomed the idea of Dominion status for India, which was formally proposed by the outgoing viceroy and governor-general of India, Lord Irwin (1881–1959), in October 1929. Headley was also aghast that the former Conservative prime minister Stanley Baldwin (1867–1947) endorsed Irwin's proposal, and he was alarmed at the rise of Indian nationalism, which threatened to push India even further from what he considered to be benevolent British rule and exasperate conflict between the Hindu majority and minority religious communities, especially Muslims. Indeed, at the end of 1929, Congress declared that its primary goal was complete independence, and it set 26 January 1930 as Independence Day. Shortly afterwards, Gandhi commenced a campaign of civil disobedience which further undermined British authority in India and united more Indians, including Muslims, in the movement for Independence.¹⁸

Congress boycotted the first of three Round Table Conferences on India which were organized by the British government and held in London in November 1930. The Round Tables (1930–32) were designed to discuss constitutional reform in India with delegates from Britain and across India, including representatives of the British provinces and the numerous princely states, including Hyderabad.

Marmaduke Pickthall was a secretary of the Hyderabad delegation and the only 'Woking' Muslim present at the first Round Table (he did not attend the subsequent conferences). The Aga Khan led the British Indian delegation. Headley met many of the Muslim delegates as they arrived in London and was reunited with Pickthall, who also attended MSGB events while he was in town.[19]

Just before the first Round Table Conference began, Headley issued a statement to the press, which was published internationally, appealing to 'Jews, Christians and Moslems to unite in a determined effort to stem the torrent of Communism', which was partly a dig at the new Labour government but was also responsible, he implied, for the 'the recent disturbances' in India.[20] 'It is,' Headley argued, 'obviously unreasonable to find fault with laws which have brought prosperity to India. [. . .] Islam and anarchy never did and never can go hand in hand.'[21] Headley believed that most of the Indians at the first Round Table Conference 'are as anxious as we all are for peace and quiet, and the maintenance of the law and order, on which the prosperity of the vast [Indian] peninsula depends'.[22]

The first Round Table Conference was adjourned in January 1931 having reached an agreement that India would acquire a form of Dominion status as a democratic All-India Federation comprising the British provinces and princely states. Shortly afterwards, Lord Irwin had a series of meetings with Gandhi which resulted in the Gandhi–Irwin Pact of 1931. The Pact suspended Congress's civil disobedience campaign and Gandhi agreed to attend the second Round Table Conference in London (September to December 1931) in return for the release of around 19,000 political prisoners and the relaxation of some of the government's emergency coercive powers.

In Britain, disaffected Conservatives determined to prevent Indian independence rallied around a former secretary of state for the colonies, Winston Churchill (1874–1965). Churchill accepted that a measure of self-government at provincial level was inevitable, but he publicly opposed the idea of an All-India Federation with self government at the centre, and he lambasted the government's policy in India. Churchill had served in India as a subaltern in the British army while Headley was working in Jammu and Kashmir. Churchill arrived in Bombay in autumn 1896 and completed his tour of duty in spring 1899. Not unlike Headley, Churchill had what the historian Warren Dockter has described as a 'Victorian conception of the [British] Empire relative to India'.[23] In his 1930 autobiography, Churchill described the India of the 1890s as 'perfection' while he recalled the 'good old days' of being 'waited on and relieved of home worries' by a retinue of servants.[24] Like Churchill, Headley considered that the British Empire was a means to spread and defend civilization and, as was highlighted in Chapter 6, he firmly believed that British rule in India guaranteed good government and the protection of all citizens, especially religious minorities. However, as Dockter has argued in relation to Churchill, 'If there was one thing that Churchill disliked more than the government's policies [. . .] and the timidity of the Conservatives' by 1930, 'it was Hinduism and Gandhi'.[25] Dockter has attributed Churchill's position not only to his 'quasi-racist views and limited grasp of empire', but also to a 'hierarchy of civilization', in which 'Islam, with its shared Judeo-Christian traditions and monotheistic structure, was understood to be infinitely more civilizing than polytheistic Hinduism'.[26]

In March 1931, just days after the Gandhi–Irwin Pact was signed, Headley went to the Royal Albert Hall in London to hear Churchill speak about India. Churchill argued that 'To abandon India to the rule of the Brahmins would be an act of cruel and wicked negligence', and he launched a bitter personal attack on Gandhi and his 'seditious' movement which, in his view, brutally oppressed India's loyal Muslim subjects and thereby created ongoing conflict between Hindus and Muslims.[27] Churchill proposed to circumvent rising Indian nationalism and protect British rule in India by promoting Indian Muslims as a bulwark against Gandhi and the Hindu-controlled Congress.

Headley was captivated by Churchill and his message. He swiftly wrote to Churchill 'to express my gratitude for all you have recently done for us – particularly with respect to India & the danger of arousing the anger of the Muslims who are opposed to Sedition'.[28] Headley also penned a personal press statement – independent of the MSGB[29] – that applauded Churchill's 'admirable exposition of the causes which have led to the present astounding situation as regards India'.[30] Echoing the public statements he had made just before the outbreak of war in 1914 (see Chapter 5), Headley said that the Qur'an forbade sedition:

> I am a Muslim, and I try to follow the teachings of our scared book, and I find in the Koran that all Sedition [is] expressly forbidden.
>
> I am also an Englishman and I and my family have for hundreds of years been most loyal supporters of the Crown and Constitution of our great country.
>
> As there are 110 Millions of my brother Muslims owing allegiance to our King, and as we may claim to be the greatest Muslim Nation in the world, I am not unreasonable in supposing that I must for two reasons condemn Sedition which leads to breaking the Law. Gandhi and Mrs Besant[31] seem to me to have forfeited any right to be heard. They are dangerous Sedition-Mongers of a very contemptible type, exploiting the ignorant for their own Vanity or gain. Away with them, neither they nor their pernicious teachings will ever help our dear Sister India to keep going on the road to prosperity in which she has been started by the most beneficent rule ever meted out to any country on the face of this Earth.[32]

In reply, Churchill assured Headley that 'I shall do all in my power to save India from the perils which threaten her at the present time'.[33] Headley subsequently helped connect Churchill with the Indian Empire Society and, later, the Indian Defence League, both of which opposed substantial self-government for India.[34]

In May 1931, Headley stepped up his role in Churchill's campaign by writing a number of letters to the British and Irish press appealing for England to 'wake up' with regards to Indian nationalism and Gandhi. Headley said that he had visited India in recent years and met there 'quite a number of Indians who were loud in their praises of the wonderful effects produced by nearly 200 years of beneficent British Rule and Influence in India':

> It appeared to me that as peaceful citizens they were satisfied with their lot, and not very particularly anxious for change or better government than they have at present. I think they would like to have it appear that they were self-governing, but would not wish to be saddled with the responsibility of keeping order or 'running the show.' I may be wrong, but it seems to me that they would say to the British Raj – 'Please allow us to appear like a self-governing country, but you must give us your guarantee against annexation by any other great power which may have its eye on our fertile plains.'
>
> It is, I think, highly probable that the leaders of sedition such as Gandhi and many others with distorted visions, may have argued that if a little country like Ireland, quite close to the shores of England, could dictate terms and cut itself adrift – surely a big country should find no difficulty in effecting a separation from England so many thousands of miles distant?[35]

Amid rioting and rising Hindu–Muslim violence in March and April 1931, Headley wrote:

> Oil and water will not mix, neither will Hindus and Moslems ever truly coalesce, because their religions are as far apart as the poles. The present lamentable state of affairs in India is mainly due to an ill-timed application of clemency which was at once put down to fear by every section of the law-breakers. It seems, indeed, that since the extreme urbanity lately shown to Gandhi there have not been wanting signs that the British Raj is actually afraid of the Mahatma. It is also possible that certain loyal Moslems may think that they are being thrown over in order to placate their political and religious enemies.
>
> [. . .] For many years past Gandhi and Mrs. Besant have proved themselves to be the most dangerous of all who have encouraged disobedience to the law [. . .] But for Gandhi's criminally conceived 'Civil Disobedience' campaign there might have been far less rioting and, perhaps, no loss of life. As [the Khilafat leader] Shaukat Ali[36] is reported to have said the other day at the All-India

conference at Delhi: 'Neither Hindus nor Moslems have any confidence in each other, and Moslems will not accept dictation or bullying.' He is perfectly right.[37]

In line with his belief that the British Empire protected the rights of minorities, Headley added that 'Under Hindu rule it seems possible that the Christians and Moslems might not receive very much better treatment' than the 'Untouchables, who are regarded as outcasts and dogs'.[38]

When, in May 1931, the recently retired viceroy, Lord Irwin, reportedly suggested that 'the policy of the strong hand' in India 'was "out of date and out of harmony with present day facts"', Headley wrote another letter to the press in which he said he wanted to

> humbly point out that the Laws exist for the protection of the people and their property, and that all law-abiding citizens should welcome the presence of the strong hand which should never be absent. Only malefactors have any reason to be afraid of the Law.
>
> The repetition of platitudes respecting 'civil disobedience' and 'passive resistance' – when it is well known that the specious catchwords lead up to breaches of the peace and massacres – can hardly be condoned; certainly they have led to a condition in which the arm of the lawbreaker has been allowed to grow longer and stronger than that of the Law itself.[39]

The second Round Table Conference opened in London in September 1931 with Gandhi the sole official representative of Congress. Headley kept a keen eye on developments through his involvement with the National League in London, a 'non-Party' but avowedly anti-Bolshevist and anti-Zionist organization that aimed at 'furthering understanding and cooperation between the Anglo-Moslem worlds'.[40] In October 1931, Headley and his wife joined a meeting organized by the National League in the House of Commons when MPs heard from Muslim delegates from the second Round Table Conference. They included the Aga Khan, Shaukat Ali of the Khilafat Movement, whom Headley had mentioned in his letter to the *Yorkshire Post* quoted earlier, and Sir Muhammad Iqbal and Sir Mian Muhammad Shafi, both of whom Headley had met in Lahore four years earlier (Chapter 8). Shafi told the MPs that 'The Moslems of India firmly believed that the future of India lay within the British Commonwealth of Nations and was attainable only through mutual cooperation between Great Britain and India'.[41] However, he also warned the House of Commons:

> Their present policy would be continued unless Britain herself brought it home to them that the British Government would not recognize their legitimate rights and interests, unless they followed methods adopted in other countries. [. . .]

As India was a vast continent and not a country, and was inhabited by races of differing cultures, self-government must be based on a federal system.[42]

After October 1931, Headley was almost totally silent on the issue of India. This seems curious because, although he was beleaguered by ill-health, he was still fairly active and vocal about other political issues, from the 'threat' of communism throughout the world (in his opinion, another reason to keep good – British – governance in India) to the campaign in the early 1930s for the reform of laws that regulated lotteries in order to benefit hospitals and charities.[43] Perhaps Headley had no more to say on the issue and left it to statesmen like Churchill to lead on an issue that, frankly, did not resonate strongly with a largely complacent British general public. In this period, Headley lost some of his closest friends and allies who might have supported him or taken their own stand on India: Syed Ameer Ali had died in 1928 and Kamal-ud-Din, Quilliam/Léon and Abbas Ali Baig all died in 1932. Or perhaps Headley realized by the time of the second Round Table Conference that he had underestimated the determination of British politicians across parties that the British Empire was an organism that had to change in order to survive. More likely, Headley understood that he (like Churchill) had underestimated the strength of Indian nationalism, even among some Muslims. Headley, Churchill and others who shared similar views about the future of India in the early 1930s had failed to comprehend the complexity of the issues on the ground in India.

The second Round Table Conference was quickly derailed as a result of squabbles about the balance of electoral power, specifically the reservation of seats for religious minorities. As Lawrence James has argued, the failure of the second and third[44] Round Table Conferences to produce a workable constitution 'placed the onus on the British Parliament' to find a solution to the problem.[45] Between 1932 and 1934, the future governance of India was 'decided by Parliamentary committees', culminating in the India Bill of 1934, which was passed the following year.[46] Under the terms of the Government of India Act, the provinces of British India became self-governing and there was provision for an Indian Federation if and when the rulers of the princely states agreed to join.

The Nizamiah Mosque scheme revived

While Headley's energy for saving the British Raj might well have dipped, the one cause to which he remained wholly committed later in life was the Nizamiah Mosque scheme. Having put it on hold again for a few months in 1930, Headley approached a well-known architect, Sir Alfred Brumwell Thomas (1868–1948), to prepare a series of initial architectural drawings. Headley showed the drawings to the many Indian Muslims who visited London in November 1930 for the first Round Table Conference.[47] Although he failed to secure donations from the delegates, Headley remained optimistic that the scheme would be realized. He told the press that a 'small but capable committee' would be formed to approve plans, including the mosque architecture, 'which, I think, should be Indo-Saracenic, since most of the money will probably come from India'.[48]

Headley anticipated that further funds would, as the Nizam had assured him in 1928, come from Hyderabad. In July 1931, Headley wrote to his granddaughter Vivienne, who was still living at the proposed mosque site in West Kensington, that he had arranged to meet 'two Hyderabadi Princes' there 'to have a look at the site and perhaps plant a tree. I fear we shall not be able to lay a foundation stone this time but we may manage it later on – perhaps in October.'[49] The princes were the elder sons of the Nizam of Hyderabad: Azam Jah (1907–70) and Moazzam Jah (1907–87). In summer 1931, Pickthall accompanied the Nizam's sons on a tour of Europe, which ended in France in the autumn, when both princes were married in a double wedding ceremony.[50] It is not clear whether Pickthall went with the princes to the West Kensington site, but it seems likely that he continued to act as liaison between the Nizam and Headley in relation to the mosque scheme.[51]

In November 1931, Headley and other trustees of the Nizamiah Mosque Trust Fund formally met with Brumwell Thomas to discuss plans, and he was appointed architect for the scheme.[52] The following April, Brumwell Thomas's designs for a grandiose mosque with a large onion dome were exhibited in the Architectural Room of the Royal Academy in London. As one newspaper noted:

> Sir Brumwell Thomas has travelled extensively in the East examining mosque architecture, and his design looks very grand. He plans the Nizamiah Mosque [...] and its minaret on the monumental scale of the mosques and minarets throughout Islam, and in many points – the cupola, for instance – it will reproduce the Taj Mahal. [. . .] The Academy watercolour [of the proposed Nizamiah Mosque] shows the minaret and great gateway leading into the colonnaded garden court before the mosque entrance. The mosque will include a hostel with dining hall, library and lecture rooms for the use of students and other Muslims as well as for the imam of the mosque and other members of staff.[53]

Donations were still not forthcoming from India or elsewhere. Headley's call for Muslims around the world to support the mosque scheme was, nevertheless, endorsed by Adil Arslan (c.1882–1954), a Lebanese Druze Amir and leader, who lived in Egypt and Iraq in the early 1930s.[54] Arslan had met Headley at Woking mosque during a visit to England in 1930. Writing in the Salafi magazine *al-Fath* in September 1932, Arslan urged the Muslim press to back Headley's scheme for a mosque that would, he believed, become a meeting place for Muslims across Europe.[55] Within two months of the publication of Arslan's article, however, the British press reported that the mosque scheme had stalled again due to the difficulty of securing donations during the Depression.[56] Frustrated with the delay, in 1933 Brumwell Thomas took legal action against Headley and the other trustees of the Mosque Fund. The architect claimed more than £10,000 for services rendered and associated fees. A settlement was reached in the High Court with an assurance from Headley that the Nizamiah Mosque scheme had

Figure 15 Lord Headley at *'Id al-Adha*, Woking, April 1932. Abdullah Yusuf Ali is just visible, sitting to the lower right of Headley.
Source: Courtesy of Janet Webb / The Estate of Fifth Lord Headley.

not been abandoned. However, the legal costs depleted the already struggling Trust Fund and, despite all his efforts to push the scheme forward, Headley was unable make any further progress in his lifetime.⁵⁷

Final year: 1934–35

Headley told reporters on the occasion of his seventy-sixth birthday in January 1931 that his prescription for a long and healthy life was 'Never use the word hopeless. It is a poor word, and will never get you anywhere. With it you can do nothing; without it you can do much.'⁵⁸ He added rather wistfully that he had reluctantly given up boxing in the 1920s and, 'Now Anno Domini is creeping along I can just manage to crawl around a golf course'.⁵⁹ Headley was enjoying his semi-retirement in the country. He seldom wrote articles for *The Islamic Review* or other Muslim publications in the 1930s. Although he was in demand from the general press for his views on all sorts of topics – from the afterlife and heaven to the conversion to Islam of Her Highness the Dayang Muda of Sarawak on board a cross-Channel aeroplane – he was more selective in obliging reporters and editors with interviews or statements.⁶⁰

The MSGB was reorganized in October 1932. Its new joint-secretaries, the Woking imam Maulana Abdul Majid and a British Muslim convert, Arthur/Ahmad Bennett, said that the reorganization would allow 'the infusion of new blood into the Society'.⁶¹ The MSGB was henceforth advertised as being 'representative of Muslim interests irrespective of sect, in this country and abroad, propagating authentic knowledge of Islam'.⁶² Headley remained president while William Burchell/Bashyr Pickard (1889–1973), a veteran of the Somme who had converted to Islam in 1922,⁶³ became the first MSGB chairman. Thereafter, Headley continued to attend MSGB meetings but was more often absent than he had been over the previous two decades.

Accompanied by Catharine, Headley attended *'Id*s and special events at Woking as well as meetings in London when he was not in Wiltshire or wintering in the south of France or Egypt. Notably, in June 1934, twelve years after first receiving him at Woking, Headley, accompanied by Catharine, welcomed back to the mosque Abdullah I, the Amir of Transjordan, during his state visit to Britain.⁶⁴ That Headley was still well regarded by Muslims across the world was evidenced a few months later when Adil Arslan's brother, the exiled Lebanese Druze Amir, politician and writer Shakib Arslan (1869–1946), invited him to attend a European Muslim Congress in Geneva.⁶⁵

Shakib Arslan organized the European Muslim Congress with a view to bringing together Muslim leaders and activists from across Europe to discuss issues affecting Islam and Muslims in the modern world. Since the end of the First World War, Arslan had campaigned for Muslim and Arab liberation and independence. Headley was therefore rather unsettled to receive an approach from a staunch pan-Islamist and anti-imperialist like Arslan. He hastily consulted Whitehall officials, who expressed their concerns about Arslan and the 'political flavour' of the proposed Congress. In contrast to his standing among Muslims in different parts of the world, Headley was evidently still unpopular in Whitehall: a civil servant at the Foreign Office noted that 'Lord Headley is a foolish old man and counts for little except his title'.[66] Headley was persuaded not to attend the European Muslim Congress, which was, in any case, postponed by a year to September 1935.[67]

Headley spent the remainder of 1934 with Catharine in London and Wiltshire. They attended the usual society events in town, as well as a meeting of the National League, when Lady Evelyn Cobbold showed a film of the 1933 Hajj to promote her new book, *Pilgrimage to Mecca*.[68] Headley also wrote an article for *The Islamic Review*, his first since contributing a short tribute to Kamal-ud-Din, which was published in spring 1933, and only his third article for *The Islamic Review* since the 1920s. Entitled 'Christians and Muslims: Where We Differ and Why We Differ', the article was published in January 1935. Headley repeated his attack against 'the establishment of certain dogmas invented by Monks and Priests in the Middle Ages' and lamented the prevalence of 'superstition and sacerdotalism' in modern Christianity.[69]

Although Headley had simply summarized in his article thoughts and arguments originally written more than twenty years earlier in *Thoughts for the Future* (1913), he seemed revitalized as the year 1935 began. He celebrated 'Id al-Fitr at Woking on 6 January and presided at a meeting of the MSGB in London three days later. In his opening speech, Headley noted with satisfaction that the Society's membership had increased from thirty when the BMS was founded in 1914 to over 200 in 1935. The speech was reported in *The Times*, which highlighted that Headley also attempted to revive interest in the Nizamiah Mosque project: 'The time had come to make a determined effort to complete the fund. The trustees had always held that they should begin to build only when sufficient funds were available, and thus avoid having an incomplete or inadequate building on their hands.'[70] During January and February, Headley also corresponded with Margaret Brooke, Ranee[71] of Sarawak (1849–1936), who had proposed the idea of producing a number of specially bound copies of the Qur'an 'for presentation purposes' among Muslims in Sarawak.[72] Headley recommended Maulana Muhammad Ali's English edition as 'perhaps the best of the several available'.[73]

Headley returned to Woking on 16 March to celebrate *'Id al-Adha* with over 600 Muslims who packed into the mosque grounds. He spoke about the sensational events of the previous day, when King Ibn Sa'ud and one of his sons had survived an assassination attempt in Mecca. Headley moved a resolution on behalf of the many Muslims present at Woking to express their 'deep sense of horror and indignation at the dastardly attempt on the lives of His Majesty King Ibn Sa'ud and the Crown Prince of Saudi Arabia and wishes to congratulate them on their providential escape'.[74]

Headley did not return to Wiltshire after the *'Id*. He was taken ill in London and his health deteriorated. He was unable to join the MSGB's annual celebration of Muhammad's birthday, which he had attended almost every year since his conversion to Islam. He underwent an operation and was moved to a nursing home in north London. He died there on 22 June 1935 of nephritis (inflammation of the kidneys) and prostate obstruction.

According to *The Islamic Review*, 'A few minutes before he breathed his last, Lord Headley scribbled a note for his son and heir and which ran: "means permitting I should like to be buried with my brother Khwaja [Kamal-ud-Din]".'[75] Kamal-ud-Din, however, had died in India and was buried in Lahore. Catharine arranged for her husband to be buried in the Muslim section of Brookwood Cemetery, near Woking. The funeral took place on 25 June 1935, beginning with prayers led by imam Maulana Aftab-ud-Din Ahmad (1901–56) at Woking mosque. It was not a pleasant summer day: the press reported that, en route to the grave, the cortege 'countered a violent storm which drenched mourners'.[76] Catharine and three of her four stepsons (John Allanson-Winn was away, working in Australia) were joined by around 100 mourners, most of them Muslims, including representatives of the Turkish Embassy and the Albanian and Persian Legations, as well as Khwaja Nazir Ahmad, Sir Hubert Omar Rankin and Lady Helen/Khalida Buchanan-Hamilton (1856–1942), who had converted to Islam in 1929.[77] Headley was buried in a grave near his friend Quilliam/Léon.[78] In subsequent years, other Muslim comrades were buried close by, including Pickthall (1936), Archibald Hamilton (1939) and Yusuf Ali (1953).

Tributes and legacies

Headley's death was as widely reported as his conversion to Islam had been more than twenty years earlier, with notices and obituaries published in newspapers, magazines and journals worldwide.[79] The *Straits Times* of

Singapore lamented that 'the Muslim world has been deprived of the services of a great missionary and a staunch champion of Islam'.[80] The Woking and Lahori Ahmadiyya Muslim communities also published warm tributes. The *Islamic Review* wrote:

> Next to Khwaja Kamal-ud-Din, Lord Headley was the one personality who may rightly be described as the founder of the Woking Mission. [...] It is difficult to write adequately of him who has gone. Our praise seems trite and trivial, our most heartfelt tribute all unworthy in face of the colossal fact of his immense and unique personality. Lord Headley's death has left a gap which time alone can fill. To say that he was popular would be belittling his character.[81]

It added:

> The whole of the Muslim world has mourned the passing away of one of its most distinguished sons and condolence meetings have been held from Japan to America, messages of sympathy and condolences have reached us and glowing tributes have been paid to the memory of the dead – a wonderful recognition of his services indeed, but would it make up the loss the Muslim Community has suffered?[82]

In Lahore, the Ahmadi *Young Islam* newspaper concluded:

> His Lordship did most energetically and actively plunge himself into the service of the cause. Indeed it is not the slightest exaggeration to say that the acceleration which the organised movement of propagation of Islam achieved in England in its very infancy is due mostly to the great personality of Lord Headley.[83]

On 15 July 1935, the Aga Khan presided at a meeting of Muslims in the Savoy Hotel in London 'to mourn the loss of Lord Headley'. The meeting was attended by Catharine and Rowland 'Paddy' Allanson-Winn (1901–69), who had succeeded his father to become the sixth Baron Headley. The meeting concluded with the formation of a 'Headley Memorial Council', which would 'determine the best form of permanent memorial and to collect funds for the purpose'.[84] However, for reasons unknown, nothing came of the initiative and a permanent memorial to Headley was not realized.

The failure of the Headley Memorial Council might well have been linked to disagreements among some of Headley's close Muslim friends immediately after his death. We have seen that, despite the disputes about the Ahmadiyya among British Muslims, Headley largely managed to keep the BMS/MSGB unified. The year before Headley's death and after the Society was reorganized with Bashyr Pickard as chairman, Ahmad Bennett had resigned as joint-secretary. Bennett said he had resigned due to 'indirect Ahmadi influence' at Woking.[85] But matters truly came to a head only after Headley died in summer 1935. His friend, Sir Hubert Omar Rankin, became MSGB president and promptly called for the Society to be completely disassociated from the Ahmadiyya.[86] At a meeting in December 1935, the majority of MSGB members rejected Rankin's proposal on the grounds that, in the spirit of Headley, the Society strived to represent the collective interest of all Muslims in Britain irrespective of theological, ethnic or other differences. According to *The Times*, 'Sir Hubert and several other members walked out' of the meeting; Rankin resigned from the MSGB and said that he would establish 'a new Muslim society in this country which would be orthodox and non-sectarian' but, shortly afterwards, he joined Sheldrake's WIA.[87] The MSGB was reconstituted with Lady Buchanan-Hamilton as president, Pickard and Lovegrove as vice-presidents and a new executive committee which included Lady Evelyn Cobbold and, symbolically, a non-Muslim: Catharine, Dowager Lady Headley.[88]

Headley's widow attempted to revive interest in the Nizamiah Mosque, which might well have become, indirectly, the permanent memorial to Headley that the Aga Khan and others sought. Indeed, soon after Headley's death, prospects for the mosque looked promising. Although Headley had failed in his lifetime to advance the scheme, the Trust Fund continued to accrue interest. New trustees were appointed and, in 1937, seven years after he had first visited the West Kensington site with Headley, the Nizam's heir-apparent, Prince Azam Jah, returned to formally lay the foundation stone for the Nizamiah Mosque.[89] It was reported in the newspapers that the trustees planned 'to build the essential parts of the mosque, leaving room for expansion when more funds became available'.[90] However, further progress was not made before the outbreak of war in 1939 and the Nizam refused to allow the funds to be made available for other mosque projects in London.

Ironically, during the Second World War, the British government came to support the idea of building a central London mosque and invoked arguments Headley had first made for a mosque in the First World War (Chapter 5). Writing to the secretary of state for India in 1940, George Ambrose Lloyd (1879–1941), who was secretary of state for the colonies, argued that it was 'really a scandal that an Empire which has more Muslims in it than Christians should not have in its capital a place of worship for Mohammedans worthy of the Empire'.[91] The British government subsequently allocated £100,000 towards the construction of a mosque in central London as a tribute to the Indian Muslims who had died defending the British Empire. After the war, London County Council issued a compulsory purchase order to acquire the West Kensington site and compensation was paid to the Nizamiah Mosque Trust Fund. The compensation and assets from the Trust Fund were eventually transferred to the government-backed London Central Mosque Trust and thereby contributed to financing the mosque that stands next to Regent's Park today.[92]

Epilogue

Following the failure of the Aga Khan's 'Headley Memorial Council' in 1935, Lord Headley's life and work disappeared from the public consciousness. Headley was, arguably, no less deserving of a memorial in his lifetime than many other influential men and women of the early twentieth century. Headley will not be remembered as a Muslim scholar or intellectual. But his contribution to the development and institutionalization of Islam in Britain, specifically through the transnational Woking Muslim Mission almost from its inception until his death twenty years later, was significant. Headley was a stalwart of the WMM and founding president of the British Muslim Society, a prolific writer and speaker about Islam and, especially, practical issues that affected Western Muslims. He was a pioneering – but not a faultless – Muslim who publicly defended his religion, encouraged others to consider Islam as a viable faith, and showed them how they might live as a Muslim in the West.

Indeed, as soon as he converted to Islam, Headley articulated the challenges of practising his faith in a Western country. Over the following two decades he regularly returned to the practical problems of, for example, praying five times daily and, more controversially, adhering to Islamic prohibitions such as abstaining from alcohol. A century on and with the limitations of surviving primary source material, it is difficult to know what other Muslims – at Woking and elsewhere in the UK and overseas – really thought about Headley's subsequent and oft-repeated call for the 'Westernization' of Islam. We have seen that some Qadiani Ahmadis in England and Muslims in India were vexed that Headley proposed 'insignificant modifications of forms or ceremonies' such as prayer in the West. However, we do not know what Headley's Muslim friends like Abdullah Quilliam/Léon or Abdullah Yusuf Ali thought (or if they questioned his qualifications to make statements about complex issues), let alone his mentor Khwaja Kamal-ud-Din, who had first presented to Headley an Islam that was 'elastic' and adaptable to the Western cultural environment.

What is clear is that, like Quilliam/Léon and other converts of the period, after his religious conversion Headley simply did not consider himself to be divorced from his Christian Western background. As a Muslim, he highlighted the commonalities between the 'sister religions' of Christianity and Islam, as well as the religious and material continuities between his life before and after his conversion to Islam. It therefore followed that Headley felt able to defend Islam against attack from, especially, Christian clergy and missionaries, and engage in Muslim–Christian dialogue, though not always successfully as he was inevitably forced onto the defensive. Moreover, it gave Headley the confidence to speak and write about Western Muslim identity and the Westernization of Muslim practice and Islam as part of a genuine desire to broaden its appeal, to indigenize and institutionalize it in Britain, and thereby secure its future in the West. These challenges continue to resonate with Muslims in the Global West.

That Headley was not a flawless Muslim made him all the more human in the eyes of his co-religionists, but also vulnerable to attack from his many critics, including Christian adversaries and other Muslims. It appears that Headley was well respected by Muslims connected with the WMM and he went unchallenged as president of the British Muslim Society/Muslim Society of Great Britain. Headley was not, nor did he claim to be, a leader of all Muslims in Britain. There is little evidence that he, or, for that matter, most of his predominantly middle-class Muslim contemporaries in London and Woking, interacted with the historic, working-class Muslim communities in, for example, East London, South Shields, Cardiff or Glasgow.

If Headley's world was predominantly middle- and upper-middle class, it was not by any means a wholly conventional white English one. Headley's social and moral outlook was in many respects extremely conservative, but he appears to have mixed easily with Muslims and non-Muslims of diverse ethnicities. In his capacity as a trustee of the WMM and president of the BMS/MSGB, Headley met countless delegations of Muslims from across Asia, Africa and Europe in England and overseas.[1] In Britain, he forged close relationships with, especially, Indian Muslims like Kamal-ud-Din and the many subsequent imams of Woking mosque, Abdullah Yusuf Ali, Syed Ameer Ali, Abbas Ali Baig and the Aga Khan, Sir Sultan Mahomed Shah. Those relationships also underline the fact that Headley embraced Muslims from different branches of Islam and schools of thought: Sunnis and Shi'is, Sufis, Isma'ilis and Ahmadis. He initially attempted to build bridges with Qadiani Ahmadis in Britain but was not wholly successful and, though he largely kept a lid on differences between Muslims in the BMS/MSGB, he increasingly faced criticism, especially from Qadianis and Muslims in India during the 1920s and 1930s.

That said, Headley was not only remarkably well known but also generally respected and connected with Muslims across the world between the two world wars. While he had little contact with Muslims in other parts of Western Europe or North America, Headley knew or was acquainted with some of the early twentieth century's most prominent Muslims within the British Empire and parts of the former Ottoman Empire where Britain had territorial and strategic interests and ambitions. In addition to those already mentioned, they included the King of the Hijaz, Hussein ibn Ali al-Hashimi, and his son, the Amir of Transjordan, Abdullah I; the King of Egypt and Sudan, Fuad I; the Begum of Bhopal, Sultan Jahan (1858–1930); the Nizam of Hyderabad, Asaf Jah VII; and the Grand Mufti of Jerusalem, Mohammed Amin al-Husseini. They also included Muslim activists, intellectuals and politicians such as Maulana Muhammad Ali, Sir Muhammad Iqbal, Sir Mian Muhammad Shafi, Inayat Khan, Sirdar Ikbal Ali Shah, Dusé Mohamed Ali, Marmaduke Pickthall, Mohamed and Shaukat Ali, Muhammad Rashid Rida, Vakkom Moulavi and Adil and Shakib Arslan. Looking at Headley's connections and interactions with these and many other Muslims sheds light on the extent to which their concerns and struggles in the early twentieth century were globalized.[2]

Headley undoubtedly benefited from white male class and colonial privilege throughout his life, and not least after he converted to Islam and in his interactions with Muslims in a globalized world. Notably, most of the Muslims cited earlier were colonial subjects. Colonial privilege was not, in Headley's case, necessarily a one-sided affair. Headley was not a passive figure, but his colonial privilege could and sometimes did work to the advantage of his Asian or African associates. To highlight two examples discussed in this book: Headley no doubt became a public Muslim figurehead of the WMM and president of the BMS partly because he was a white British, titled man, but we have seen that this worked to Kamal-ud-Din's advantage as he sought to propagate Islam in Britain, promote the WMM internationally and enhance his own position in the world. Likewise, Headley was given special privilege and dispensation when he made the Hajj as a guest of King Hussein in 1923, but the latter also made great capital of his British Muslim *Hajji* at a time when diplomatic relations between the governments of the Hijaz and Britain were strained, and Headley returned to Britain an advocate of Hussein and his fragile government.

Despite his early involvement in politics, Headley was never a significant voice in British political life. After his religious conversion, Headley's attempt to avoid political issues was probably well intentioned but frequently contradicted by his words and actions. A traditional Conservative, he could not resist dipping into political issues, especially as they affected the stability of the British Crown and Empire. It follows that, despite his concerns about the deterioration of the *umma* and belief in religious solidarity, Headley was not wholly comfortable with pan-Islamic politics and the pan-Islamic aim to liberate the so-called Muslim world[3] from European domination. Consequently, Headley's position on political issues was at times ambiguous, and this put him at odds with some of his closest Muslim friends and associates. We have seen, for example, that his support for the Ottoman Caliphate was tentative and wavering, and he belatedly switched to the unfashionable idea of an Arab Caliphate; and he simply avoided the Khilafat Movement delegation when they visited England in the 1920s. Ultimately, Headley was not an effective political lobbyist.

Although the initiative for a Headley Memorial quickly floundered in 1935, Headley was not, of course, entirely forgotten by Muslims after his death. Notably, the WMM republished his first book, *A Western Awakening to Islam*, in 1949 and, into the 1950s, new Muslim converts continued to state that they had been influenced by Headley and inspired by his books and articles in *The Islamic Review*.[4] Many years after Headley's death, the grand imam of al-Azhar, Shaykh Abdel-Halim Mahmoud (1910–78), cited Headley as 'an exemplary European Muslim who rendered a great service to Islam in Europe'.[5]

However, it is the case that, beyond certain Muslim circles, Headley was, indeed, forgotten and, perhaps, *conveniently* forgotten in his home country. He knew or came into contact with many influential British politicians and establishment figures after 1913. Yet, Headley's public conversion to Islam and his subsequent defence and promotion of that religion were neither welcomed nor ever wholly accepted by the British establishment or colonial authorities. Notes about Headley in official government files, some of them quoted in this book, reveal a deep disdain for the 'English pervert to Islam' as a British intelligence officer described him in 1923. Most British government ministers, senior officials and their administrators in Whitehall and in consulates overseas did not understand why Headley had converted to an apparently inferior religion like Islam and they were annoyed that he consistently lobbied their departments on behalf of Muslims in Britain and the British Empire. Headley faced an uphill challenge because most of his compatriots did not respect Islam, much less have an interest in converting to it.

On balance, it is, perhaps, because of Headley's tenacity as a public Muslim figure when Islam was popularly derided, as well as his contribution to the institutionalization of Islam in Britain, that he is remembered today. Headley is commemorated by the international Lahori Ahmadiyyat, which has a comprehensive section dedicated to him on its UK branch website: 'The pride of place among Woking's converts goes to Lord Headley.'[6] Headley's life and work is also slowly being revived and invoked by other Muslims and non-Muslims keen to reclaim and document the history of Islam in the West. All of Headley's books have been reprinted in recent years and his lecture transcripts and articles published in *The Islamic Review* and *The Light* are freely available online.[7] He may not ever be celebrated in quite the same way as the pioneering Quilliam/Léon or the scholarly Pickthall, but, especially through social media, Headley is gradually being recognized as an important figure in the history of Islam in Britain and the Global West.[8]

Notes

Introduction

1 *The Light* (hereafter *TL*), 16 April 1926, 3.
2 Office for National Statistics (UK), 'Muslim Population in the UK', 2 August 2018. Available online: https://www.ons.gov.uk/aboutus/transparencyandgovernance/ freedomofinformationfoi/muslimpopulationintheuk/ (accessed 18 October 2019); Humayun Ansari, *'The Infidel Within': Muslims in Britain since 1800*, new edn (London: Hurst, 2018), xviii.
3 See, for example, Yvonne Yazbeck Haddad (ed.), *Muslims in the West: From Sojourners to Citizens* (New York: Oxford University Press, 2002); Ansari, *'The Infidel Within'* (2004/2018); Nathalie Clayer and Eric Germain (ed.), *Islam in Inter-War Europe* (London: Hurst, 2008); David Motadel (ed.), *Islam and the European Empires* (Oxford: Oxford University Press, 2014); Edward E. Curtis (ed.), *The Bloomsbury Reader on Islam in the West* (London: Bloomsbury, 2015); Ron Geaves, *Islam and Britain: Muslim Mission in an Age of Empire* (London: Bloomsbury, 2018).
4 Marmaduke Pickthall, *The Meaning of the Glorious Koran: An Explanatory Translation* (London: Alfred A. Knopf, 1930).
5 On Quilliam, see Ron Geaves, *Islam in Victorian Britain: The Life and Times of Abdullah Quilliam* (Markfield: Kube, 2010); Jamie Gilham and Ron Geaves (ed.), *Victorian Muslim: Abdullah Quilliam and Islam in the West* (London: Hurst, 2017). On Pickthall, see Anne Fremantle, *Loyal Enemy* (London: Hutchinson, 1938); Peter Clark, *Marmaduke Pickthall: British Muslim* (London: Quartet, 1986); Geoffrey P. Nash (ed.), *Marmaduke Pickthall: Islam and the Modern World* (Leiden and Boston, MA: Brill, 2017).
6 Headley has been name-checked, in passing, in popular books about Islam in contemporary Britain, for example, James Fergusson, *Al-Britannia: A Journey through Muslim Britain* (London: Bantam Press, 2017), 315; Sayeeda Warsi, *The Enemy Within: A Tale of Muslim Britain* (London: Allen Lane, 2017), 11, 19. By contrast, he is not mentioned in the recent scholarly survey by Martin Pugh, *Britain and Islam: A History from 622 to the Present Day* (New Haven and London: Yale University Press, 2019), and features little beyond also being name-checked in Ansari, *'The Infidel Within'*, 130, 132–4, 396. The only substantive work on Headley is an article written while researching this book: Jamie Gilham, 'The British Muslim

Baron: Lord Headley and Islam, 1913-35', *Common Knowledge* 23, no. 3 (2017): 468–95. Headley also figures more prominently in Jamie Gilham, *Loyal Enemies: British Converts to Islam, 1850-1950* (London: Hurst, 2014), chapters 4–6; Umar Ryad, 'Salafiyya, Ahmadiyya and European Converts to Islam in the Interwar Period', in *Muslims in Interwar Europe: A Trans-Cultural Historical Perspective*, ed. Agai Bekim, Umar Ryad and Sajid Mehdi (Leiden and Boston, MA: Brill, 2015), 47–87; Geaves, *Islam and Britain*, chapters 7–8. In 2004, Headley was added to the *Oxford Dictionary of National Biography*: see Jason Tomes, 'Winn, Rowland George Allanson Allanson-', in *Oxford Dictionary of National Biography*, ed. H. C. G. Matthew and Brian Harrison, vol. 59 (Oxford: Oxford University Press, 2004), 744–6.
7   Gilham, *Loyal Enemies*, 13–15.
8   Brian Taylor, 'Conversion and Cognition: An Area for Empirical Study in the Microsociology of Religious Knowledge', *Social Compass* 23, no. 1 (1976): 16–21; Brian Taylor, 'Recollection and Membership: Converts' Talk and the Ratiocination of Commonality', *Sociology* 12, no. 2 (1978): 316–24; James A. Beckford, 'Accounting for Conversion', *British Journal of Sociology* 29, no. 2 (1978): 249–62.
9   Beckford, 'Accounting for Conversion', 260.
10 John Lofland and Norman Skonovd, 'Conversion Motifs', *Journal for the Scientific Study of Religion* 20, no. 4 (1981): 373–85.
11 Lewis R. Rambo, *Understanding Religious Conversion* (New Haven: Yale University Press, 1993), 137–9.

Chapter 1

1   See A. L. Macfie, *The Eastern Question 1774–1923*, rev. edn (Harlow: Longman, 1996).
2   This and the following short history of the Barons Allanson and Winn is based primarily on information from H. A. Doubleday, Duncan Warr and Lord Howard De Walden (ed.), *The Complete Peerage, or a History of the House of Lords and All Its Members from the Earliest Times*, vol. 2 (London: The St. Catherine Press, 1926), 429–31; Arthur G. M. Hesilrige (ed.), *Debrett's Peerage and Titles of Courtesy* (London: Dean and Son, 1921), 463–4; Charles Kidd and David Williamson (ed.), *Debrett's Peerage and Baronetage* (London: Debrett's Peerage Ltd./Macmillan, 1990), 599.
3   Doubleday et al., *The Complete Peerage*, 431; NUI Galway, 'Connacht and Munster Landed Estates'. Available online: http://landedestates.nuigalway.ie/LandedEstates/jsp/estate-show.jsp?id=1822 (accessed 10 June 2018).
4   Quoted in ibid.

5   Anon, 'English Tourists in Ireland', *The Dublin Review* 3, no. 6 (1837): 414.
6   Ibid., 425.
7   Quoted in ibid., 425–6.
8   Mark Bence-Jones, *A Guide to Irish Country Houses*, new edn (London: Constable, 1988), 136.
9   See the Irish Government National Inventory of Architectural Heritage website. Available online: http://buildingsofireland.ie/niah/search.jsp?type=record&county=KE&regno=21306301 (accessed 10 June 2018).
10 *Daily British Colonist* (Victoria, British Columbia), 22 May 1886, 2.
11 On Charlie Winn, see obituaries in *The Kerry Evening Post* (hereafter *KEP*), 15 January 1913, 2 and 16 July 1913, 4; *The Essex County Chronicle*, 24 January 1913, 3.
12 Doubleday et al., *The Complete Peerage*, 431.
13 Kidd and Williamson, *Debrett's*, 559.
14 The National Archives, London (hereafter TNA), 'Census of England, Wales and Scotland 1871'.
15 A[llanson]. W[inn]., *Thoughts for the Future* (London and Felling-on-Tyne: The Walter Scott Publishing Co., 1913), 47. The hymn, written in the first decade of the twentieth century, continues: 'I knew not then, as now I know / That she was made an angel fair, / Too bright to stay with us below, / Her feet were on the golden stair.'
16 *The Islamic Review* (hereafter *IR*) 14, no. 9 (1926): 349.
17 Ibid., 348.
18 Ibid., 349.
19 Ibid., 350.
20 Ibid.
21 Author's interview with fifth Lord Headley's great-granddaughter, Berkshire, 14 February 2003.
22 J. A. Venn (ed.), *Alumni Cantabrigienses*, part 2, vol. 6 (Cambridge: Cambridge University Press, 1954), 540.
23 Private Collection (hereafter PC), Papers of Ivy Davis (hereafter PID), Birth Certificate of Laura Davis, 20 January 1875.
24 Anon, *Who's Who 1914* (London: Adam and Charles Black, 1914), 960.
25 For example, PC, Papers of Rowland George Allanson-Winn, fifth Lord Headley (hereafter PLH), Hon. Rowland Allanson-Winn to Rowland George Allanson-Winn (hereafter RGAW), 12 July 1876.
26 Ibid., 28 October 1876.
27 Ibid.
28 Ibid., 10 December 1876.
29 Ibid., 30 April 1877.
30 'Pendragon' (pseudonym of the journalist Henry Sampson, 1841–91), editor of *The Referee* magazine, noted in 1889 that he remembered seeing Rowland 'ruled out, or

at any rate made the loser of his bout, in a heavy-weight Queensbury competition because he was hitting his opponent hard enough to hurt him' (*The Referee*, 1 December 1889, 2).
31 *The Cambridge Independent Press*, 2 February 1878, 5.
32 PLH, Hon. Rowland Allanson-Winn to RGAW, 22 February (*c.*1879).
33 PLH, Margaretta Allanson-Winn to RGAW, 29 April (*c.*1879).
34 See, for example, PLH, Hon. Rowland Allanson-Winn to RGAW, 11 January 1882.
35 The British Newspaper Archive, 'Salisbury and Winchester Journal'. Available online: https://www.britishnewspaperarchive.co.uk/titles/salisbury-and-winchester-journal (accessed 14 June 2018).
36 PLH, Hon. Rowland Allanson-Winn to RGAW, 30 November 1882.
37 Ibid., 24 December 1883.
38 Ibid.
39 RGAW quoted in ibid.
40 Ibid., 9 September 1885.
41 Ibid., 26 October 1885.
42 Ibid.
43 *Daily British Colonist*, 22 May 1886, 2.
44 *The Western Times*, 28 July 1887, 4; *Daily British Colonist*, 22 May 1886, 2; *The Hemel Hempstead Gazette*, 26 June 1886, 3.
45 *Daily British Colonist*, 22 May 1886, 2. It was also reported that 'On the occasion of Lord Headley's last visit to Ireland, he being a magistrate held at court at Tralee, and while he was sitting upon the bench a bailiff stood guarding the door, lest the magistrate might escape the service of eight writs, which his creditors had procured against him. There was but one exit from the building, and the baron failing to tire the bailiff out, was finally compelled to adjourn the court, which he did after dark, and ran the gauntlet. The writs were duly served, and Lord Headley disappeared from Tralee on the following morning, since which time he has not regarded Ireland as a pleasant place of residence' (ibid.).
46 Ibid.
47 Anon, 'Statesmen No. 613: Sir Frederick Seager Hunt, Bart.', *Vanity Fair*, 18 May 1893, n.p.
48 Hunt was, by all accounts, a genial man. *Vanity Fair* noted that 'he is so good a fellow that, even in [the] Westminster bear-garden, no decent man has found a word to say against him. He is generous; and, despite the fact he is a distiller, he is a gentleman. He knows a good cigar when he gets it' (ibid).
49 *The Times*, 27 January 1887, 10.
50 See, for example, *KEP*, 29 January 1887, 3.
51 *The Northern Daily Mail and South Durham Herald*, 4 July 1892, 2.
52 *The Freeman's Journal*, 26 January 1887, 5.

53 *Illustrated London News*, 29 January 1887, 1.
54 *The Times*, 25 January 1887, 10. See also *The Globe*, 25 January 1887, 6. Rowland senior also had a right to reply in *The Times*, in which he set out the circumstances that led to the evictions: see *The Times*, 27 January 1887, 10.
55 *The Aberdeen Journal*, 9 June 1887, 4.
56 The *Times* letter was repr. in *KEP*, 29 February 1888, 4.
57 Rowland senior appeared to be in good health until he was struck down by angina while addressing a meeting of shareholders of the Metropolitan District Railway at the Cannon Street Hotel, London, in February 1888. It was thought that he was recovering well and, in March, he returned home to recuperate. See *St. James's Gazette*, 28 February 1888, 11; *The Morning Post*, 10 May 1888, 5.
58 R. G. Allanson-Winn, *Boxing* (London: George Bell and Sons, 1889).
59 Ibid., 1.
60 *St. James's Gazette*, 21 November 1889, 26.
61 R. G. Allanson-Winn and C. Phillipps-Wolley, *Broadsword and Singlestick: With Chapters on Quarter-Staff, Bayonet, Cudgel, Shillalah, Walking-Stick, Umbrella and Other Weapons of Self-Defence* (London: George Bell and Sons, 1890), n.p. (preface).
62 *The Globe*, 14 November 1890, 6.
63 Allanson-Winn and Phillipps-Wolley, *Broadsword*, 2–3.
64 *St. James's Gazette*, 4 December 1890, 28.
65 *The Scotsman*, 17 November 1890, 3.
66 Ernest Bell (ed.), *Handbook of Athletic Sports*, vol. 3 (London: George Bell and Sons, 1890).
67 *KEP*, 14 November 1891, 3.
68 On Census day 1891 (5 April), Rowland was registered at the Duke Street address and his profession given as 'Magistrate for County Kerry, law student and secretary': TNA, 'Census of England, Wales and Scotland 1891'.
69 *KEP*, 23 January 1892, 4.
70 Ibid.
71 Ibid.
72 Ibid.
73 See, for example, *The Morning Post*, 2 May 1892, 2.
74 *The Canterbury Journal and Farmer's Gazette*, 28 May 1892, 5.
75 Ibid. See also *The Primrose League Gazette*, 18 June 1892, 14.
76 *KEP*, 18 June 1892, 2.
77 Repr. in *KEP*, 25 June 1892, 4; see, for example, *The Northern Daily Mail and South Durham Herald*, 4 July 1892, 2.
78 *The Cork Constitution*, 8 July 1892, 3.
79 *KEP*, 9 July 1892, 4.
80 *The Irish Times*, 4 July 1892, 6.

81 *KEP*, 6 July 1892, 3.
82 Ibid.
83 *The Irish Times*, 13 July 1892, 3.
84 Ibid.
85 Ibid.
86 *KEP*, 13 July 1892, 3.
87 In 1892, a third Kerry South candidate, representing the Irish National League, polled 225 votes (9.3 per cent). See Anon, *The Popular Guide to the New House of Commons and Record of the Election of 1892, July 1 to July 29*, 2nd edn (London: Pall Mall Gazette, 1892), 76.
88 *KEP*, 20 July 1892, 3.
89 Ibid.
90 Ibid.

Chapter 2

1 See Kartar Lalvani, *The Making of India: The Untold Story of British Enterprise* (London: Bloomsbury, 2016), chapter 7.
2 Anon, *The Cyclopedia of India*, vol. 2 (Calcutta: Cyclopedia Publishing Company, 1908), 379.
3 *The Courier and Advertiser* (Dundee; hereafter *TCA*), 23 January 1929, 12.
4 *The Homeward Mail from India, China, and the East* (hereafter *HM*), 14 September 1892, 1176.
5 Lord Headley, 'Pilgrimage to Mecca', *Journal of the Central Asian Society* 11, no. 1 (1924): 24.
6 *HM*, 25 October 1892, 1371.
7 Anon, *A Handbook for Travellers in India and Ceylon* (London: John Murray, 1891), xv.
8 The *tonga* journey from Rawalpindi to Srinagar, albeit in 1897 (by which time the road had been improved), is detailed in John Collett and A. Mitra, *A Guide for Visitors to Kashmir*, new edn (Calcutta: W. Newman and Co., 1898), 14–26.
9 On Kashmir as a 'resort of the Raj', see Brigid Keenan, *Travels in Kashmir: A Popular History of Its People, Places and Crafts* (Delhi: Oxford University Press, 1989), chapter 3.
10 Collett and Mitra, *Guide for Visitors*, 50.
11 The first and most important division in the *umma* occurred after the death of Muhammad in relation to his successor. Unlike the vast majority of Muslims (Sunnis), Shi'is believe in the succession of the direct descendants of Muhammad through the line of the Prophet's cousin and son-in-law Ali ibn Talib (601–61) rather than the Caliphate.

12 Collett and Mitra, *Guide for Visitors*, 69; Anon, *The Imperial Gazetteer of India*, new edn, vol. 15 (Oxford: Clarendon Press, 1908), 99.
13 Collett and Mitra, *Guide for Visitors*, 68.
14 E. F. Knight, *Where Three Empires Meet: A Narrative of Recent Travel in Kashmir, Western Tibet, Gilgit, and the Adjoining Countries* (1893; repr., London: Longmans, Green and Co., 1905), 75–6.
15 For contemporaneous images, see Arthur Neve, *Picturesque Kashmir* (London: Sands and Company, 1900).
16 Anon, *Imperial Gazetteer*, 72–3.
17 Collett and Mitra, *Guide for Visitors*, 1.
18 Ibid., 17.
19 Knight, *Where Three Empires Meet*, 9.
20 Ibid., 22.
21 Ibid., 22–3.
22 Ibid., 20.
23 Anon, *Imperial Gazetteer*, 79; Collett and Mitra, *Guide for Visitors*, 16.
24 Probably Henry Mitchell, senior partner of Spedding and Company: see Anon, *The Cyclopedia of India*, 37.
25 *HM*, 15 August 1893, 1030–1.
26 Quoted in R. G. Allanson-Winn, 'Notes on Road Construction', *Transactions of the Institution of Civil Engineers of Ireland* 28 (1898–1901): 261–2.
27 Ibid., 263
28 Ibid., 260.
29 *HM*, 27 August 1894, 1129.
30 Quoted in Allanson-Winn, 'Notes on Road Construction', 262.
31 Ibid., 236–7.
32 Ibid., 262–3.
33 Quoted in ibid., 261.
34 Ibid., 261–2.
35 Collett and Mitra, *Guide for Visitors*, 21–2.
36 Anon, *Imperial Gazetteer*, 77; Knight, *Where Three Empires Meet*, 35.
37 Ibid., 37.
38 Ibid., 37–8.
39 Collett and Mitra, *Guide for Visitors*, 10.
40 Charles Allen, *Plain Tales from the Raj: Images of British India in the Twentieth Century*, new edn (1975; repr., London: Abacus, 2000), 64.
41 Ibid., 231.
42 He mentioned this to an Egyptian reporter in 1923: see Ryad, 'Salafiyya', 56.
43 Allen, *Plain Tales*, 153.
44 Ibid.
45 Collett and Mitra, *Guide for Visitors*, 109–12.

46 Lieutenant-Colonel H. H. Godwin-Austin, 'Obituary: Mr. W. H. Johnson', *Proceedings of the Royal Geographical Society and Monthly Record of Geography* 5, no. 5 (1883): 291.
47 Person of status; ruler.
48 Godwin-Austin, 'Obituary', 292.
49 Major-General Sir Henry C. Rawlinson, 'On the Recent Journey of Mr. W. H. Johnson from Leh, in Ladakh, to Ilchi in Chinese Turkestan', *Proceedings of the Royal Geographical Society* 11, no. 1 (1866): 6.
50 Peter Hopkirk, *Foreign Devils on the Silk Road: The Search for the Lost Treasures of Central Asia* (London: John Murray, 1980), 39.
51 British Library (hereafter BL), India Office Records (hereafter IOR), British India Office Births and Baptisms Ecclesiastical Returns (hereafter BIOBBER), Parish Register Transcripts from the Presidency of Bengal (Baptisms), N-1-146, 3 December 1873.
52 BL, IOR, British India Office Deaths and Burials Ecclesiastical Returns, Parish Register Transcripts from the Presidency of Bengal (Burials), N-1-183, 5 February 1883.
53 Godwin-Austin, 'Obituary: Mr. W. H. Johnson', 291.
54 Ibid.
55 BL, IOR, British India Office Marriages Ecclesiastical Returns, Parish Register Transcripts from the Presidency of Bengal, N-1-201, 3 September 1887. Cooke became a commissioned officer in October 1861 and retired in the 1880s as a Major in the 3rd (Prince of Wales's) Dragoon Guards: BL, IOR, *The Quarterly Indian Army List for April 1, 1891* (Calcutta: Military Department/Office of the Superintendent of Government Printing, India, 1891), 163.
56 BL, IOR, BIOBBER, Roman Catholic Returns of Baptisms, Marriages and Burials (Baptisms), N-3-RC, 22 August 1844. John's father, also John, was a musician in the 1st Bombay Fusiliers.
57 BL, IOR, BIOBBER, Parish Register Transcripts from the Presidency of Bengal (Baptisms), N-1-221, 4 May 1892. Cyril's birth date as stated on his baptism record is contradicted by some sources. While army and merchant navy records give the year as 1892, the Census of Ireland for 1901 and again for 1911 give 1893 (see TNA, British Army Service Records, WO 363, First World War Service Record for Cyril Norman Johnson-Winn, 1915–1919; TNA, Merchant Navy Seamen Records, BT 349/CR1, Record for Cyril Norman Johnson-Winn, 1923).
58 I have been unable to find a definite death or burial record for John Cooke. He was listed as a retired Major in the British government's official *Quarterly Indian Army List* for April 1891, but was not included in the April 1894 edn. When Teresa married Rowland in 1899, her given surname was Johnstone rather than Cooke and she was listed as a 'spinster' rather than a widow: General Record Office (England), Marriage Certificate of Rowland George Allanson-Winn and Teresa St. Josephine Johnson, 27 October 1899.

59 R. G. Allanson-Winn, *Boxing* (London: A. D. Innes and Company, 1897).
60 Ibid., n.p.
61 *The Graphic*, 1 January 1898, 12. See also *The Scots Magazine*, 2 May 1898, 474; *The Birmingham Daily Post*, 28 October 1897, 8.
62 *The Referee*, 9 January 1898, 1.
63 *HM*, 25 January 1897, 128.
64 *The Colonies and India* (London), 30 January 1897, 28; *HM*, 25 January 1897, 128. 'Cooke' is misspelt 'Coode' in *The Colonies and India*, but not in *HM*.
65 The allegations and counter-allegations are summarized in *The Times*, 28 June 1900, 3.
66 The reason for Rowland's return to India in autumn 1897 is unclear, and his travel arrangements must have changed as he was officially recorded as a passenger on three different steamships due to sail from London to Bombay between August and October 1897: the SS *India* (August), the SS *Britannia* (September) and the SS *Carthage* (October): *HM*, 19 July 1897, 977; 31 August 1897, 1176; and 2 October 1897, 1437. He left Bombay on the SS *Caledonia* on 25 December 1897, and returned to London in January 1898: *HM*, 7 January 1898, 61.
67 See R. G. Allanson-Winn, 'The Constructive Power of the Sea', *Transactions of the Institution of Civil Engineers of Ireland* 28 (1902): 125–6.
68 *The Irish Builder and Engineer* (hereafter *IBE*), 2 June 1906, 426.
69 Ibid.
70 Allanson-Winn, 'The Constructive Power', 143.
71 Ibid., 144.
72 *Bexhill-on-Sea Observer*, 1 July 1899, 2.
73 R. G. Allanson-Winn, *Sea-Coast Erosion and Remedial Works* (London: St. Bride's Press, n.d. [1904]), 32. See, for example, reports of the paper in *The Yorkshire Post* (hereafter *TYP*), 6 June 1899, 6 and *The Norfolk Chronicle and Norwich Gazette*, 10 June 1899, 12.
74 Allanson-Winn, *Sea-Coast Erosion*, n.p. (introduction).
75 *The Times*, 4 October 1899, 2; *KEP*, 23 October 1899, 2 and 25 October 1899, 3. The *Times* letter was republished in newspapers across the UK, for example *The Liverpool Mercury*, 27 October 1899, 8. See also government correspondence about the proposal in Allanson-Winn, 'The Constructive Power', 161–3.
76 General Record Office, Marriage Certificate of RGAW and Teresa Johnson, 27 October 1899.

Chapter 3

1 *The Daily Telegraph* (London), 1 January 1900, 9.
2 The matter was settled in court. Following a short hearing, the judge successfully convinced Rowland and Lord Headley to settle the matter privately: *The Times*, 28 June 1900, 3 and 29 June 1900, 16.

3. The National Archives of Ireland (hereafter TNAI), 'Census of Ireland 1901'. Available online: http://www.census.nationalarchives.ie/pages/1901/Dublin/Dalkey/Sorrento_Road/1317259/ (accessed 25 March 2018).
4. Allanson-Winn, *Sea-Coast Erosion*, 32.
5. R. G. Allanson-Winn, 'Harnessing the Sea: A New Method of Coast Protection', *Pearson's Magazine* (UK edn) 9, no. 50 (1900): 183–8, and (USA edn), 3, no. 4 (1900): 363–7; *North Otago Times* (New Zealand), 10 August 1900, 1.
6. Allanson-Winn, 'The Constructive Power of the Sea', 124–85.
7. R. G. Allanson-Winn, 'The Youghal Foreshore Protection Works; and Deep-Sea Erosion on the East Coast of England', *Transactions of the Institution of Civil Engineers of Ireland* 30 (1904): 144–75.
8. R. G. Allanson-Winn, 'The Protection and Improvement of Foreshores by the Utilization of Tidal and Wave Action', *Transactions of the American Society of Civil Engineers* 50, paper 944 (1903): 66–94.
9. R. G. Allanson-Winn and C. E. Walker, *Self-Defence, Being a Guide to Boxing, Quarter-Staff and Bayonet Practice, the Walking-Stick Cudgel, Fencing, etc.* (London: Lawrence and Bullen, 1903).
10. *IBE*, 22 October 1904, 713.
11. Allanson-Winn, *Sea-Coast Erosion*. Other papers and articles included R. G. Allanson-Winn, 'Foreshore Protection and Public Health', *Contract Journal and Specification Record* 45 (1901–2): 377; R. G. Allanson-Winn, 'Some Recent Developments in the Design and Construction of Groynes', *Fielden's Magazine* 5 (1901–2): 539.
12. *IBE*, 22 September 1906, 774.
13. *IBE*, 27 January 1906, 49.
14. *IBE*, 22 September 1906, 774.
15. *IBE*, 20 April 1907, 298.
16. *IBE*, 4 May 1907, 314.
17. Ibid., 317.
18. *IBE*, 1 June 1907, 401.
19. *IBE*, 11 August 1906, 653.
20. *The Times*, 6 November 1907, 3.
21. A. W., *Thoughts*, 48.
22. PLH, RGAW to Lord Headley, 8 June 1911.
23. TNAI, 'Census of Ireland, 1911'. Available online: http://www.census.nationalarchives.ie/pages/1911/Dublin/Dalkey/Coliemore_Road/98044/ (accessed 25 March 2018).
24. PLH, RGAW to Lord Headley, 3 May 1911.
25. Ibid.
26. A. W., *Thoughts*, 49.

27 TNAI, 'Census of Ireland, 1911'. Available online: http://www.census.nationalarchives.ie/pages/1911/Dublin/Dalkey/Coliemore_Road/98044/ (accessed 25 March 2018).
28 TNAI, 'Census of Ireland, 1911'. Available online: http://www.census.nationalarchives.ie/pages/1911/Dublin/Rathmines___Rathgar_West/Grove_Park/65386/ and http://www.census.nationalarchives.ie/pages/1911/Dublin/Arran_Quay/Richmond_Male_Asylum/49504/ (accessed 25 March 2018).
29 See Brendan D. Kelly, 'One Hundred Years Ago: The Richmond Asylum, Dublin in 1907', *Irish Journal of Psychological Medicine* 24, no. 3 (2007): 108–14.
30 TNAI, 'Census of Ireland, 1911'. Available online: http://www.census.nationalarchives.ie/reels/nai000097802/ (accessed 25 March 2018).
31 Quoted in Kelly, 'One Hundred Years', 112.
32 Ibid., 111.
33 PLH, RGAW to Lord Headley, 3 May 1911.
34 Ibid.
35 Ibid.
36 Ibid., 8 June 1911.
37 Ibid., 6 May 1911.
38 Ibid., 3 May 1911.
39 Ibid., 6 May 1911.
40 Ibid. and 3 May 1911.
41 Ibid., 6 May 1911.
42 Ibid., 3 May 1911.
43 Ibid., 6 May 1911.
44 Ibid.
45 Ibid., 8 June 1911.
46 Ibid., 29 August 1911.
47 Ibid., 3 May 1911.
48 The beneficiary of her will was a Mr George T. Rowe. See TNAI, 'Calendars of Wills and Administrations 1858–1922'. Available online: http://www.willcalendars.nationalarchives.ie/reels/cwa/005014924/005014924_00831.pdf (accessed 25 March 2018).
49 Author's interview with the fifth Lord Headley's granddaughter, Surrey, 11 January 2018.
50 TNA, Merchant Navy Seamen Records, BT 349/CR1, Record for Cyril Norman Johnson-Winn, 1923; PID, Lord Headley to Vivienne (surname unknown), 14 July 1931; author's interview with the fifth Lord Headley's granddaughter, Surrey, 11 January 2018. A 'Cyril N. Johnson' was born in 1892 and died in Surrey in 1957, though it is unclear if this was Teresa's son.
51 *Muslim India and Islamic Review* (hereafter *MIIR*) 1, no. 12 (1914): 444; A. W., *Thoughts*, 14.

52 Ibid.
53 Ibid., 24.
54 Ibid., 32.
55 Ibid., 25.
56 Ibid., 29.
57 PLH, Undated note written by RGAW.
58 Ibid.
59 'Who among you fears the Lord / and obeys the voice of his servant? / Let him who walks in darkness / and has no light / trust in the name of the LORD / and rely on his God' (Isaiah, 50:10).
60 An editorial comment in *Islamic Review and Muslim India* (hereafter *IRMI*) in 1914 suggested that Headley wrote the introduction to *Thoughts for the Future* 'some eight or nine years ago' (*IRMI* 2, no. 4 [1914]: 139), but it seems likely that he wrote it in the summer of 1913, *after* he had begun corresponding with a Muslim missionary (see Chapter 4). The precise publication date of *Thoughts for the Future* is unknown, though the British Library – the national legal deposit library – received a copy on 5 November 1913.
61 Charlie Allanson-Winn died in Dublin on 13 January 1913: see *The Times*, 14 January 1913, 9.
62 A. W., *Thoughts*, 8.
63 *IR* 23, no. 9 (1935): 323.
64 See, for example, his 1923 interview with an Egyptian journalist quoted in Ryad, 'Salafiyya', 56.
65 On Quilliam and his Muslim community, see Geaves, *Islam in Victorian Britain*; Gilham and Geaves, *Victorian Muslim*.
66 A. W., *Thoughts*, 7.
67 Ibid., 9–10.
68 Ibid., 10–11.
69 Ibid., 11–12.
70 Ibid., 12–13.
71 The *shahada* is as follows: 'I declare that there is no god but God and I declare that Muhammad is His Messenger'. The other 'pillars' are worship/ritual prayer (*salat*); almsgiving (*zakat*); fasting/abstinence during Ramadan, the Muslim month of fasting (*sawm*); and pilgrimage to Mecca (Hajj).
72 A. W., *Thoughts*, 15–17.
73 Ibid., 21.
74 Ibid., 22–3.
75 Ibid., 59.
76 Ibid., 64.

Chapter 4

1. W. E. Gladstone, *Bulgarian Horrors and the Question of the East* (London: John Murray, 1876), 9.
2. See Clinton Bennett, *Victorian Images of Islam* (London: Grey Seal, 1992); K. H. Ansari, 'Attitudes to Islam and Muslims in Britain: 1875–1924', *Indo-British Review* 23, no. 2 (2001): 58–74.
3. See Philip C. Almond, *Heretic and Hero: Muhammad and the Victorians* (Wiesbaden: Harrassowitz, 1989); Bennett, *Victorian Images*.
4. Clinton Bennett, 'Is Isaac without Ishmael Complete? A Nineteenth-Century Debate Revisited', *Islam and Christian-Muslim Relations* 2, no. 1 (1991): 42–55; Bennett, *Victorian Images*.
5. Syed Ameer Ali, *The Spirit of Islam, Or the Life and Teachings of Mohammed*, new edn (Calcutta: S. K. Lahiri, 1902).
6. On the history of Islam in Britain, see Nabil Matar, *Islam in Britain, 1558–1685* (Cambridge: Cambridge University Press, 1998); Jerry Brotton, *This Orient Isle: Elizabethan England and the Islamic World* (London: Allen Lane, 2016); Ansari, '*The Infidel Within*'; Gilham, *Loyal Enemies*.
7. Ibid., 53, 57.
8. Jamie Gilham, 'Britain's First Muslim Peer of the Realm: Henry, Lord Stanley of Alderley and Islam in Victorian Britain', *Journal of Muslim Minority Affairs* 33, no. 1 (2013): 93–110.
9. Ibid., 107. Quilliam claimed after Stanley's death that the latter had visited the Liverpool Muslim Institute 'two or three times' in disguise (*Moslem Chronicle and Muhammadan Observer*, 23 January 1904, 55). However, Quilliam was prone to exaggeration and his claim has not been corroborated.
10. See Jamie Gilham, 'Abdullah Quilliam, First and Last "Sheikh-ul-Islam of the British Isles"', in *Victorian Muslim*, ed. Gilham and Geaves, 97–112.
11. Gilham, *Loyal Enemies*, 95–8.
12. Francis Robinson, 'The British Empire and the Muslim World', in *The Oxford History of the British Empire, Volume IV: The Twentieth Century*, ed. Judith M. Brown and Wm. Roger Louis (Oxford: Oxford University Press, 1999), 402; Gilham, *Loyal Enemies*, 109.
13. Cited in Nathalie Clayer and Eric Germain, 'Introduction', in *Islam in Inter-War Europe*, ed. Clayer and Germain, 8.
14. See, for example, *The Crescent* (hereafter *TC*), 12 February 1896, 526 and 27 May 1896, 262–3.
15. *TC*, 10 June 1896, 791.
16. See John Keay, *Eccentric Travellers*, new edn (London: John Murray, 2001), chapter 7.

17 G. W. Leitner, *Muhammadanism* (Woking: The Oriental Nobility Institute, 1889), 12.
18 G. W. Leitner, 'Correspondence, Notes and News', *Imperial and Asiatic Quarterly Review* 4 (third series) (1897): 182.
19 *Pall Mall Gazette* (hereafter *PMG*), 30 November 1893, 11.
20 *TC*, 16 December 1893, 383.
21 An *anjuman* is an organization or association.
22 Anon, 'The Central Islamic Society' leaflet (London: Central Islamic Society, 1916), n.p.
23 *MIIR* 1, no. 11 (1913): 427. On Quilliam's change of identity, see Geaves, *Islam in Victorian Britain*, 260–1; Gilham, *Loyal Enemies*, 76–8.
24 *TC*, 21 February 1906, 121.
25 *The Review of Religions* (hereafter *RoR*) 11, no. 9 (1912): 395–6.
26 On Ahmad and the history of the Ahmadiyya, see Spencer Lavan, *The Ahmadiyah Movement: A History and Perspective* (Delhi: Manohar, 1974); Yohanan Friedmann, *Prophecy Continuous: Aspects of Ahmadi Religious Thought and Its Medieval Background*, new edn (1989; repr., New Delhi: Oxford University Press, 2003); Francis Robinson, 'Ahmad and the Ahmadiyya', *History Today* 40, no. 6 (1990): 42–7.
27 Attributed to the Sufi Shaykh Ahmad Sirhindi (1564–1624). A Sufi is a follower of Sufism or Islamic mysticism.
28 Geaves, *Islam and Britain*, chapter 2.
29 Ibid., 29–30, 46.
30 Ibid., 48–50.
31 Ibid., 43, 50.
32 On the Ahmadi mission in the United States, see Kambiz GhaneaBassiri, *A History of Islam in America* (New York: Cambridge University Press, 2010), 207–18; Patrick D. Bowen, *A History of Conversion to Islam in the United States, Volume 1: White American Muslims before 1975* (Leiden and Boston, MA: Brill, 2015), chapter 7.
33 See Geaves, *Islam and Britain*, 40.
34 Quoted in *RoR* 12, no. 12 (1911): 522.
35 Geaves, *Islam and Britain*, 98.
36 Ibid., 101.
37 TNA, Treasury Solicitor Records, TS27/520 (1910–13). See also London Mosque Fund minutes (1912) in Humayun Ansari (ed.), *The Making of the East London Mosque, 1910–1951* (Cambridge: Cambridge University Press/Royal Historical Society, 2011), 102–3.
38 *MIIR* 1, no. 1 (1913): 3.
39 Lit. 'master'; a title given to a Muslim religious scholar.
40 *IRMI* 3, no. 12 (1915): 608–20.

41 *MIIR* 1, no. 6 (1913): 238.
42 Geaves, *Islam and Britain*, 112; Gilham, *Loyal Enemies*, 143.
43 *MIIR* 1, no. 11 (1913): 405.
44 Quoted in *The Comrade*, 29 November 1913, 374.
45 *RoR* 12, no. 12 (1913): 520.
46 Ibid., 519–20.
47 On the differences between the Lahori and Qadiani Ahmadis, see Friedmann, *Prophecy Continuous*, chapter 5.
48 See Gilham, *Loyal Enemies*, 138–40; Geaves, *Islam and Britain*, 111–14.
49 On these issues, see David Powell, *The Edwardian Crisis: Britain, 1901–1914* (Basingstoke: Palgrave Macmillan, 1996).
50 Gilham, *Loyal Enemies*, p.129.
51 *IRMI* 4, no. 1 (1916): 2; *IRMI* 3, no. 11 (1915): 551.
52 Qur'an, 2:256. See also *MIIR* 1, no. 9 (1913): 336–8.
53 *The Moslem World* (hereafter *TMW*) 8, no. 2 (1918): 204.
54 Ibid.
55 *KEP*, 16 July 1913, 4; 13 August 1913, 2; 29 November 1913, 2; and 30 May 1914, 4.
56 Anon, *Who's Who 1914*, 960.
57 Quoted in *Badr*, 2 October 1913, 2, trans. from the original Urdu into English by Zahid Aziz for the Ahmadiyya Anjuman Isha'at Islam Lahore (UK) website. Available online: http://www.wokingmuslim.org/pers/headley/islam.htm (accessed 12 August 2017). All subsequent quotations from *Badr* were translated by Dr Zahid Aziz.
58 See Headley's 1923 Egyptian press interview quoted in Ryad, 'Salafiyya', 56.
59 *Paigham Sulh* (hereafter *PS*), 2 December 1913, 3, trans. from the original Urdu into English by Zahid Aziz for the Ahmadiyya Anjuman Isha'at Islam Lahore (UK) website. Available online: http://www.wokingmuslim.org/pers/headley/islam.htm (accessed 12 August 2017). All subsequent quotations from *PS* were translated by Dr Zahid Aziz.
60 *Badr*, 6/13/20 November 1913, 4.
61 Quoted in *PS*, 2 December 1913, 3.
62 *Badr*, 6/13/20 November 1913, 4.
63 *MIIR* 1, no. 9 (1913): 355–7.
64 *MIIR* 1, no. 10 (1913): 370.
65 Ibid., 379–80.
66 Ibid., 380.
67 Ibid., 382.
68 *IRMI* 3, no. 1 (1915): 9. Ivy's granddaughter recalled that Headley, whom she knew as a child, often had 'psychiatric care' (Author's interview with the fifth Lord Headley's great-granddaughter, Berkshire, 14 February 2003).

69 *IRMI* 2, no. 3 (1914): 81.
70 *MIIR* 1, no. 10 (1913): 382.
71 *IR* 21, no. 4–5 (1933): 109.
72 See also Gilham, *Loyal Enemies*, chapter 4.
73 See also Lord Headley, *A Western Awakening to Islam* (hereafter *AWAI*), new edn (1914; repr., Woking: Woking Muslim Mission and Literary Trust, 1949), 22. *AWAI* was first published in 1914. All subsequent quotations from *AWAI* are from the 1949 edn.
74 Headley, *AWAI*, 72–3.
75 *The Observer* (hereafter *TO*), 23 November 1913, 4.
76 Dusé Mohamed Ali, *Duse Mohamed Ali (1866–1945): The Autobiography of a Pioneer Pan African and Afro-Asian Activist*, ed. Mustafa Abdelwahid (Trenton, NJ: The Red Sea Press, 2011), chapter 21.
77 On Ali's life and work, see Mustafa Abdelwahid, 'Introduction', in Ali, *Duse Mohamed Ali*, 1–30; Ian Duffield, 'Dusé Mohamed Ali and the Development of Pan-Africanism' (PhD thesis, Edinburgh University, Edinburgh, 1971).
78 Quoted in Duffield, 'Dusé Mohamed Ali', 420–1. Ali also mocked Kamal-ud-Din in his memoirs, referring to the latter as 'a rather heavy, bearded Indian, oozing perspiration from his every pore': Ali, *Duse Mohamed Ali*, 155.
79 Ibid., 156.
80 *Manchester Guardian*, repr. in *MIIR* 1, no. 11 (1913): 411–12.
81 Quoted in, among many other newspapers on the same day, *The Evening Telegraph and Post* (Dundee), 17 November 1913, 4.
82 *MIIR* 1, no. 11 (1913): 427–30.
83 Ibid., 429.
84 Ali, *Duse Mohamed Ali*, 157.
85 Quoted in Duffield, 'Dusé Mohamed Ali', 423.
86 *The New York Times*, 16 November 1913, 1.
87 *The Times*, 17 November 1913, 11.
88 Ali, *Duse Mohamed Ali*, 157.
89 Duffield, 'Dusé Mohamed Ali', 423.
90 Ali, *Duse Mohamed Ali*, 157.
91 *PS*, 4 December 1913, 4.
92 *MIIR* 1, no. 11 (1913): 401.
93 Ali, *Duse Mohamed Ali*, 157.
94 *PS*, 6 January 1914, 4.
95 Quoted in Maulana Hafiz Sher Mohammad, *Dr. Sir Muhammad Iqbal and the Ahmadiyya Movement*, trans. Zahid Aziz (1995). Available online: http://callinghome.blogspot.com/2004/10/dr-sir-muhammad-iqbal-and-ahmadiyya.html (accessed 11 April 2019).

96　Ibid. See also *HM*, 13 December 1913, 1570.
97　*PS*, 25 November 1913, quoted in Mohammad, *Dr. Sir Muhammad Iqbal*.
98　Ibid.
99　See ibid.
100　*RoR* 12, no. 12 (1913): 519.
101　*MIIR* 1, no. 12 (1914): 462.
102　Ibid., 441.
103　*The Sketch*, 26 November 1913, 248; *Northampton Daily Echo*, 17 November 1913, 2.
104　See Gilham, *Loyal Enemies*, 107–11.
105　Reprinted in *MIIR* 1, no. 11 (1913): 410.
106　*Arkansas Gazette* (Sunday Magazine), 30 November 1913, 1.
107　*The Leeds Mercury*, 20 November 1913, 4.
108　*Daily Sketch*, 17 November 1913, repr. in *MIIR* 1, no. 11 (1913): 405–6.
109　Ibid., 405.
110　*The Comrade*, 6 December 1913, 394.
111　*Manchester Dispatch*, 18 November 1913, repr. in *MIIR* 1, no. 11 (1913): 404. Note that this report was reprinted in *MIIR*, suggesting that Kamal-ud-Din did not realize his mistake until after that issue had gone to print in December 1913.
112　*Arkansas Gazette* (Sunday Magazine), 30 November 1913, 1. John Horace Savile (1843–1916), the fifth Earl of Mexborough, publicly announced his conversion to Buddhism in 1896: see *TYP*, 10 June 1916, 6.
113　*PMG*, 17 November 1913, 8.
114　*Jewish World*, repr. in *MIIR*, 1, no. 11 (1913): 411.
115　The Aliens Act 1905 introduced immigration controls to Britain, ostensibly to prevent the entry of 'undesirable immigrants' (paupers, criminals), but the restrictions were mostly levied against Jewish and Eastern European immigrants: see Jill Pellew, 'The Home Office and the Aliens Act, 1905', *The Historical Journal* 32, no. 2 (1989): 369–85.
116　*Jewish World*, repr. in *MIIR* 1, no. 11 (1913): 411.
117　*The Evening Telegraph and Post*, 17 November 1913, 4; *PMG*, 18 November 1913, 6.
118　*PMG*, 3 December 1913, 6.
119　*The Sketch*, 24 December 1913, 354. 'Al-Farooq' was the epithet given to the second Caliph, Umar b. al-Khattab (*c*.583–644), meaning 'he who distinguishes between right and wrong'.
120　*The Tablet*, 13 December 1913, 34.
121　Quoted in *PMG*, 3 December 1913, 6.
122　*TO*, 23 November 1913, 4.
123　Ibid.
124　*MIIR* 1, no. 10 (1913): 381.

125 Quoted in, among many other newspapers on the same day, *The Evening Telegraph and Post*, 17 November 1913, 4.
126 Ibid. Headley's claim that he had lived in 'many Roman Catholic countries' was an exaggeration.
127 *The Evening Telegraph and Post*, 17 November 1913, 4.
128 Reprinted in *IRMI* 2, no. 3 (1914): 98–9.
129 Ibid., 99.
130 *TO*, 23 November 1913, 4.
131 A reform movement within Sunni Islam that originated in Egypt in the nineteenth century as a response to Western imperialism.
132 *The Comrade*, 20 December 1913, 422–3; *al-Manar* 17, no. 1 (1913): 34–40. On Rida, see Umar Ryad, *Islamic Reformism and Christianity: A Critical Reading of the Works of Muhammad Rashid Rida and His Associates (1898–1935)* (Leiden and Boston, MA: Brill, 2009).
133 *TO*, 23 November 1913, 4.
134 Ibid.
135 Ibid.
136 Ibid.
137 *IRMI* 4, no. 4 (1916): 147–50.
138 *TO*, 23 November 1913, 4.
139 *PMG*, 17 November 1913, 8.
140 *PMG*, 18 November 1913, 6.
141 *IR* 15, no. 7 (1927): 242.
142 *Aberdeen Press and Journal*, 20 November 1913, 5.
143 *The East and the West* 12 (1914): 100–1.
144 *PMG*, 20 November 1913, 8.
145 *PMG*, 22 November 1913, 6. The correspondence between Headley and Berlyn was partially reproduced in *MIIR* 1, no. 11 (1913): 407–8. It concluded in the *PMG*, 24 November 1913, 6, with the addition of two further correspondents, both of whom challenged Berlyn's claims.
146 *TMW* 4, no. 2 (1914): 201.
147 *The Hendon and Finchley Times*, 5 December 1913, 10.
148 *MIIR* 1, no. 12 (1914): 448.
149 Ibid., 449.
150 *TO*, 23 November 1913, 4.
151 Quoted in *KEP*, 19 November 1913, 3.
152 *TL*, 1 July 1927, 5.
153 Al-Hajj Lord Headley, *The Affinity between the Original Church of Jesus Christ and Islam* (Woking: Trust for the Encouragement and Circulation of Muslim Religious Literature, 1927), 11.

154 PLH, Helen Allanson-Winn to Lord Headley, 23 October (no year).
155 Ibid., 26 October (no year).

Chapter 5

1. On the year 1913, see Charles Emmerson, *1913: The World Before the Great War* (London: Vintage, 2013).
2. See A. L. Macfie, *The End of the Ottoman Empire, 1908–1923* (Harlow: Longman, 1998).
3. Quoted in Emmerson, *1913*, 448.
4. *IRMI* 2, no. 1 (1914): 1.
5. On these communities, see Richard I. Lawless, *From Ta'izz to Tyneside: An Arab Community in the North-East of England during the Early Twentieth Century* (Exeter: Exeter University Press, 1995); Mohammad Siddique Seddon, *The Last of the Lascars: Yemeni Muslims in Britain, 1836–2012* (Markfield: Kube, 2014).
6. *RoR* 12, no. 12 (1913): 529–30.
7. *Yorkshire Telegraph and Star*, 29 November 1913, 4.
8. *PS*, 6 January 1914, 4.
9. Ibid.
10. Ibid.
11. *PS*, 13 January 1914, 3.
12. Kamal-ud-Din quoting Headley in *PS*, 27 January 1914, 1. Joseph Rudyard Kipling (1865–1936), Indian-born British writer whose poem 'The Ballad of East and West' (1889) began with the line 'Oh, East is East, and West is West, and never the twain shall meet'.
13. On this issue in the nineteenth century, see Gilham, *Loyal Enemies*, chapters 1–2.
14. *The Nottingham Daily Express*, 18 November 1913, 2.
15. *The Nottingham Evening Post*, 28 November 1913, 3; *The Leeds Mercury*, 28 November 1913, 5.
16. *MIIR* 1, no. 11 (1913): 425.
17. *IRMI* 3, no. 6 (1915): 296; *IR* 15, no. 1 (1927): 30.
18. *IRMI* 3, no. 6 (1915): 277.
19. For example, ibid., 301–2.
20. On dogma, for example, see *IRMI* 2, no. 10 (1914): 492.
21. These included 'Why I became a Muslim', 'Warning against Drink' and 'What do we Believe?'
22. Headley, *AWAI*, 58.
23. Ibid., 36–7.
24. Ibid., 38. He had first proposed these ideas when he spoke at the CIS in November 1913: see *MIIR* 1, no. 11 (1913): 428.

25 Ali, *Duse Mohamed Ali*, 156.
26 Headley, *AWAI*, 196–7.
27 Ibid., 198–9.
28 *The Near East*, 30 July 1915, 355.
29 *TMW* 5, no. 2 (1915): 201.
30 Jose Abraham, *Islamic Reform and Colonial Discourse on Modernity in India: Socio-Political and Religious Thought of Vakkom Moulavi* (New York: Palgrave Macmillan, 2014), 42–3.
31 A copy is held in the British Library: Lord Headley, *Garp'ta Müslimanlık cereyanı* (*A Treatise on Islam and Its Practice in the West*), trans. Ömer Rıza (Istanbul: Amedi Matbaası, 1927).
32 *IRMI* 2, no. 4 (1914): 171–3.
33 *IRMI* 3, no. 1 (1915): 16.
34 *IR* 17, no. 6 (1929): 192.
35 See *MIIR* 1, no. 12 (1914): 443. Headley likewise joined congregational prayers at the WMM's subsequent London premises, at Bedford Square and Campden Hill Road, Notting Hill Gate.
36 For example, Khwaja Kamal-ud-Din, *Islam and the Muslim Prayer* (Woking: Salter and Co., 1914), which was republished many times. Later editions included photographs of WMM Muslims, including Headley, demonstrating prayer positions: see Al-Hajj Khwaja Kamal-ud-Din, *Islam and the Muslim Prayer*, ed. Nasir Ahmad, 7th rev. edn (Lahore: The Woking Muslim Mission and Literary Trust, 1960).
37 *IRMI* 3, no. 1 (1915): 14.
38 Ibid.
39 *IRMI* 4, no. 1 (1916): 20.
40 Ibid.
41 *IRMI* 4, no. 4 (1916): 146; *The Daily Mirror*, 24 June 1916, 10.
42 BL, IOR, L/MIL/7/18861, 'Proposal for the Erection of a Mosque in or Near London' (1914–18), A. Hirtzel file note, 31 March 1916.
43 Ibid.
44 Ibid., Lord Headley to the Rt. Hon. Austin Chamberlain, India Office, 23 March 1916.
45 Ibid.
46 See Gilham, *Loyal Enemies*, 189.
47 Hajj is the greater of the two pilgrimages to Mecca, undertaken during the last month of the Islamic calendar. 'Umrah, the lesser pilgrimage, can be made at any time of the year.
48 Headley, 'Pilgrimage', 20.
49 *IRMI* 2, no. 3 (1914): 99.
50 This was also the case in the nineteenth century: see Gilham, *Loyal Enemies*, 58, 99–100 and, on Headley's contemporaries in the twentieth century, 239–41.

51 *IR* 14, no. 9 (1926): 350.
52 Gilham, *Loyal Enemies*, 192.
53 *IRMI* 3, no. 1 (1915): 13.
54 *IRMI* 2, no. 3 (1914): 123.
55 Ibid.
56 Ibid., 124.
57 *IRMI* 3, no. 1 (1915): 12.
58 Ibid., 12–13.
59 *IRMI* 4, no. 11 (1916): 512.
60 Sadr-ud-Din returned to Woking in 1919 and left in 1922 to lead the Lahore Ahmadi mission in Berlin. He became head of the Lahori Ahmadiyya in 1951.
61 Gilham, *Loyal Enemies*, 141–2, 173–6.
62 *IRMI* 2, no. 1 (1914): 32.
63 *IRMI* 3, no. 1 (1915): 9–11.
64 Ibid., 11, 16.
65 *IRMI* 2, no. 6 (1914): 294.
66 *The Scotsman*, 25 September 1914, 6.
67 TNA, FO371/2202, 'The War: Copy of Resolution Passed by British Muslim Society', September 1914.
68 *IRMI* 2, no. 8 (1914): 384.
69 See for example, ibid., 395; *IRMI* 2, no. 9 (1914): 439–46.
70 Ibid., 422.
71 Ibid., 421–2.
72 *IRMI* 2, no. 10 (1914): 493.
73 Ibid., 509.
74 See Gilham, *Loyal Enemies*, 75–84.
75 *IR* 11, no. 11 (1923): 391. See Geoffrey Nash, 'Abdullah Quilliam, Marmaduke Pickthall and the Politics of Christendom and the Ottoman Empire', in *Victorian Muslim*, ed. Gilham and Geaves, 79–95.
76 *IRMI* 2, no. 11–12 (1914): 588.
77 Ibid.
78 *IRMI* 3, no. 1 (1915): 12.
79 *The Irish Independent*, 20 January 1915, 4.
80 *IRMI* 3, no. 1 (1915): 12.
81 Ibid.
82 Ibid.
83 Ibid.
84 TNA, FO371/2146, 'Moslems and Turkey', Henri M. Léon to Arthur Field (AOS hon. secretary), 5 November 1914; Gilham, *Loyal Enemies*, 81–4.
85 On these wartime activities, see ibid., 217–25.

86 Marmaduke Pickthall, *Muslim Interests in Palestine* (Woking and London: The Gresham Press, 1917), 1.
87 TNA, FO371/3406, 'Moslem Interests in Palestine', 1918.
88 TNA, FO371/4233, 'Sheikh Kidwai', Undated file minutes, 1919.
89 *IRMI* 3, no. 5 (1915): 237. See also *IRMI* 3, no. 3 (1915): 113–17.
90 *The Belfast News Letter*, 30 October 1914, 5; *The Globe*, 27 August 1915, 9.
91 *The Globe*, 28 October 1914, 6.
92 *Reading Mercury*, 29 May 1915, 6.
93 Ibid.
94 Panikos Panayi, 'The British Empire Union in the First World War', *Immigrants and Minorities* 8, no. 1–2 (1989): 124–5.
95 E. D. Morel, *Truth and the War* (London: The National Labour Press, 1916), 215. For the impact of these organizations on Germans, see Stella Yarrow, 'The Impact of Hostility on Germans in Britain, 1914–1918', *Immigrants and Minorities* 8, no. 1–2 (1989): 97–112.
96 *The Shepton Mallet Journal*, 17 September 1915, 7.
97 *The Washington Post*, 17 December 1915, 6.
98 *The Globe*, 8 October 1915, 5; *TYP*, 22 October 1915, 10; *Daily Record and Mail*, 26 October 1915, 4; *The [Hull] Daily Mail*, 3 November 1915, 5.
99 *The Washington Post*, 17 December 1915, 6.
100 *TYP*, 3 November 1915, 8; *The Bath Chronicle*, 18 December 1915, 2.
101 Richmond upon Thames Local Studies and Library and Archive, Douglas B. W. Sladen Papers, SLA/68/361, Undated open letter from Douglas B. W. Sladen, 1915.
102 Ibid., SLA/68/332, Lord Headley to Douglas B. W. Sladen, 2 October 1915.
103 *IRMI* 3, no. 11 (1915): 599.
104 Ibid., 602.
105 Lord Headley, 'Trust in God – But Tie Your Camel', *The Suffragette* 4, no. 115 (1915): 277; Lord Headley, 'More about the Naturalisation Farce', *Britannia* 5, no. 1 (1915): 8.
106 *The Daily Express*, 25 January 1916, 6; *The Otago Daily Times* (New Zealand), 19 June 1916, 8.
107 Lord Headley, 'The British Workman', *The Aeroplane* 9, no. 21 (1915): 640.
108 *The Coventry Standard*, 14–15 July 1916, 9.
109 Headley did not feature at all in the BEU *Monthly Record*, which commenced publication in December 1916, nor was he listed as a member of the BEU Grand Council for 1917 (or thereafter).
110 *The Times*, 11 December 1916, 5; quoted in *The Globe*, 12 January 1917, 6.
111 *The Times*, 11 December 1916, 5.
112 Ibid.
113 Ibid.

114 Ibid.
115 *The East and the West* 15 (1917): 108.
116 Quoted in *The Globe*, 12 January 1917, 6. See also *The Irish Independent*, 13 January 1917, 2.
117 *PMG*, 12 January 1917, 9.
118 *IRMI* 5, no. 10 (1917): 422.
119 *IRMI* 5, no. 5 (1917): 189.
120 *IRMI* 5, no. 2-3 (1917): 106. On Stephen, see the obituary written by Quilliam/Léon in *The Physiologist* 5, no. 21 (1928): 199–200.
121 *IRMI* 5, no. 5 (1917): 212.
122 *IRMI* 5, no. 10 (1917): 421–8.
123 Ibid., 421.
124 Ibid., 424.
125 Ibid., 428.
126 *IRMI* 6, no. 2 (1918): 69.
127 Gilham, *Loyal Enemies*, 43, 64, 209.
128 Tomes, 'Winn, Rowland George Allanson Allanson-', 745.
129 *IRMI* 6, no. 2 (1918): 70.
130 Ibid., 79.
131 Ibid., 80.

Chapter 6

1 See Sally Krimmer and Alan Lawson (ed.), *Barbara Baynton* (St. Lucia, Queensland: University of Queensland Press, 1980); Penne Hackforth-Jones, *Barbara Baynton: Between Two Worlds*, new edn (1989; repr., Carlton, Victoria: Melbourne University Press, 1995).
2 Ibid., 106–7.
3 See ibid., 93; Krimmer and Lawson, *Barbara Baynton*, 314.
4 Hackforth-Jones, *Barbara Baynton*, 123, 129.
5 Ibid., 136.
6 Ibid., 137.
7 Quoted in ibid., 119.
8 Ibid., 135.
9 A point made by Baynton's grandson in the 1960s: H. B. Gullett, 'Memoir of Barbara Baynton', in Barbara Baynton, *Bush Studies*, new edn (1902; repr., Sydney: Angus and Robertson, 1965), 19.
10 For example, *Larne Times and Weekly Telegraph*, 22 November 1913, 11.
11 See his letters on the subject in *TYP*, 9 June 1919, 3; 2 July 1919, 5; and 4 July 1919, 5.

12 *The Freeman's Journal*, 27 October 1919, 3.
13 During the war, he had advocated transport reform: see Lord Headley, 'Introduction', in *How to Make the Railways Pay for the War; Or, the Transport Problem Solved*, ed. Roy Horniman (London: George Routledge and Sons, 1916), vii–xi; Lord Headley, 'Complacineptitude', *The Commercial Motor*, 13 December 1917, 2. Lord Headley (R. G. Allanson-Winn), *Boxing*, new edn (London: G. Bell and Sons, 1920).
14 *The Devon and Exeter Gazette*, 15 February 1921, 6.
15 *The Mail* (Adelaide), 12 February 1921, 1.
16 Ibid.
17 Ibid.
18 *Birmingham Daily Gazette*, 14 February 1921, 3.
19 Quoted in *The Mail* (Adelaide), 12 February 1921, 1; *The Shields Daily News*, 8 February 1921, 2.
20 *The Graphic*, 8 April 1922, 14. In 1922, Headley was also part of an unsuccessful bid to recover treasure from a Spanish Armada galleon which reportedly sank at Tobermory Bay in the Scottish Inner Hebrides: see *The Midland Daily Telegraph*, 22 August 1922, 3; *The Graphic*, 5 August 1922, 203.
21 *Birmingham Daily Gazette*, 14 February 1921, 1; *The Mail* (Adelaide), 12 February 1921, 1.
22 See Tom Doyle, *The Civil War in Kerry* (Cork: Mercier Press, 2008).
23 *Sheffield Daily Telegraph*, 12 July 1922, 3.
24 Quoted in *The Sunday Times* (Perth), 18 September 1921, 23.
25 Ibid.
26 Hackforth-Jones, *Barbara Baynton*, 146.
27 Ibid., 149.
28 *Irish Society and Social Review*, 27 May 1922, 1.
29 Martin Mills, *Brangane: A Memoir* (London: Constable and Co., 1926). It was published as *The Aristocrat* in the United States.
30 Mills, *Brangane*, 135–6.
31 Ibid., 38.
32 Ibid., 139–41.
33 *The Londonderry Sentinel*, 21 October 1922, 6.
34 Mills, *Brangane*, 143.
35 Ibid., 144–5.
36 *Malaya Tribune*, 26 June 1922, 2; *The Londonderry Sentinel*, 21 October 1922, 6; LHP, Lord Headley to The Lord Chamberlain's Office, Undated draft (February 1932).
37 *The Scotsman*, 28 June 1922, 7; *The Northern Whig and Belfast Post*, 23 May 1922, 6. See also *Belfast News Letter*, 8 June 1922, 5.

38 *The Scotsman*, 28 June 1922, 7. By 'Gilbertian', Headley meant that the situation was as ludicrous or paradoxical as might be found in the comic operas of the popular English writer, W. S. Gilbert (1836–1911).
39 *The Northern Whig and Belfast Post*, 31 October 1922, 5 and 13 December 1924, 6.
40 *The Ealing Gazette*, 21 October 1922, 1.
41 See the case file in TNAI, FIN/COMP/2/8/406, Department of Finance, 'William H. Giles, Agent for Lord Headley, Aghadoe House, Killarney', 1922. Headley publicly denounced the compensation settlement of £4,500, claiming that the actual cost of rebuilding Aghadoe House would be around £36,000: see *The Northern Whig and Belfast Post*, 13 December 1924, 6.
42 Besides his return to Irish issues and the campaign for divorce law reform, in the years immediately after the war Headley also spoke out against the idle 'British workman' and the 'tyranny' of the trade unions at a time when the economy needed a boost through increased production and exports: see, *TYP*, 9 October 1919, 5; *Norwood News*, 14 April 1922, 10.
43 Quoted in Muhammad Yusuf Abbasi, *London Muslim League (1908–1928): An Historical Study* (Islamabad: National Institute of Historical and Cultural Research, 1988), 362.
44 Ibid., 344–6. See also Conor Meleady, 'Negotiating the Caliphate: British Responses to Pan-Islamic Appeals, 1914–1924', *Middle Eastern Studies* 52, no. 2 (2016): 182–97.
45 Abbasi, *London Muslim League*, 344.
46 A branch of the Shi'a, who do not believe in the finality of Muhammad's prophethood.
47 See Gilham, *Loyal Enemies*, 227–8.
48 Abbasi, *London Muslim League*, 346.
49 Quoted in ibid., 351–2. Muslim signatories also included the Aga Khan, Ameer Ali, Ispahani, Pickthall and Sheldrake.
50 *The Times*, 2 August 1919, 11.
51 See Jamie Gilham, 'Marmaduke Pickthall and the British Muslim Convert Community', in *Marmaduke Pickthall*, ed. Nash, 58–61.
52 *IRMI* 7, no. 11 (1919): 406.
53 Ibid., 407.
54 *The Times*, 22 December 1919, 6.
55 See Afzal Iqbal, *The Life and Times of Mohamed Ali: An Analysis of the Hopes, Fears and Aspirations of Muslim India from 1878 to 1931*, 2nd rev. edn (Lahore: Institute of Islamic Culture, 1979), chapter 7.
56 Not to be confused with Dusé Mohamed Ali (see Chapters 4 and 5) or the Ahmadi scholar and translator of the Qur'an, Maulana Muhammad Ali (see Chapter 8).
57 British Pathé, 'Mohamed Ali at Woking Mosque' Newsreel, 1920, British Pathé

58 *Daily Herald*, 22 March 1920, 1.
59 Iqbal, *The Life and Times of Mohamed Ali*, 208.
60 M. Naeem Qureshi, *Pan-Islam in British Indian Politics: A Study of the Khilafat Movement, 1918–1924* (Brill: Leiden and Boston, MA, 1999), 417.
61 Khwaja Kamal-ud-Din, *India in the Balance: British Rule and the Caliphate* (Woking: The Islamic Review, n.d. (*c*.1921/22), 155–6.
62 *IR* 9, no. 3 (1921): 82.
63 *IR* 10, no. 5 (1922): 199.
64 *IR* 10, no. 11 (1922): 451. See also *The Times*, 22 September 1922, 12.
65 On Pickthall and the Armenian massacres/genocide, see Clark, *Marmaduke Pickthall*, 30–3.
66 *The Western Morning News and Mercury*, 8 October 1925, 8.
67 Ibid.
68 See Abbasi, *London Muslim League*, 369–79.
69 Lord Headley, *The Three Great Prophets of the World: Moses, Jesus and Muhammad* (Woking: The Islamic Review, 1923).
70 Ibid., 30.

Chapter 7

1 See Pitts's account in Paul Auchterlonie (ed.), *Encountering Islam. Joseph Pitts: An English Slave in 17th-Century Algiers and Mecca* (London: Arabian Publishing, 2012).
2 Richard F. Burton, *Personal Narrative of a Pilgrimage to El-Medinah and Meccah*, 3 vols (London: Longman, Brown, Green and Longmans, 1855–1856); Mary S. Lovell, *A Rage to Live: A Biography of Richard and Isabel Burton* (London: Abacus, 1999), 85, 120–5.
3 They were Alfred H./Abdullah Browne (*c*.1812–1907), who made the Hajj in *c*.1875/76, before he converted to Islam; William Richard/Abdullah Fazil Williamson (1872–1958) in 1894; and Hedley/Mahmoud Mobarek Churchward (1862–1929), apparently without disguise, in 1910. On Browne, see *TC*, 9 October 1907, 237–8; on Williamson, see Stanton Hope, *Arabian Adventurer: The Story of Haji Williamson* (London: Robert Hale, 1951); on Churchward, see Eric Rosenthal, *From Drury Lane to Mecca*, new edn (1931; repr., Cape Town: Howard Timmins, 1982).
4 *The Egyptian Gazette*, 24 August 1923, 7.

5 Eldon Rutter, *The Holy Cities of Arabia*, new edn (1928; repr., London: Arabian Publishing, 2015); Lady Evelyn Cobbold, *Pilgrimage to Mecca* (London: John Murray, 1934); H. St. J. B. Philby, *A Pilgrim in Arabia* (The Golden Cockerel Press, 1943); Muhammad Asad, *The Road to Mecca* (London: Max Reinhardt, 1954).
6 Title given to a military commander, governor or prince; leader.
7 See Joshua Teitelbaum, *The Rise and Fall of the Hashimite Kingdom of Arabia* (London: Hurst, 2001).
8 TNA, FO686/134, 'Pan-Islamism in Egypt', Headley to British Consul, Jidda, 21 May 1923.
9 Ibid. On Abdullah's 1922 visit to England, see Elizabeth Monroe, *Philby of Arabia* (1973; repr., Reading: Ithaca, 1998), 114–15.
10 TNA, FO686/134, British Agency Mecca to Headley, 10 June 1923.
11 Ibid., Shaykh Fu'ad al-Khatib, secretary of state for Foreign Affairs in Mecca, to Kamal-ud-Din, 9 June 1923.
12 Ibid.
13 John Slight, *The British Empire and the Hajj, 1865–1956* (Cambridge, MA: Harvard University Press, 2015), 243.
14 Headley, 'Pilgrimage', 22.
15 TNA, FO371/8954, 'Message for Lord Headley', Undated memorandum by Lancelot Oliphant (1923).
16 TNA, FO686/134, Shaykh Fu'ad al-Khatib to Kamal-ud-Din, 9 June 1923.
17 *The Egyptian Gazette*, repr. in *IR* 11, no. 9 (1923): 315.
18 Headley, 'Pilgrimage', 20.
19 TNA, FO371/8954, Undated memorandum by Lancelot Oliphant (1923).
20 *IR* 11, no. 6–7 (1923): 206.
21 Britain also continued to directly govern the Sudan, which had been controlled as part of an Anglo-Egyptian condominium since 1889.
22 TNA, FO686/134, British Intelligence Report, Cairo, 22 June 1923.
23 The leader of the Wafd Party – and briefly Egyptian prime minister in 1924 – was Saad Zaghloul (1859–1927).
24 TNA, FO686/134, Viscount Allenby, High Commissioner for Egypt and the Sudan, to Marquess Curzon, Foreign Secretary, 13 July 1923.
25 TNA, FO371/8990, 'Visit of Lord Headley to Egypt', July 1923.
26 *IR* 11, no. 9 (1923): 302.
27 *New York Times*, 21 October 1923, 3.
28 Headley, 'Pilgrimage', 21.
29 *IR* 11, no. 9 (1923): 302.
30 Ibid., 303.
31 Reprinted in *IR* 11, no. 8 (1923): 270.
32 Headley, 'Pilgrimage', 21.

33. *IR* 11, no. 9 (1923): 303.
34. Ibid.
35. Ibid., 304.
36. Headley, 'Pilgrimage', 21.
37. Quoted in Ryad, 'Salafiyya', 56.
38. Ibid.
39. Karl Baedeker, *Egypt and the Sudan: Handbook for Travellers*, 7th edn (London: T. Fisher Unwin, 1914), 55.
40. Headley, 'Pilgrimage', 22.
41. *IR* 11, no. 9 (1923): 304.
42. Quoted in *The Egyptian Gazette*, repr. in ibid.: 313–14.
43. *TL*, 16 August 1923, 1.
44. *IR* 11, no. 9 (1923): 305.
45. Ibid.
46. Headley, 'Pilgrimage', 22.
47. *IR* 11, no. 9 (1923): 307.
48. Headley, 'Pilgrimage', 23.
49. TNA, FO686/134, Allenby to Curzon, 13 July 1923.
50. Ibid.
51. Ibid.
52. Headley, 'Pilgrimage', 23.
53. Ibid.
54. TNA, FO371/8946, 'Situation at Jeddah, 1 July – 29 July 1923', 6.
55. Cobbold, *Pilgrimage*, 7.
56. Quoted in Lawrence James, *The Golden Warrior: The Life and Legend of Lawrence of Arabia* (1990; repr., London: Abacus, 1995), 164.
57. Headley, 'Pilgrimage', 24.
58. Ibid., 23.
59. Reader Bullard, *Two Kings in Arabia: Letters from Jeddah, 1923–5 and 1936–9*, ed. E. C. Hodgkin (Reading: Ithaca, 1993), 5–6. See also TNA, FO371/8946, 'Situation at Jeddah, 1 July – 29 July 1923'.
60. Bullard, *Two Kings*, 6.
61. Ibid.; TNA, FO371/8946, 'Situation at Jeddah, 30 May – 30 June 1923'.
62. *The Times*, 30 August 1923, 7.
63. TNA, FO686/134, Shaykh Fu'ad al-Khatib to Kamal-ud-Din, 9 June 1923.
64. Quoted in *The Franklin Times* (North Carolina), 21 January 1924, 6.
65. Headley, 'Pilgrimage', 25.
66. Ibid.
67. Ibid.
68. Ibid., 26.

69 Ibid., 25–6. In his memoir, written in the 1960s, the British diplomat and former vice-consul in Jidda, Laurence Grafftey-Smith (1892–1989), suggested that Headley arrived in Jidda wearing *ihram*. According to Grafftey-Smith's account, as Headley disembarked from the ship that had brought him from Suez, 'a non-Moslem nail caught the lower towel and held it, without his noticing this; and his descent of the next few steps was spectacular.' Grafftey-Smith also claimed that Headley drank whisky in the company of Kamal-ud-Din at the British consulate in Jidda. See Laurence Grafftey-Smith, *Bright Levant* (1970; repr., London: Stacey International, 2002), 162.
70 Rutter, *The Holy Cities*, 133.
71 Bullard, *Two Kings*, 6.
72 Ibid.
73 TNA, FO371/8946, 'Situation at Jeddah, 1 July – 29 July 1923', File minutes.
74 Headley, 'Pilgrimage', 26.
75 *The Franklin Times*, 21 January 1924, 6.
76 Headley, 'Pilgrimage', 25.
77 Ibid.
78 Rutter, *The Holy Cities*, 256.
79 A conservative Islamic reform movement founded by Muhammad ibn Abd al-Wahhab (1703–92) and followed by Ibn Sa'ud and his successors.
80 Cobbold, *Pilgrimage*, 172. Rutter was even more distressed at the destruction of Jannat al-Baqi: 'All over the cemetery nothing was to be seen but little indefinite mounds of earth and stones, pieces of timber, iron bars, blocks of stone, and a broken rubble of cement and bricks, strewn about. It was like the broken remains of a town which had been demolished by an earthquake' (Rutter, *The Holy Cities*, 459).
81 Headley, 'Pilgrimage', 25.
82 Qur'an, 2:124.
83 On the history of Mecca, see Ziauddin Sardar, *Mecca: Sacred City* (London: Bloomsbury, 2014).
84 Qur'an, 2:196. On the Hajj, see Venetia Porter (ed.), *Hajj: Journey to the Heart of Islam* (London: The British Museum Press, 2012).
85 Headley, 'Pilgrimage', 25.
86 Eldon Rutter, 'The Holy Cities of Arabia', *Journal of the Central Asian Society* 16, no. 2 (1929): 200.
87 Cobbold, *Pilgrimage*, 131–2.
88 Headley's short account of 21 July 1923 was published in *IR* 11, no. 11 (1923): 417–18. The *muezzin* is a Muslim elected to call others to prayer.
89 Cobbold, *Pilgrimage*, 133.
90 Headley, 'Pilgrimage', 26.

91 Ibid., 27.
92 Ibid.
93 Ibid.
94 Cobbold, *Pilgrimage*, 158.
95 Headley, 'Pilgrimage', 27.
96 Ibid., 27–8.
97 Ibid., 28.
98 Ibid.
99 Headley said that 70,000 pilgrims had made the Hajj in 1923; Bullard thought the number was around 80,000 'from overseas' plus 'scores of thousands from the desert' (Bullard, *Two Kings*, 10). Drawing on pilgrimage reports from the British consulate in Jidda, John Slight estimates that there were 100,000 pilgrims at Arafat during the 1923 Hajj (Slight, *The British Empire*, 243–4).
100 Headley, 'Pilgrimage', 21.
101 Ibid., 28.
102 Ibid., 28–9.
103 Ibid., 29.
104 *The Times*, 30 August 1923, 7.
105 Headley, 'Pilgrimage', 26.
106 Lord Headley, 'Within the Holy City of Mecca', *The Sphere*, 29 September 1923, 405–7; Sir John Hammerton (ed.), *Countries of the World*, vol. 1, new edn (London: Amalgamated Press, n.d. [*c*.1937]), 77–94.
107 *The Times*, 30 August 1923, 7.
108 Headley, 'Pilgrimage', 29.
109 Bullard, *Two Kings*, 8.
110 TNA, FO371/8946, 'Situation at Jeddah, 1 – 29 November 1923', Report by Bullard.
111 TNA, FO371/8946, 'Situation at Jeddah, 1 – 29 May 1924', Report by Bullard.
112 Bullard, *Two Kings*, 51.
113 *The Times*, 30 August 1923, 7.
114 *The Radio Times*, 30 November 1923, 339. Radio was in its infancy in Britain in 1923, and it was a sign of the novelty of Headley's Hajj that he was asked to speak about it on air. Alas, the broadcast was not recorded for posterity, and the transcript has not survived.
115 *PMG*, 26 October 1923, 8.
116 Headley, 'Pilgrimage', 29.
117 *The Times*, 31 August 1923, 12; and see, for example, *The Ogden Standard-Examiner* (Utah), 9 December 1923, 32.
118 *The Reading Eagle* (Pennsylvania), 23 September 1923, 8; *The Pukekohe and Waiuku Times* (South Auckland), 21 January 1924, 6; *The Greencastle Herald* (Indiana), 12 November 1923, 2.

119 *The Franklin Times*, 21 January 1924, 6.
120 Headley, 'Pilgrimage', 29.
121 Ibid., 22.
122 Ibid., 32.
123 *The Times*, 30 August 1923, 7.
124 The report was printed in scores of British provincial newspapers, such as *Aberdeen Press and Journal*, 17 September 1923, 5.
125 Headley, 'Pilgrimage', 34.
126 TNA, FO372/2068, 'Request for Permission to Wear the Order of Nahda (First Class)', Headley to Foreign Office, 22 September 1923.
127 Ibid., Undated file minutes, September/October 1923.
128 Quoted in ibid., Headley to Foreign Office, 4 October 1923.
129 Ibid.
130 Ibid., Undated file minutes, October 1923. Stubborn as ever, Headley continued to bother the Foreign Office, unsuccessfully asking for 'restricted permission' to wear the medal. When, in 1924, he wrote a character reference for the imam of Woking mosque, a Foreign Office official noted that Headley's 'recent bombardment of this office to be allowed to receive a decoration from the King of the Hejaz [. . .] shows him to be very small minded' (TNA, FO371/10223, 'Proposed Journey to Near East of Imam of Mosque at Woking', File minutes, 16 May 1924).
131 Newcastle University, Gertrude Bell Archive, Gertrude Bell to Sir Hugh Bell, 5 December 1923. Available online: http://www.gerty.ncl.ac.uk/letter_details.php?letter_id=661 (accessed 10 May 2017).
132 *The Northern Whig and Belfast Post*, 17 March 1924, 7.

Chapter 8

1 Middle East Centre Archive, St Anthony's College, University of Oxford (hereafter MECA), Harry St John Bridger Philby Collection, GB165-0229 (hereafter Philby Collection), 2/3/4/8/Correspondence, Lord Headley to Harry St John Bridger Philby, 22 August 1926.
2 *Sheffield Daily Telegraph*, 8 April 1924, 6.
3 Ibid.
4 PLH, Rev. Charles H. Lodge to Lord Headley, 6 November 1925.
5 See *The Daily Herald*, 9 January 1924, 3; *IR* 12, no. 2 (1924): 41–2.
6 See Gilham, *Loyal Enemies*, 175, 179; *IR* 17, no. 1 (1929): frontispiece.
7 *The Physiologist* 1 (new series) (1917): 1. See also see Gilham, *Loyal Enemies*, 78–9.
8 See ibid., 162, 164.
9 Details of the College's activities are listed in its journal *The Physiologist*.

10 Headley, *The Affinity*, 140, 149. See also his discussion of Spiritualism in Lord Headley, 'Presidential Address', in *The Society of Engineers (Incorporated) Transactions for 1921* (London: The Society of Engineers, 1921), 7–30.
11 *The Times*, 10 March 1923, 12.
12 *IR* 11, no. 4 (1923): 136.
13 *IR* 11, no. 5 (1923): 174.
14 On Muslim missions and communities in Germany between the wars, see Clayer and Germain, *Islam in Inter-War Europe*; Gerdien Jonker, *The Ahmadiyya Quest for Religious Progress: Missionizing Europe 1900-1965* (Leiden and Boston, MA: Brill, 2016); Gerdien Jonker, 'In Search of Religious Modernity: Conversion to Islam in Interwar Berlin', in *Muslims in Interwar Europe*, ed. Agai, Ryad and Sajid, 18–46.
15 *IR* 16, no. 9 (1928): 326. On the Paris Mosque and Muslims in France between the wars, see Moustafa Bayoumi, 'Shadows and Light: Colonial Modernity and the Grande Mosquée of Paris', *The Yale Journal of Criticism* 13, no. 2 (2000): 267–92; Naomi Davison, 'Muslim Bodies in the Metropole: Social Assistance and "Religious" Practice in Interwar Paris', in *Muslims in Interwar Europe*, ed. Agai, Ryad and Sajid, 105–24.
16 See Brent D. Singleton, 'Abdullah Quilliam's International Influence: America, West Africa and Beyond', in *Victorian Muslim*, ed. Gilham and Geaves, 113–31.
17 Bowen, *A History of Conversion to Islam*, 225–9.
18 Ibid., 253. See also a letter from the American Islamic Association in *IR* 21, no. 11 (1933): 391–2.
19 Founded by Rida's contemporary, the Syrian Salafi writer and activist Muhibb-ud-Din al-Khatib (1886–1969).
20 Ryad, 'Salafiyya', 51, 53.
21 Ibid., 56.
22 Ibid., 57; see also Ryad, *Islamic Reformism*, 167–9.
23 Donald McCormick, *The Mask of Merlin: A Critical Biography of David Lloyd George* (New York: Holt, Rinehart and Winston, 1964), 168–71; Bejtullah Destani and Jason Tomes (ed.), *Albania's Greatest Friend: Aubrey Herbert and the Making of Modern Albania. Diaries and Papers 1904–1923* (London: I.B. Tauris, 2011), 316, 326–31.
24 *Belfast Telegraph*, 19 April 1924, 6.
25 Quoted in *Belfast News Letter*, 29 January 1925, 7.
26 Quoted in *The Sunday Post*, 1 February 1925, 9.
27 Hackforth-Jones, *Barbara Baynton*, 150.
28 See *The Leeds Mercury*, 31 December 1923, 13.
29 Quoted in Brenda Niall, *Martin Boyd: A Life* (Carlton, Victoria: Melbourne University Press, 1988), 228.
30 *The Register* (Adelaide), 8 May 1924, 11.

31 Quoted in Hackforth-Jones, *Barbara Baynton*, 151.
32 *The Sunday Post*, 4 October 1925, 9.
33 Quoted in *The Examiner* (Launceston, Tasmania), 3 December 1927, 2.
34 Hackforth-Jones, *Barbara Baynton*, 163.
35 Quoted in *Belfast News Letter*, 29 January 1925, 7.
36 Quoted in *The Sunday Post*, 1 February 1925, 9.
37 *MIIR* 1, no. 10 (1913): 383.
38 *IRMI* 2, no. 5 (1914): 218.
39 Lord Headley, 'Foreword', in Maulvi Muhammad Ali, *Islam: The Religion of Humanity* (n.pl.: n.pub., n.d. [*c.*1917]), n.p.
40 Geaves, *Islam and Britain*, 120.
41 Cited in ibid., 116.
42 TNA, FO371/1973, 'Protectorate in Egypt', Khalid Sheldrake to Sir Edward Grey, Foreign Office, 19 December 1914.
43 BL, IOR, L/PS/11125, 3273, Metropolitan Police Report, 6 September 1915.
44 Repr. in *IRMI* 8, no. 10 (1920): 365.
45 Ibid., 365–6.
46 See *IR* 12, no. 1 (1924): 1.
47 Ibid., 2.
48 *The Straits Times*, 1 October 1924, 15.
49 Lord Headley, 'Foreword', in Khwaja Kamal-ud-Din, *The Ideal Prophet* (Woking: The Woking Muslim Mission and Literary Trust, 1925), v.
50 Headley, *The Affinity*, 8.
51 See Ephraim C. Mandivenga, 'The Cape Muslims and the Indian Muslims of South Africa: A Comparative Analysis', *Journal of Muslim Minority Affairs* 20, no. 2 (2000): 347–52.
52 See *IR* 14, no. 5 (1926): 163–4.
53 Ibid., 165.
54 See the reports reproduced in ibid., 163–77 and *IR* 14, no. 6 (1926): 206–13.
55 See *IR* 14, no. 7 (1926): 264–70. See also Headley's article for *Moslem Outlook* (Cape Town) entitled 'When Intellectual Darkness Faced Europe', repr. in Khwaja Kamal-ud-Din, *Open Letters to the Bishops of Salisbury and London* (Woking: The Trust for the Encouragement and Circulation of Muslim Religious Literature, 1926), 142–7.
56 *Indian Opinion*, 12 March 1926, 80.
57 *TL*, 16 October 1926, 5.
58 Headley, *The Affinity*, frontmatter. One of the few reviews of Headley's final book appeared in the *Nottingham Journal*: 'He shows the tendency of most over-zealous converts, of seeing all the splendour of the new love in contrast to the unattractiveness of the old. [. . .] Doubtless Christians need to know more of

Mahomet and his teaching, but not more than Lord Headley needs to know of the religion he renounced' (*The Nottingham Journal*, 28 May 1927, 5). A relative who read the book subsequently wrote to Headley 'with "infinite sorrow and distress"' because, although she felt that Headley was 'sincere', he was 'absolutely ignorant about Divine things' (*IR* 15, no. 9 [1927]: 312). Headley replied thus: 'I suppose you mean that I am ignorant of your particular views on Divine things?' (ibid., 314).

59 *TL*, 16 August 1926, 4.
60 Repr. in *TL*, 16 October 1926, 5.
61 Gilham, *Loyal Enemies*, 140, 173–4.
62 Ibid., 201.
63 See correspondence in TNA, FO 371/13871, 'Western Islamic Association', 1929.
64 Bowen, *A History of Conversion to Islam*, 249–56.
65 Lawless, *From Ta'izz to Tyneside*, chapters 5–6. Sheldrake lived out his days in relative obscurity: see Max Everest-Phillips, 'The Suburban King of Tartary', *Asian Affairs* 21, no. 3 (1990): 324–35.
66 Sirdar Ikbal Ali Shah, 'Ferments in the World of Islam' (with Discussion), *Journal of the Central Asian Society* 14, no. 2 (1927): 130–46.
67 Ibid., 141.
68 Ibid., 142.
69 Ibid.
70 Ibid., 143.
71 Ibid.
72 Ibid., 145.
73 Ibid., 145–6.
74 *IR* 15, no. 7 (1927): 234–46. A short version was published in *TL*, 1 July 1927, 5–7.
75 *IR* 15, no. 7 (1927): 237–8.
76 Ibid., 238.
77 Ibid., 238–9.
78 Ibid., 245–6.
79 Ibid., 245.
80 Repr. in *IR* 15, no. 11 (1927): 420.
81 Ibid., 421–2.
82 It was certainly not a role sanctioned by the British authorities. For example, when Headley wrote a character reference for Khwaja Nazir Ahmad in 1924, a Foreign Office official wrote that 'his recommendation counts for nothing' (TNA, FO371/10223, 'Proposed Journey to Near East of Imam of Mosque at Woking', File minutes, 16 May 1924).
83 See Nishant Kumar, 'Laws and Colonial Subjects: The Subject-Citizen Riddle and the Making of Section 295(A)', in *Subjects, Citizens and Law: Colonial and*

Independent India, ed. Gunnel Cederlöf and Sanjukta Das Gupta (Abingdon: Routledge, 2017), chapter 4.
84 *IR* 15, no. 9 (1927): 320–1; *TL*, 16 September 1927, 1–8. The Government of India duly enacted a new law prohibiting insults aimed at founders and leaders of religious communities. The publisher of *Rangila Rasul* was acquitted in 1929, but he was assassinated shortly afterwards.
85 *TL*, 16 June 1927, 7.
86 *IR* 15, no. 12 (1927): 435.
87 Ibid., 435–6.
88 *The Singapore Free Press and Mercantile Advertiser*, 2 January 1928, 15.
89 *IR* 16, no. 3 (1928): 82, 87.
90 The speech was repr. in ibid., 88–120.
91 Ibid., 88, 93.
92 Ibid., 105.
93 Ibid., 118–19.
94 Ibid., 119.
95 Ibid., 120.
96 Ibid., 116.
97 *TL*, 5 January 1928, 3.
98 *TL*, 22 December 1927, 7.
99 *TL*, 5 January 1928, 3.
100 Ibid., 6.
101 *Malaya Tribune*, 23 February 1928, 5.
102 Ibid.
103 Ibid.
104 *TL*, 26 January 1928, 6.
105 *TL*, 9 February 1928, 6.
106 Headley and Pickthall were old friends but, by the late 1920s, they had diametrically opposed views about India and its future. Headley championed the British administration of India and the British Empire more broadly. Pickthall, on the other hand, became a close ally of Gandhi when the latter sought to build bridges with Muslims by supporting the Khilafat Movement in the early 1920s. Consequently, Pickthall came to 'believe in Non-Co-operation thoroughly. [. . .] It is liberty. It is a national resurrection, postulating only the destruction of such things and influences as are positively noxious to the growth of a healthy Asiatic life': Marmaduke Pickthall, 'Foreword', in Anon, *Non-Co-operation in Congress Week* (Bombay: The National Literature Publishing Company, n.d [1921]), 4. Pickthall resigned from the *Bombay Chronicle* after it was sold and the new owners insisted on an editorial policy hostile to Gandhi.
107 *The Times*, 27 February 1928, 11; *IR* 16, no. 4–5 (1928): 122.

108 See correspondence in Ansari, *The Making of the East London Mosque*, 137–9.
109 *Malaya Tribune*, 20 September 1929, 13.
110 *IR* 16, no. 9 (1928): 326.
111 Princeton Theological Seminary Library, Robert Elliott Speer Manuscript Collection, Series V, Scrapbooks, Box 69, File 69:1: Comparative Religions, vol. 1, W[illiam]. H[enry]. T[emple]. G[airdner]., 'Lord Headley and Islam', Unreferenced newspaper article (1928).
112 Ibid.
113 Ibid.
114 Ibid.
115 Ibid.
116 Ibid.
117 Ibid.
118 *IR* 16, no. 9 (1928): 322–33.
119 Ibid., 322.
120 Ibid., 323.
121 Ibid., 324–5, 329.
122 Ibid., 325.
123 Ibid., 329.
124 Quoted in *The Daily Herald*, 4 September 1928, 2.
125 Ibid.
126 See the friendly letter from Headley to Field in MECA, Philby Collection, 2/3/4/8/ Correspondence, Lord Headley to Arthur Field, 20 July 1926.
127 Repr. in *TMW* 19, no. 1 (1929): 75–6.
128 Ibid.
129 Ibid.
130 *TL*, 31 January 1929, 4.
131 *IR* 17, no. 12 (1929): 426–7.
132 *The Northern Whig and Belfast Post*, 19 August 1929, 14.
133 *The Singapore Free Press and Mercantile Advertiser*, 12 September 1929, 6.
134 *IR* 18, no. 8 (1930): 275.
135 *IR* 18, no. 10 (1930): 374.

Chapter 9

1 *TCA*, 12 September 1929, 12. See also *The Western Gazette*, 2 August 1929, 6.
2 PC, Papers of Catharine, Lady Headley (hereafter PCLH), Statutory Declaration by Mrs Catharine Bashford, 27 August 1925.
3 *The Daily Herald*, 1 August 1929, 7.

4 Author's interviews with the fifth Lord Headley's great-granddaughter, Berkshire, 14 February 2003 and 3 March 2017. The few surviving letters from Headley to Vivienne are affectionate: PC, PID, Headley to Vivienne (surname unknown), 22 January 1930 and 14 July 1931.
5 *TCA*, 12 September 1929, 12; *IR* 17, no. 10 (1929): 382–4.
6 *TCA*, 12 September 1929, 12.
7 *TCA*, 20 December 1929, 14.
8 *East London Observer*, 21 July 1928, 6.
9 Repr. in *IR* 17, no. 11 (1929): 424.
10 Ibid., 422.
11 Ibid., 424.
12 Ibid.
13 *IR* 18, no. 6 (1930): 222.
14 Ibid.
15 Ibid.
16 Ibid., 223.
17 Ibid., 215.
18 For a summary of the events of 1929–30, see Lawrence James, *Raj: The Making and Unmaking of British India* (1997; repr., London: Abacus, 1998), 519–34.
19 *The Times*, 21 July 1933, 4; *IR* 18, no. 11 (1930): 423.
20 Repr. in *The Scotsman*, 3 November 1930, 11.
21 Repr. in *The Singapore Free Press and Mercantile Advertiser*, 13 November 1930, 5.
22 Repr. in *The Scotsman*, 3 November 1930, 11.
23 Warren Dockter, *Churchill and the Islamic World: Orientalism, Empire and Diplomacy in the Middle East* (London: I.B. Tauris, 2015), 200.
24 Quoted in ibid., 200–1.
25 Ibid., 203.
26 Ibid., 201.
27 Quoted in ibid., 203; see also 204–8.
28 Churchill Archives Centre, Churchill College, University of Cambridge (hereafter CAC), The Papers of Sir Winston Churchill, Chartwell Papers (hereafter CHAR), CHAR2/180B/116, Lord Headley to Winston Churchill, 22 March 1931.
29 I have not found evidence that British Muslim converts supported Headley in 1931 or later.
30 CAC, Papers of Churchill, CHAR2/180B/117, Copy of undated statement on India by Lord Headley, sent to Winston Churchill, March 1931.
31 Annie Besant (1847–1933) was a British-born theosophist and politician in India. She was President of the Indian National Congress in 1917.
32 CAC, Papers of Churchill, CHAR2/180B/117, Undated statement on India by Lord Headley.

33 CAC, Papers of Churchill, CHAR2/180B/124, Winston Churchill to Lord Headley, 24 March 1931.
34 Dockter, *Churchill*, 209.
35 *Belfast News Letter*, 8 May 1931, 11.
36 Shaukat Ali (1873–1938) was the elder brother of Mohamed Ali (see Chapter 6) and a founder and leader of the Khilafat Movement.
37 *TYP*, 9 April 1931, 4.
38 Ibid.
39 *TYP*, 21 May 1931, 4.
40 *The Times*, 7 November 1934, 19.
41 *The Times*, 2 October 1931, 7.
42 Ibid.
43 On Headley's views about communism, see *TYP*, 27 September 1932, 7. In 1931, Headley became a patron of the Lottery Laws Reform Association: see *The Nottingham Evening Post*, 30 March 1931, 6.
44 Most of the main Indian political leaders boycotted the third Round Table Conference (November and December 1932).
45 James, *Raj*, 532.
46 Ibid.
47 *The Times*, 21 July 1933, 4.
48 *IR* 18, no. 12 (1930): 426.
49 PC, PID, Headley to Vivienne (surname unknown), 14 July 1931.
50 See M. A. Sherif, 'Pickthall's Islamic Politics', in *Marmaduke Pickthall*, ed. Nash, 128–32.
51 Pickthall certainly acted as intermediary between the Nizam of Hyderabad and Lord Lamington and others in London who, also in the early 1930s, sought funding for a mosque and religious school in the East End: see Gilham, 'Marmaduke Pickthall', 59.
52 *TYP*, 21 July 1933, 6.
53 *TYP*, 30 April 1932, 10. An image of Brumwell Thomas's design is reproduced in Shahed Saleem, *The British Mosque: An Architectural and Social History* (Swindon: Historic England, 2018), 135.
54 See Sami Moubayed, *Steel and Silk: Men and Women who Shaped Syria, 1900–2000* (Seattle: Cune Press, 2006), 140–2.
55 Ryad, 'Salafiyya', 60.
56 *The Lancashire Daily Post*, 14 November 1932, 4.
57 *Belfast News Letter*, 22 July 1933, 1; *The Times*, 21 July 1933, 4.
58 *Northern Daily Mail*, 19 January 1931, 2.
59 *Sheffield Daily Telegraph*, 20 January 1931, 4.
60 On Headley's views about heaven, see *The Straits Times*, 19 April 1930, 6. The Dayang Muda was the British-born Gladys Milton Brooke (1884–1952). Headley said that

her religious conversion, which was overseen by Khalid Sheldrake, was 'liable to be misconstrued as a desire for notoriety, even as a somewhat freakish departure from good taste. I am afraid that it will hurt the feelings of many Moslems all over the world' (*The Auckland Star*, 9 April 1932, 3; *New York Times*, 20 February 1932, 17).

61 *IR* 21, no. 8 (1933): 269.
62 MECA, Philby Collection, 6/5/4/10/Correspondence (Islam), Muslim Society of Great Britain, *Muslim Society of Great Britain Bulletin* 1 (n.d. [c. August 1933]), 1.
63 See *IR* 10, no. 4 (1922): 146.
64 See *IR* 22, no. 9 (1934): 301–3. Headley and Abdullah had previously met at Woking in autumn 1922 (see Chapter 7).
65 See Martin Kramer, *Islam Assembled: The Advent of the Muslim Congresses* (New York: Columbia University Press, 1986), 142–53.
66 TNA, FO371/17831, 'Forthcoming European Moslem Congress at Geneva', Undated file minutes, 1934.
67 Kramer, *Islam Assembled*, 146.
68 *The Times*, 7 November 1934, 19. On Cobbold's Hajj, see Chapter 7.
69 *IR* 23, no. 1 (1935): 3–6.
70 *The Times*, 10 January 1935, 12.
71 Queen consort. Margaret, Lady Brooke, was married to the second 'White Raja' of Sarawak, Charles Brooke (1829–1917).
72 The Brooke Heritage Trust Digital Archive, MPS83.b15.2.H1, Lord Headley to Margaret, Lady Brooke, 28 January 1935. Available online: http://archive.brooketrust.org/DA/showObject.php?id=MPS83.b15.2.H1 (accessed 12 March 2020).
73 The Brooke Heritage Trust Digital Archive, MPS83.b15.2.H4, Lord Headley to Margaret, Lady Brooke, 26 February 1935. Available online: http://archive.brooketrust.org/DA/showObject.php?id=MPS83.b15.2.H4 (accessed 12 March 2020).
74 *IR* 23, no. 5 (1935): 162.
75 *IR* 23, no. 9 (1935): 324.
76 *The Singapore Free Press and Mercantile Advertiser*, 2 July 1935, 6.
77 Ibid.; *The Times*, 26 June 1935, 19.
78 The precise location of Quilliam/Léon's (unmarked) grave within the Muslim burial area is currently unknown.
79 For example, *The Brooklyn Daily Eagle*, 22 June 1935, 11; *The Egyptian Gazette*, 24 June 1935, 6; *The Advertiser* (Adelaide), 24 June 1935, 15; *The Gazette* (Montreal), 24 June 1935, 7.
80 *The Straits Times*, 5 July 1935, 16.
81 *IR* 23, no. 9 (1935): 324.
82 Ibid., 325.
83 *The Young Islam* (Lahore), 1 July 1935, 2.
84 *The Times*, 16 July 1935, 13.

85 *Genuine Islam* (Singapore) 1, no. 1 (1936): 28.
86 *The Times*, 11 November 1935, 10.
87 *The Times*, 12 December 1935, 18. Rankin converted from Islam to Buddhism in the 1940s: see Anon, *Who Was Who, Volume 8, 1981–1990* (London: A. and C. Black, 1991), 624.
88 After Headley's death, Catharine continued to live at Portland Place and expanded her property portfolio. She also retained Ashton Gifford House in Wiltshire and lived there until 1940, when, due to wartime provisions, it became a school. Catharine died in Hampshire in 1947 (see *The Liverpool Echo*, 8 January 1947, 3). According to her wishes, she was cremated and her ashes scattered at a local crematorium (PCLH, Copy of the Will of Catharine, Dowager Lady Headley, 29 May 1946). She bequeathed a portrait of Lord Headley, still hanging at her Portland Place apartment in 1947, to the 'British Muslim Society' (which had become the MSGB), and it was sent to the Society care of the imam at Woking. It is unclear what became of the portrait (PCLH, John Turing [solicitor] to Margaret Higgins [Dowager Lady Headley's personal assistant], 13 May 1947).
89 Photographs of the event were published in *IR* 25, no. 8 (1937): frontispieces.
90 *TMW* 27, no. 4 (1937): 421.
91 Quoted in Ansari, *The Making of the East London Mosque*, 25.
92 See ibid., 15–26; Anon, 'The London Mosque', *Journal of the Royal Central Asian Society* 27, no. 2 (1940): 221–3; A. L. Tibawi, 'History of the London Central Mosque and the Islamic Cultural Centre, 1910–1980', *Die Welt des Islams* 21, no. 1–4 (1981): 197–208.

Epilogue

1 Photographs of these meetings were published regularly in *The Islamic Review*.
2 On the emerging field of transnational European Muslim history, see Götz Nordbruch and Umar Ryad (ed.), *Transnational Islam in Interwar Europe: Muslim Activists and Thinkers* (New York: Palgrave Macmillan, 2014).
3 A contested but popular term that describes an imagined global Muslim unity that is typically contrasted with a putative (and, in the nineteenth century, a broadly Christian) 'West'. Cemil Aydin has argued that the idea of a 'Muslim world' does not derive from *umma*; rather, 'Muslims did not imagine belonging to a global political unity *until* the peak of European hegemony in the late nineteenth century, when poor colonial conditions, European discourses of Muslim racial inferiority, and Muslims' theories of their own apparent decline nurtured the first arguments for pan-Islamic solidarity': Cemil Aydin, *The Idea of the Muslim World: A Global Intellectual History* (Cambridge, MA: Harvard University Press, 2017), 3.

4 See, for example, the conversion testimony of Mahmud Gunnar Erikson, who converted in Sweden in the early 1950s, in S. A. Khulusi (ed.), *Islam Our Choice*, new edn (Woking: The Woking Muslim Mission and Literary Trust, 1961), 207–8.
5 Ryad, 'Salafiyya', 83.
6 Ahmadiyya Anjuman Isha'at Islam Lahore (UK) website. Available online: http://wokingmuslim.org/pers/headley/ (accessed 3 October 2019).
7 Headley's *Thoughts for the Future* and his three books on Islam have been republished by various presses in the United States.
8 See, for example, the short film 'Baron Headley', part of the ILM Film 'Great Muslim Lives' series on YouTube, available online: https://www.youtube.com/watch?v=-iTV4ol6tFc (accessed 26 October 2019); 'Famous Islamic Figures' Facebook post. Available online: https://www.facebook.com/132290866861580/photos/pb.132290866861580.-2207520000.1456089820./416432831780714/?type=3 (accessed 10 October 2019); Regular Joe Blog, 'The Irish Lord who Converted to Islam'. Available online: http://josefoshea.blogspot.com/2014/ (accessed 23 October 2019). Headley featured in the BBC television documentary 'Great British Islam' (2012). Available online: https://www.bbc.co.uk/programmes/p00vynh7 (accessed 20 October 2019); he is also included in the 'Muslim Heritage Trail' (2019), designed by the Everyday Muslim Heritage and Archive Initiative. Available online: https://www.everydaymuslim.org/projects/woking-mosque-project/muslim-heritage-trail-woking/ (accessed 12 October 2019).

Select bibliography

I Primary sources

Unpublished sources

British Library (BL), London, UK
Archive of the Royal Literary Fund (Loan 96 RLF).

Churchill Archives Centre (CAC), Churchill College, University of Cambridge, UK
The Papers of Sir Winston Churchill, Chartwell Papers (CHAR).

General Record Office (England), Southport, UK
Marriage Certificate of Rowland George Allanson-Winn and Teresa St. Josephine Johnson, 27 October 1899.

India Office Records (IOR), Asia, Pacific and Africa Collections, British Library, London, UK
Births and Baptisms Ecclesiastical Returns, Parish Register Transcripts from the Presidency of Bengal.
Births and Baptisms Ecclesiastical Returns, Roman Catholic Returns of Baptisms, Marriages and Burials.
Deaths and Burials Ecclesiastical Returns, Parish Register Transcripts from the Presidency of Bengal.
Marriages Ecclesiastical Returns, Parish Register Transcripts from the Presidency of Bengal.
Military Department Records (L/MIL).
Political and Secret Department Papers (L/PS).
The Quarterly Indian Army List for April 1, 1891. Calcutta: Military Department/Office of the Superintendent of Government Printing, India, 1891.

Middle East Centre Archive (MECA), St Antony's College, University of Oxford, UK
Harry St John Bridger Philby Collection (GB165-0229), Correspondence.

Princeton Theological Seminary Library, Princeton, USA
Robert Elliott Speer Manuscript Collection, Series V, Scrapbooks.

Private Collections and Archives (PC), UK
Papers of Ivy Davis (PID).
Papers of Catharine, Lady Headley (PCLH).
Papers of Rowland George Allanson-Winn, fifth Lord Headley (PLH).

Richmond upon Thames Local Studies and Library and Archive, London, UK
Douglas B. W. Sladen Papers (SLA).

The Brooke Heritage Trust Digital Archive, London, UK
Papers of Margaret, Lady Brooke and Ranee of Sarawak, Correspondence transcribed by Margaret Noble.

The National Archives (TNA), London, UK
British Army Service Records (WO).
Census of England, Wales and Scotland 1871.
Census of England, Wales and Scotland 1891.
Foreign Office Records (FO).
Merchant Navy Seamen Records (BT).
Treasury Solicitor Records (TS).

The National Archives of Ireland (TNAI), Dublin, Ireland
Calendars of Wills and Administrations 1858-1922.
Census of Ireland 1901.
Census of Ireland 1911.
Department of Finance, Compensation Records (FIN/COMP).

Published sources

Works of reference and edited collections

Ahmad, Nasir (ed.). *Eid Sermons at the Shah Jehan Mosque Woking, England, 1931-1940*. Lahore: Aftab-ud-Din Memorial Benevolent Trust, 2002.
Anon. *A Handbook for Travellers in India and Ceylon*. London: John Murray, 1891.
Anon. *The Popular Guide to the New House of Commons and Record of the Election of 1892, July 1 to July 29*. 2nd edn. London: Pall Mall Gazette, 1892.
Anon. *The Cyclopedia of India*, vol. 2. Calcutta: Cyclopedia Publishing Company, 1908.
Anon. *The Imperial Gazetteer of India*. New edn. Oxford: Clarendon Press, 1908.
Anon. *Who's Who 1914*. London: Adam and Charles Black, 1914.
Anon. *Who's Who 1919*. London: A. and C. Black, 1919.
Anon. *Who's Who 1926*. London: A. and C. Black, 1926.
Anon. *Who's Who 1935*. London: A. and C. Black, 1935.
Anon. *Who Was Who 1929-1940*. London: A. and C. Black, 1947.
Anon. *Who Was Who, Volume 8, 1981-1990*. London: A. and C. Black, 1991.
Ansari, Humayun (ed.). *The Making of the East London Mosque, 1910-1951*. Cambridge: Cambridge University Press/Royal Historical Society, 2011.
Baedeker, Karl. *Egypt and the Sudan: Handbook for Travellers*. 7th edn. London: T. Fisher Unwin, 1914.
Doubleday, H. A., Duncan Warr and Lord Howard De Walden (ed.). *The Complete Peerage, or a History of the House of Lords and All Its Members from the Earliest Times*, vol. 2. London: The St. Catherine Press, 1926.

Hesilrige, Arthur G. M. (ed.). *Debrett's Peerage and Titles of Courtesy*. London: Dean and Son, 1921.
Kidd, Charles and David Williamson (ed.). *Debrett's Peerage and Baronetage*. London: Debrett's Peerage Ltd./Macmillan, 1990.
Venn, J. A. (ed.). *Alumni Cantabrigienses*, part 2, vol. 6. Cambridge: Cambridge University Press, 1954.

Newspapers, magazines and journals

The Aberdeen Journal.
Aberdeen Press and Journal.
African Times and Orient Review.
al-Manār (Cairo).
Arkansas Gazette.
The Auckland Star.
Badr (Lahore).
The Bath Chronicle.
The Belfast News-Letter.
Belfast Telegraph.
Bexhill-on-Sea Observer.
Birmingham Daily Gazette.
The Birmingham Daily Post.
The Brooklyn Daily Eagle.
The Cambridge Independent Press.
The Canterbury Journal and Farmer's Gazette.
The Colonies and India (London).
The Comrade (Delhi).
The Cork Constitution.
The Courier and Advertiser (Dundee).
The Coventry Standard.
The Crescent (Liverpool).
Daily British Colonist (Victoria, Canada).
The Daily Express.
The Daily Herald.
The Daily Mail (Hull).
The Daily Mirror.
Daily Record and Mail.
Daily Sketch.
The Daily Telegraph.
The Devon and Exeter Gazette.
The Ealing Gazette.
The East and the West (London).
East London Observer.

The Egyptian Gazette.
The Essex County Chronicle.
The Evening Telegraph and Post (Dundee).
The Examiner (Launceston, Australia).
The Franklin Times (North Carolina).
The Freeman's Journal.
The Gazette (Montreal).
Genuine Islam (Singapore).
The Globe.
The Graphic.
The Greencastle Herald (Indiana).
The Hemel Hempstead Gazette.
The Hendon and Finchley Times.
The Homeward Mail from India, China, and the East.
Illustrated London News.
Indian Opinion (Johannesburg).
The Irish Builder and Engineer.
The Irish Independent.
Irish Society and Social Review.
The Irish Times.
The Islamic Review.
Islamic Review and Muslim India.
Jewish World.
The Kerry Evening Post.
The Lancashire Daily Post.
Larne Times and Weekly Telegraph.
The Leeds Mercury.
The Light (Lahore).
The Liverpool Echo.
The Liverpool Mercury.
The Londonderry Sentinel.
The Mail (Adelaide).
Mulaya Tribune.
Manchester Dispatch.
Manchester Guardian.
The Midland Daily Telegraph.
The Morning Post.
Moslem Chronicle and Muhammadan Observer.
The Moslem World.
Muslim India and Islamic Review.
The Near East (London).
The New York Times.

The Norfolk Chronicle and Norwich Gazette.
North Otago Times.
Northampton Daily Echo.
The Northern Daily Mail and South Durham Herald.
The Northern Whig and Belfast Post.
Norwood News.
The Nottingham Daily Express.
The Nottingham Evening Post.
The Nottingham Journal.
The Observer.
The Ogden Standard-Examiner (Utah).
The Otago Daily Times.
Paigham Sulh (Lahore).
Pall Mall Gazette.
The Physiologist.
The Primrose League Gazette.
The Pukekohe and Waiuku Times (South Auckland).
The Radio Times.
The Reading Eagle (Pennsylvania).
Reading Mercury.
The Referee.
The Register (Adelaide).
The Review of Religions (Qadian).
The Scots Magazine.
The Scotsman.
Sheffield Daily Telegraph.
The Shepton Mallet Journal.
The Shields Daily News.
The Singapore Free Press and Mercantile Advertiser.
The Sketch.
St. James's Gazette.
The Straits Times.
The Sunday Post.
The Sunday Times (Perth).
The Tablet.
The Times.
Vanity Fair.
The Washington Post.
The Western Gazette.
The Western Morning News and Mercury.
The Western Times.
The Yorkshire Post.

Yorkshire Telegraph and Star.
The Young Islam (Lahore).

Autobiographies, memoirs, obituaries and published diaries and letters

Ali, Dusé Mohamed. *Duse Mohamed Ali (1866-1945): The Autobiography of a Pioneer Pan African and Afro-Asian Activist*, edited by Mustafa Abdelwahid. Trenton, NJ: The Red Sea Press, 2011.

Boyd, Martin. *Such Pleasure*. London: Cresset Press, 1949.

Bullard, Reader. *Two Kings in Arabia: Letters from Jeddah, 1923–5 and 1936–9*, edited by E. C. Hodgkin. Reading: Ithaca, 1993.

Destani, Bejtullah and Jason Tomes (ed.). *Albania's Greatest Friend: Aubrey Herbert and the Making of Modern Albania. Diaries and Papers 1904–1923*. London: I.B. Tauris, 2011.

Fremantle, Anne. *Loyal Enemy*. London: Hutchinson, 1938.

Godwin-Austin, Lieutenant-Colonel H. H. 'Obituary: Mr. W. H. Johnson'. *Proceedings of the Royal Geographical Society and Monthly Record of Geography* 5, no. 5 (1883): 291–3.

Grafftey-Smith, Laurence. *Bright Levant*. 1970. Reprint, London: Stacey International, 2002.

Gullett, H. B., 'Memoir of Barbara Baynton'. In Barbara Baynton, *Bush Studies*, 1–25. 1902. Reprinted with notes and introduction. Sydney: Angus and Robertson, 1965.

Books, pamphlets and articles

Addison, James Thayer. 'The Ahmadiya Movement and Its Western Propaganda'. *Harvard Theological Review* 22, no. 1 (1929): 1–32.

Ahmad, Khwaja Nazir (ed.). *Charms of Islam: A Collection of Writings of Some of the Eminent Scholars*. Woking and Lahore: The Woking Muslim Mission and Literary Trust, 1935.

A[llanson]. W[inn]. *Thoughts for the Future*. London and Felling-on-Tyne: The Walter Scott Publishing Co., 1913.

Allanson-Winn, R. G. *Boxing*. London: George Bell and Sons, 1889.

Allanson-Winn, R. G. *Boxing*. London: A. D. Innes and Company, 1897.

Allanson-Winn, R. G. 'Notes on Road Construction'. *Transactions of the Institution of Civil Engineers of Ireland* 28 (1898–1901): 236–69.

Allanson-Winn, R. G. 'Harnessing the Sea: A New Method of Coast Protection'. *Pearson's Magazine* (UK edn) 9, no. 50 (1900): 183–8.

Allanson-Winn, R. G. 'Foreshore Protection and Public Health'. *Contract Journal and Specification Record* 45 (1901–1902): 377.

Allanson-Winn, R. G. 'Some Recent Developments in the Design and Construction of Groynes'. *Fielden's Magazine* 5 (1901–1902): 539.

Allanson-Winn, R. G. 'The Constructive Power of the Sea'. *Transactions of the Institution of Civil Engineers of Ireland* 28 (1902): 124–85.

Allanson-Winn, R. G. 'The Protection and Improvement of Foreshores by the Utilization of Tidal and Wave Action'. *Transactions of the American Society of Civil Engineers* 50, paper 944 (1903): 66–94.

Allanson-Winn, R. G. *Sea-Coast Erosion and Remedial Works*. London: St. Bride's Press, n.d. (1904).

Allanson-Winn, R. G. 'The Youghal Foreshore Protection Works; and Deep-Sea Erosion on the East Coast of England'. *Transactions of the Institution of Civil Engineers of Ireland* 30 (1904): 144–75.

Allanson-Winn, R. G. and C. Phillipps-Wolley. *Broadsword and Singlestick. With Chapters on Quarter-Staff, Bayonet, Cudgel, Shillalah, Walking-Stick, Umbrella and Other Weapons of Self-Defence*. London: George Bell and Sons, 1890.

Allanson-Winn, R. G. and C. E. Walker, *Self-Defence, Being a Guide to Boxing, Quarter-Staff and Bayonet Practice, the Walking-Stick Cudgel, Fencing etc*. London: Lawrence and Bullen, 1903.

Ameer Ali, Syed. *The Spirit of Islam, Or the Life and Teachings of Mohammed*. New edn. Calcutta: S. K. Lahiri, 1902.

Anon. 'English Tourists in Ireland'. *The Dublin Review* 3, no. 6 (1837): 401–27.

Anon. *The Central Islamic Society* (leaflet). London: Central Islamic Society, 1916.

Anon. 'The London Mosque'. *Journal of the Royal Central Asian Society* 27, no. 2 (1940): 221–3.

Bell, Ernest (ed.). *Handbook of Athletic Sports*, vol. 3. London: George Bell and Sons, 1890.

Cobbold, Lady Evelyn. *Pilgrimage to Mecca*. London: John Murray, 1934.

Collett, John and A. Mitra. *A Guide for Visitors to Kashmir*. New edn. Calcutta: W. Newman and Co., 1898.

Gladstone, W. E. *Bulgarian Horrors and the Question of the East*. London: John Murray, 1876.

Hammerton, Sir John (ed.). *Countries of the World*. vol. 1, new edn. London: Amalgamated Press, n.d. (c.1937).

Headley, Al-Hajj Lord. *The Affinity between the Original Church of Jesus Christ and Islam*. Woking: Trust for the Encouragement and Circulation of Muslim Religious Literature, 1927.

Headley, Al-Hajj Lord. *Is Our House in Order?* Woking: The Trust for the Encouragement and Circulation of Muslim Religious Literature, 1928.

Headley, Al-Hajj Lord. 'Introduction'. In Soorma, C. A. (ed.), *Islam's Attitude towards Women and Orphans*, n.p. Woking: The Trust for the Encouragement and Circulation of Muslim Religious Literature, 1929.

Headley, Lord. 'More about the Naturalisation Farce'. *Britannia* 5, no. 1 (1915): 8.

Headley, Lord. 'The British Workman'. *The Aeroplane* 9, no. 21 (1915): 640–2.

Headley, Lord. 'Trust in God – But Tie Your Camel'. *The Suffragette* 4, no. 115 (1915): 277.

Headley, Lord. 'Introduction'. In Roy Horniman (ed.), *How to Make the Railways Pay for the War; Or, the Transport Problem Solved*, vii–xi. London: George Routledge and Sons, 1916.

Headley, Lord. *Sister Religions*. Woking and London: The Gresham Press, 1916.

Headley, Lord. 'Complacineptitude'. *The Commercial Motor*, 13 December 1917: 334.

Headley, Lord. 'Foreword'. In Maulvi Muhammad Ali, *Islam: The Religion of Humanity*, 1–2. No place of publication: No publisher, n.d. (*c*.1917).

Headley, Lord. *Sister Religion*. Lahore: The Muslim Book Society, 1920.

Headley, Lord. 'Presidential Address'. In *The Society of Engineers (Incorporated) Transactions for 1921, 7–30*. London: The Society of Engineers, 1921.

Headley, Lord. *The Three Great Prophets of the World: Moses, Jesus and Muhammad*. Woking: The Islamic Review, 1923.

Headley, Lord. 'Within the Holy City of Mecca'. *The Sphere*, 29 September 1923: 405–7.

Headley, Lord. 'Pilgrimage to Mecca'. *Journal of the Central Asian Society* 11, no. 1 (1924): 20–35.

Headley, Lord. 'Foreword'. In Khwaja Kamal-ud-Din, *The Ideal Prophet*, v–vi. Woking: The Woking Muslim Mission and Literary Trust, 1925.

Headley, Lord. 'When Intellectual Darkness Faced Europe'. In Khwaja Kamal-ud-Din, *Open Letters to the Bishops of Salisbury and London*, 142–7. Woking: The Trust for the Encouragement and Circulation of Muslim Religious Literature, 1926.

Headley, Lord. *Garp'ta Müslimanlık cereyanı* (A Treatise on Islam and Its Practice in the West), translated by Ömer Rıza. Istanbul: Amedi Matbaası, 1927.

Headley, Lord. 'Moses, Jesus, and Mohammed'. In *Whom Do Men Say that I Am? A Collection of the Views of the Most Notable Christian and Non-Christian Modern Authors about Jesus of Nazareth*, edited by Harold Osbourne, 170–2. London: Faber and Faber, 1932.

Headley, Lord. *A Western Awakening to Islam*. New edn. 1914. Reprint, Woking: Woking Muslim Mission and Literary Trust, 1949.

Headley, Lord (R. G. Allanson-Winn). *Boxing*. New edn. London: G. Bell and Sons, 1920.

Kamal-ud-Din, Al-Hajj Khwaja. *Islam and the Muslim Prayer*, edited by Nasir Ahmad. 7th rev. edn. Lahore: The Woking Muslim Mission and Literary Trust, 1960.

Kamal-ud-Din, Khwaja. *Islam and the Muslim Prayer*. Woking: Salter and Co., 1914.

Kamal-ud-Din, Khwaja. *India in the Balance: British Rule and the Caliphate*. Woking: The Islamic Review, n.d. (*c*.1921/22).

Kamal-ud-Din, Khwaja. *The House Divided: England, India and Islam*. Woking: The Islamic Review, 1922.

Kamal-ud-Din, Khwaja. *Islam to East and West*. Woking and Lahore: The Woking Muslim Mission and Literary Trust, 1935.

Khulusi, S. A. (ed.). *Islam Our Choice*. New edn. Woking: The Woking Muslim Mission and Literary Trust, 1961.

Knight, E. F. *Where Three Empires Meet: A Narrative of Recent Travel in Kashmir, Western Tibet, Gilgit, and the Adjoining Countries*. 1893. Reprint, London: Longmans, Green and Co., 1905.

Leitner, G. W. *Muhammadanism*. Woking: The Oriental Nobility Institute, 1889.

Leitner, G. W. 'Correspondence, Notes and News'. *Imperial and Asiatic Quarterly Review* 4 (third series) (1897): 182.

Lovegrove, J. W. (Habeeb-Ullah). *What Is Islam?*. 2nd edn. Woking: The Woking Muslim Mission and Literary Trust, 1934.

Mills, Martin. *Brangane: A Memoir*. London: Constable and Co., 1926.

Morel, E. D. *Truth and the War*. London: The National Labour Press, 1916.

Pickthall, Marmaduke. *Muslim Interests in Palestine*. Woking and London: The Gresham Press, 1917.

Pickthall, Marmaduke. 'Foreword'. In Anon, *Non-Co-operation in Congress Week*, 3–5. Bombay: The National Literature Publishing Company, n.d. (1921).

Pickthall, Marmaduke. *The Meaning of the Glorious Koran: An Explanatory Translation*. London: Alfred A. Knopf, 1930.

Rawlinson, Major-General Sir Henry C. 'On the Recent Journey of Mr. W. H. Johnson from Leh, in Ladakh, to Ilchi in Chinese Turkestan'. *Proceedings of the Royal Geographical Society* 11, no. 1 (1866): 6–14.

Rutter, Eldon. *The Holy Cities of Arabia*. 1928. Reprinted with notes and introduction. London: Arabian Publishing, 2015.

Rutter, Eldon. 'The Holy Cities of Arabia'. *Journal of the Central Asian Society* 16, no. 2 (1929): 196–205.

Shah, Sirdar Ikbal Ali. 'Ferments in the World of Islam'. *Journal of the Central Asian Society* 14, no. 2 (1927): 130–46.

Internet sources

British Pathé. 'Mohamed Ali at Woking Mosque'. Newsreel, 1920. Available online: https://www.britishpathe.com/video/VLVACJNPAAY9WALLTSRMGLQVD2BSG-MOHAMED-ALI-AT-WOKING-MOSQUE/query/woking+mosque (accessed 29 August 2019).

British Pathé. 'Begum of Bhopal at Mosque'. Newsreel, 1925. Available online: https://www.britishpathe.com/video/the-begum-of-bhopal-aka-the-begum-pf-bhotal/query/bhopal (accessed 29 August 2019).

Gertrude Bell Archive, Newcastle University. Gertrude Bell to Sir Hugh Bell, 5 December 1923. Available online: http://www.gerty.ncl.ac.uk/letter_details.php?letter_id=661 (accessed 10 May 2017).

II Secondary sources

Books, pamphlets and articles

Abbasi, Muhammad Yusuf. *London Muslim League (1908-1928): An Historical Study*. Islamabad: National Institute of Historical and Cultural Research, 1988.

Abdelwahid, Mustafa. 'Introduction'. In Dusé Mohamed Ali, *Duse Mohamed Ali*, edited by Mustafa Abdelwahid, 1–30. Trenton, NJ: The Red Sea Press, 2011.

Select Bibliography

Abraham, Jose. *Islamic Reform and Colonial Discourse on Modernity in India: Socio-Political and Religious Thought of Vakkom Moulavi*. New York: Palgrave Macmillan, 2014.

Allen, Charles. *Plain Tales from the Raj: Images of British India in the Twentieth Century*. New edn. 1975. Reprint, London: Abacus, 2000.

Almond, Philip C. *Heretic and Hero: Muhammad and the Victorians*. Wiesbaden: Harrassowitz, 1989.

Ansari, Humayun. *'The Infidel Within': Muslims in Britain since 1800*. New edn. London: Hurst, 2018.

Ansari, K. H. 'Attitudes to Islam and Muslims in Britain: 1875–1924'. *Indo-British Review* 23, no. 2 (2001): 58–74.

Auchterlonie, Paul (ed.). *Encountering Islam. Joseph Pitts: An English Slave in 17th-Century Algiers and Mecca*. London: Arabian Publishing, 2012.

Aydin, Cemil. *The Idea of the Muslim World: A Global Intellectual History*. Cambridge, MA: Harvard University Press, 2017.

Beckford, James A. 'Accounting for Conversion'. *British Journal of Sociology* 29, no. 2 (1978): 249–62.

Bence-Jones, Mark. *A Guide to Irish Country Houses*. New edn. London: Constable, 1988.

Bennett, Clinton. 'Is Isaac without Ishmael Complete? A Nineteenth-Century Debate Revisited'. *Islam and Christian-Muslim Relations* 2, no. 1 (1991): 42–55.

Bennett, Clinton. *Victorian Images of Islam*. London: Grey Seal, 1992.

Bowen, Patrick D. *A History of Conversion to Islam in the United States, Volume 1: White American Muslims before 1975*. Leiden and Boston, MA: Brill, 2015.

Clark, Peter. *Marmaduke Pickthall: British Muslim*. London: Quartet, 1986.

Clayer, Nathalie and Eric Germain. 'Introduction'. In *Islam in Inter-War Europe*, edited by Nathalie Clayer and Eric Germain, 1–21. London: Hurst, 2008.

Dockter, Warren. *Churchill and the Islamic World: Orientalism, Empire and Diplomacy in the Middle East*. London: I.B. Tauris, 2015.

Emmerson, Charles. *1913: The World before the Great War*. London: Vintage, 2013.

Friedmann, Yohanan. *Prophecy Continuous: Aspects of Ahmadi Religious Thought and Its Medieval Background*. New edn. 1989. Reprint, New Delhi: Oxford University Press, 2003.

Geaves, Ron. *Islam in Victorian Britain: The Life and Times of Abdullah Quilliam*. Markfield: Kube, 2010.

Geaves, Ron. *Islam and Britain: Muslim Mission in an Age of Empire*. London: Bloomsbury, 2018.

GhaneaBassiri, Kambiz. *A History of Islam in America*. New York: Cambridge University Press, 2010.

Gilham, Jamie. 'Britain's First Muslim Peer of the Realm: Henry, Lord Stanley of Alderley and Islam in Victorian Britain'. *Journal of Muslim Minority Affairs* 33, no. 1 (2013): 93–110.

Gilham, Jamie. 'A Passage to Conversion'. In *Critical Muslim 10: Sects*, edited by Ziauddin Sardar and Robin Yassin-Kassab, 99–114. London: The Muslim Institute/Hurst, 2014.

Gilham, Jamie. *Loyal Enemies: British Converts to Islam, 1850–1950*. London: Hurst, 2014.

Gilham, Jamie. 'Abdullah Quilliam, First and Last "Sheikh-ul-Islam of the British Isles"'. In *Victorian Muslim: Abdullah Quilliam and Islam in the West*, edited by Jamie Gilham and Ron Geaves, 97–112. London: Hurst, 2017.

Gilham, Jamie. 'Marmaduke Pickthall and the British Muslim Convert Community'. In *Marmaduke Pickthall: Islam and the Modern World*, edited by Geoffrey P. Nash, 47–71. Leiden and Boston, MA: Brill, 2017.

Gilham, Jamie. 'The British Muslim Baron: Lord Headley and Islam, 1913–35'. *Common Knowledge* 23, no. 3 (2017): 468–95.

Hackforth-Jones, Penne. *Barbara Baynton: Between Two Worlds*. New edn. 1989. Reprint, Carlton, Victoria: Melbourne University Press, 1995.

Hopkirk, Peter. *Foreign Devils on the Silk Road: The Search for the Lost Treasures of Central Asia*. London: John Murray, 1980.

Iqbal, Afzal. *The Life and Times of Mohamed Ali: An Analysis of the Hopes, Fears and Aspirations of Muslim India from 1878 to 1931*. 2nd rev. edn. Lahore: Institute of Islamic Culture, 1979.

James, Lawrence. *The Golden Warrior: The Life and Legend of Lawrence of Arabia*. New edn. 1990. Reprint, London: Abacus, 1995.

James, Lawrence. *Raj: The Making and Unmaking of British India*. New edn. 1997. Reprint, London: Abacus, 1998.

Keenan, Brigid. *Travels in Kashmir: A Popular History of Its People, Places and Crafts*. Delhi: Oxford University Press, 1989.

Kelly, Brendan D. 'One Hundred Years Ago: The Richmond Asylum, Dublin in 1907'. *Irish Journal of Psychological Medicine* 24, no. 3 (2007): 108–14.

Kramer, Martin. *Islam Assembled: The Advent of the Muslim Congresses*. New York: Columbia University Press, 1986.

Krimmer, Sally and Alan Lawson (ed). *Barbara Baynton*. St. Lucia, Queensland: University of Queensland Press, 1980.

Lavan, Spencer. *The Ahmadiyah Movement: A History and Perspective*. Delhi: Manohar, 1974.

Lawless, Richard I. *From Ta'izz to Tyneside: An Arab Community in the North-East of England during the Early Twentieth Century*. Exeter: Exeter University Press, 1995.

Lofland, John and Norman Skonovd. 'Conversion Motifs'. *Journal for the Scientific Study of Religion* 20, no. 4 (1981): 373–85.

Lovell, Mary S. *A Rage to Live: A Biography of Richard and Isabel Burton*. London: Abacus, 1999.

Macfie, A. L. *The Eastern Question 1774–1923*. Rev. edn. Harlow: Longman, 1996.

Macfie, A. L. *The End of the Ottoman Empire, 1908–1923*. Harlow: Longman, 1998.

Matar, Nabil. *Islam in Britain, 1558–1685*. Cambridge: Cambridge University Press, 1998.

McCormick, Donald. *The Mask of Merlin: A Critical Biography of David Lloyd George*. New York: Holt, Rinehart and Winston, 1964.

Meleady, Conor. 'Negotiating the Caliphate: British Responses to Pan-Islamic Appeals, 1914–1924'. *Middle Eastern Studies* 52, no. 2 (2016): 182–97.

Monroe, Elizabeth. *Philby of Arabia*. New edn. 1973. Reprint, Reading: Ithaca, 1998.

Motadel, David (ed.). *Islam and the European Empires*. Oxford: Oxford University Press, 2014.

Moubayed, Sami. *Steel and Silk: Men and Women Who Shaped Syria, 1900–2000*. Seattle: Cune Press, 2006.

Nash, Geoffrey. 'Abdullah Quilliam, Marmaduke Pickthall and the Politics of Christendom and the Ottoman Empire'. In *Victorian Muslim: Abdullah Quilliam and Islam in the West*, edited by Jamie Gilham and Ron Geaves, 79–95. London: Hurst, 2017.

Niall, Brenda. *Martin Boyd: A Life*. Carlton, Victoria: Melbourne University Press, 1988.

Niall, Brenda. *The Boyds: A Family Biography*. New edn. Carlton, Victoria: Melbourne University Press, 2007.

Nordbruch, Götz and Umar Ryad (ed.). *Transnational Islam in Interwar Europe: Muslim Activists and Thinkers*. New York: Palgrave Macmillan, 2014.

Panayi, Panikos. 'The British Empire Union in the First World War'. *Immigrants and Minorities* 8, no. 1–2 (1989): 113–28.

Powell, David. *The Edwardian Crisis: Britain, 1901–1914*. Basingstoke: Palgrave Macmillan, 1996.

Qureshi, M. Naeem. *Pan-Islam in British Indian Politics: A Study of the Khilafat Movement, 1918–1924*. Brill: Leiden and Boston, MA, 1999.

Rambo, Lewis R. *Understanding Religious Conversion*. New Haven: Yale University Press, 1993.

Robinson, Francis. 'Ahmad and the Ahmadiyya'. *History Today* 40, no. 6 (1990): 42–7.

Robinson, Francis. 'The British Empire and the Muslim World'. In *The Oxford History of the British Empire, Volume IV: The Twentieth Century*, edited by Judith M. Brown and Wm. Roger Louis, 398–420. Oxford: Oxford University Press, 1999.

Ryad, Umar. *Islamic Reformism and Christianity: A Critical Reading of the Works of Muhammad Rashid Rida and His Associates (1898–1935)*. Leiden and Boston, MA: Brill, 2009.

Ryad, Umar. 'Salafiyya, Ahmadiyya and European Converts to Islam in the Interwar Period'. In *Muslims in Interwar Europe: A Trans-Cultural Historical Perspective*, edited by Agai Bekim, Umar Ryad and Sajid Mehdi, 47–87. Leiden and Boston, MA: Brill, 2015.

Sherif, M. A. 'Pickthall's Islamic Politics'. In *Marmaduke Pickthall: Islam and the Modern World*, edited by Geoffrey P. Nash, 106–36. Leiden and Boston, MA: Brill, 2017.

Slight, John. *The British Empire and the Hajj, 1865–1956*. Cambridge, MA: Harvard University Press, 2015.

Taylor, Brian. 'Conversion and Cognition: An Area for Empirical Study in the Microsociology of Religious Knowledge'. *Social Compass* 23, no. 1 (1976): 16–21.

Taylor, Brian. 'Recollection and Membership: Converts' Talk and the Ratiocination of Commonality'. *Sociology* 12, no. 2 (1978): 316–24.

Tibawi, A. L. 'History of the London Central Mosque and the Islamic Cultural Centre, 1910–1980'. *Die Welt des Islams* 21, no. 1–4 (1981): 193–208.

Tomes, Jason. 'Winn, Rowland George Allanson Allanson-'. In *Oxford Dictionary of National Biography*, edited by H. C. G. Matthew and Brian Harrison, vol. 59, 744–6. Oxford: Oxford University Press, 2004.

Unpublished theses

Duffield, Ian. 'Dusé Mohamed Ali and the Development of Pan-Africanism'. PhD thesis, Edinburgh University, Edinburgh, 1971.

Internet sources

Mohammad, Maulana Hafiz Sher. *Dr. Sir Muhammad Iqbal and the Ahmadiyya Movement*, translated by Zahid Aziz, 1995. Available online: http://callinghome.blogspot.com/2004/10/dr-sir-muhammad-iqbal-and-ahmadiyya.html (accessed 11 April 2019).

Office for National Statistics (UK). 'Muslim Population in the UK', 2 August 2018. Available online: https://www.ons.gov.uk/aboutus/transparencyandgovernance/freedomofinformationfoi/muslimpopulationintheuk/ (accessed 18 October 2019).

Index

Note: Page numbers followed by 'n' refer to notes.

Abdullah I (Amir of Transjordan, 1882–1951), son of Hussein ibn Ali al-Hashimi   125, 197
Affinity between the Original Church of Jesus Christ and Islam, The (Headley)   158, 218 n.153
African Times and Orient Review, The   70
'After the Battle of Life' (Headley)   69
Aga Khan (Sir Sultan Mahomed Shah, 1877–1957)   117, 118, 147, 159, 163, 168, 181, 184, 191, 195, 196
Aghadoe House, Killarney   9, 67, 113
AGU. *See* Anti-German Union
Ahmad, Hazrat Mirza Ghulam (1835–1908)   61, 65–7, 79, 154, 156, 161
Ahmad, Khwaja Nazir (1897–1970)   98, 157, 167, 172, 190, 234 n.82
Ahmad, Maulana Aftab-ud-Din (1901–56)   190
Ahmad, Mirza Bashir-ud-Din Mahmud (1889–1965)   156
Ahmadi disputes and rivalries   5, 62–3, 65, 66, 147, 150, 154–6, 160, 172, 192, 221 n.60
Ahmadiyya Anjuman Isha'at-e-Islam   163, 166, 215 nn.57, 59, 241 n.6
Ahmadiyya Movement   5, 61–6, 96, 147, 151, 154, 170, 191, 192
al-Azhar mosque   130, 198
Albania, King of   152–3
Alexandria   129–32
al-Fath   151, 187
Al-Fazl   154
Ali, Abdullah Yusuf (1872–1953)   97, 147, 176, 180, 190, 195, 196

Ali, Dusé Mohamed (1866–1945)   70–2, 91, 95, 97, 149, 151, 197
Ali Gate   141
Ali ibn Talib (601–61)   206 n.11
Ali, Maulana Muhammad (1874–1951)   64, 154, 166, 172, 197
Ali, Mohamed (aka Muhammad Ali Jauhar, 1878–1931)   64, 75, 79, 119, 189, 197
Ali, Prince (1879–1935), elder son of Hussein ibn Ali al-Hashimi   136, 141
Ali, Shaukat (1873–1938)   183–4, 197, 238 n.36
Aliens Act of 1905   76, 217 n.115
Allanson-Winn, Anne ('Annie,' 1908)   ix
Allanson-Winn, Charles Mark, fourth Lord Headley (1845–1913)   8, 10, 18–19, 21, 41, 44, 47–50, 53
Allanson-Winn, Charles Rowland, seventh Lord Headley (1902–94)   44, 50
Allanson-Winn, Charles, third Lord Headley (1810–77)   8–9, 23
Allanson-Winn, George Mark Arthur Way (1785–1827)   8
Allanson-Winn, Helen Margaretta (1857–1941)   11, 82, 83, 112, 204 n.33, 219 n.154
Allanson-Winn, John Valentine (1904–72)   190
Allanson-Winn, Margaretta Anne (1860–1951)   11
Allanson-Winn, Margaretta Stefana (1823–71)   8, 11, 83
Allanson-Winn, Owain Gwynedd (1906–93)   47
Allanson-Winn, Rowland George (1855–1935). *See* Headley, Lord

Allanson-Winn, Rowland Patrick ('Paddy,' 1901–69)   44, 46, 111, 191
Allanson-Winn, Stephanie (1858–1940)   11, 83
Allanson-Winn, Teresa (nee Johnson, 1871–1919)   38–42, 44, 47, 48, 50, 110, 111
Allanson-Winn, Thomas Frederick George ('Tommy,' 1903–04)   44, 46, 47, 51
Allenby, Viscount (1861–1936)   128, 131–2
Allen, Charles   37, 38
'All-England Series of Athletic Sports'   21, 22
All-India Federation   181
All-India Muslim Conference, Lucknow (1919)   118
All-India Muslim League   102
All-India Tabligh (Preaching) Conference   163, 165
al-Manar   79, 130, 151, 152
al-Qibla (or *al-Kibla*)   132
Ameer Ali, Syed (or Saiyid) (1849–1928)   58, 64, 117, 118, 147, 150, 163, 168, 185, 196
American Islamic Association   151, 159, 232 n.18
American Society of Civil Engineers   44
Amritsar massacre (Jallianwala Bagh)   118
Anglo-Ottoman Society (AOS)   101, 102, 117, 171
Anjuman-i-Islam   61
Anti-German League   104
Anti-German Union (AGU)   103–6, 109
AOS. *See* Anglo-Ottoman Society
Arabian Nights, The   56
Arnold, Thomas Walker (1864–1930)   64
Arslan, Adil (c.1882–1954)   187–9, 197
Arya Samaji (Hindu reform movement)   164
Asad, Muhammad (1900–92)   124
Asaf Jah VII, Nizam of Hyderabad (1886–1967)   167–9, 171, 186, 192, 197, 238 n.51
Aydin, Cemil   240 n.3
Azam Jah (1907–70), son of the Nizam of Hyderabad   186, 192

Baedeker, Karl   130
Baig, Abbas Ali (1859–1932)   64, 65, 97, 157, 168, 185, 196
Baldwin, Stanley (1867–1947)   180
Balfour Declaration (1917)   178, 179
Bamber, J. H.   141
bankruptcy   5, 18, 109, 115–16
Bankruptcy Act   116
Baramulla–Srinagar road   32–7, 40
Bashford, Catharine (third Lady Headley, 1865–1947)   175–7, 188–92, 240 n.88
Bashford, Radcliffe James Lindsay (1881–1921)   175
Baynton, Barbara (second Lady Headley, 1857–1929)   109–14, 175, 223 n.9
Baynton, Thomas   153
Beckford, James   3–4
Begum of Bhopal, Shahjahan (1838–1901)   60
Begum of Bhopal, Sultan Jahan (1858–1930)   197
Bekri, Syed Ihsan   130
Bell, Ernest (1851–1933)   21, 22
Bell, George (1814–90)   21
Bell, Gertrude (1868–1926)   146
Bennett, Arthur/Ahmad   188, 191–2
Bennett, James   17
Berlin Mosque and Mission   150, 151
Berlyn, Reverend   81
BEU. *See* British Empire Union
Bible   63, 65, 69, 77, 90, 106
Blennerhassett, Elizabeth ('Bessie') Housemayne (1846–1928)   10
BMS. *See* British Muslim Society
Board of Commissioners   45
Board of Trade   42
Bombay Chronicle   155, 167
Boxing (Headley)   21–2, 40–1, 111
Boyd, Martin à Beckett (1893–1972)   113–14, 115, 153
Brangane: A Memoir (Boyd)   113–14, 153
British Empire Union (BEU). *See* Anti-German Union (AGU)
British Muslim Society (BMS)   97–9, 101, 142, 147, 149, 159, 163, 170, 177–9, 181, 182, 188–92, 195–7, 240 n.88

British Red Crescent Society   148
Broadsword and Singlestick (Headley)   22
Brooke, Gladys (Dayang Muda of Sarawak, 1884–1952)   238 n.60
Brooke, Lady Margaret (Ranee of Sarawak, 1849–1936)   189
Brumwell Thomas, Sir Alfred (1868–1948)   186, 187
Buchanan-Hamilton, Khalida/Lady Helen (1856–1942)   190, 192
Buddhism   31
Bullard, Reader (1885–1976)   133, 136, 141–2
Burton, Sir Richard Francis (1821–90)   124
Bush Stories (Baynton)   109

Cairo   79, 99, 127, 129–32, 142, 169
Cavell, Edith (1865–1915)   104
Cavendish, Victor, Duke of Devonshire (1868–1938)   150
Census of 1891   31
Central Asian Society   124, 126, 140–2, 144–6, 148, 159, 161
Central Islamic Society (CIS)   61, 67, 70, 71, 73, 97, 99, 102, 117, 148, 154
Chamberlain, Austen (1863–1937)   94
Chancellor, Sir John Robert (1870–1952)   178
Charity Commission   168
Chettoe, Reverend S. E.   81
Children's Employment Act 1903   146
Christianity   13, 43, 53, 56–8, 60, 62, 63, 65, 69, 76–8, 89, 98, 130, 131, 148, 150, 158, 171, 189, 196
'Christians and Muslims: Where We Differ and Why We Differ' (Headley)   189
Churchill, Sir Winston (1874–1965)   181–3, 185
CIS. *See* Central Islamic Society
Cobbold, Lady Evelyn (1867–1963)   124, 132, 137–9, 149, 189, 192
Cochrane-Baillie, Charles   147
Collett, John   31, 32, 37
Committee of Union of Progress (CUP)   86
Comrade, The   75, 79

Conference of Lausanne (1923)   121, 123, 127
Conservative Party   23
'Constructive Power of the Sea, The' (Headley)   44
Cooke, John   39, 208 n.58
Crescent, The   59–61, 64, 107
Crimean War   7
Curzon, Lord (1859–1925)   128

Dard, Abdur Rahim (1894–1955)   156, 158–60
Davis, Laura 'Ivy,'   13, 46, 176
'Day of Hajj' (Headley)   139
'Day of Prayer for the Sultan-Caliph,'   118
Disraeli, Benjamin (1804–81)   18, 58
Dockter, Warren   181, 182
Doulie, Mohammed (aka Dollie, 1846–1906)   59–60
Duffield, Ian   72

East African Standard   150
East and the West, The   80–1, 106
Eastern Question   7, 74, 118
East India Association   148
East London Seamen's Mission   148
Ebráhim, Fátima Violet   65
Egyptian Gazette   130–1
El Bakry, Syed Ehsan   97
Erikson, Mahmud Gunnar   241 n.4
European Muslim Congress (1935)   188–9
Evolution Society   142

fatwas   100
Ferdinand, Archduke Franz (1863–1914)   99
First Anglo-Sikh War of 1845–6   30
First Balkan War (October 1912–May 1913)   85–6
First Boer War (1880–81)   21
First World War   5, 50, 85, 109, 121, 124, 149, 154, 163, 189, 192
   Muslim loyalty and politics during   98–103
France   7, 50, 59, 151, 186, 188, 232 n.15
Fuad I, King of Egypt and Sudan (1868–1936)   131, 142, 197

Gairdner, William Henry Temple (1873–1928)   169, 170
Gandhi–Irwin Pact of 1931   181, 182
Gandhi, Mahatma (1869–1948)   118, 157, 175, 180, 183
Gascoyne-Cecil, Robert, the third Marquess of Salisbury (1830–1903)   19
George, David Lloyd (1863–1945)   115, 116, 152
Gladstone, William Ewart (1809–98)   19, 58
Glenbeigh Towers   10, 113, 114, 116
'God's Chastening' (Headley)   46, 48
Godwin-Austin, Henry Haversham, Lieutenant-Colonel (1834–1923)   39
Goodwin Sands   111
Gordon, Charles, Major-General (1833–85)   21, 54
Grafftey-Smith, Laurence (1892–1989)   229 n.69
Greco-Turkish War (1919–22)   117, 119, 120

Hackforth-Jones, Penne   110, 152
Hajj (pilgrimage to Mecca)   5, 60, 94, 97, 123–46, 152, 220 n.47, 230 nn.99, 114
Hajji   142–6, 197
al-Hamid II, Sultan Abd (1842–1918)   57, 58, 85, 118
Hamilton-Gordon, George, the fourth Earl of Aberdeen (1784–1860)   7
Hamilton, Sir Abdullah Archibald (Watkin) (1876–1939)   148, 149, 152, 169, 170, 190
Headley, Lord (1855–1935)
  as ambassador for British Islam 1923-9   147–73
  antecedents   8–10
  bankruptcy   115–16
  as British Muslim leader   85–9
  childhood   10–13
  conversion to Islam 1913   57–83
    path   67–70
    reactions   72–6
    responses   76–83
  courtship in Srinagar   36–41
  crisis   46–51
  death   190
  early years (1855–92)   7–27
  in 1892 general election   22–7
  first decade as a Muslim   85–122
  Hajj   5, 60, 94, 97, 123–46, 152, 220 n.47, 230 nn.99, 114
  as imperial engineer   29–42
  marriages   5, 42, 47, 109–13, 175–7, 208 n.58
  practising Islam   92–7
  semi-retirement   175–7
  tributes and legacies   190–3
  university life   13–15
Headley Memorial Council   191, 195
Herbert, George, the thirteenth Earl of Pembroke (1850–95)   18
Hinduism   31, 110
Hirtzel, Sir Arthur (1870–1937)   94
Hopkirk, Peter   39
Hunter, Reverend Joseph Alexander   47–9
Hunt, Sir Frederick Seager (1838–1904)   19, 21, 29, 204 n.48
Husain, Khan Bahadur Pirzada Muhammad   165
al-Husayni, Musa Kazim Pasha (1853–1934)   178
Hussein ibn Ali al-Hashimi, King of the Hijaz (1853–1931)   123–5, 136, 141, 144–6, 197
al-Husseini, Mohammed Amin (c.1895–1974)   179, 197
al-Husseini, Mustafa Effendi   179

ICEI. *See* Institution of Civil Engineers of Ireland
'Id al-Adha   60, 94, 119, 180, 187, 190
'Id al-Fitr   94, 119, 189
Ideal Prophet, The (Kamal-ud-Din)   156
ihram   134–5, 229 n.69
India   235 n.84
  Amritsar massacre (Jallianwalah Bagh)   118
  Hindu–Muslim violence (1931)   183–4
  Indian Khilafat Movement (1919–24)   118–19, 198, 235 n.106

Indian National Congress   180
  and London Mosque Campaign
    1927-8   163-9
Indian Opinion of Johannesburg   157
Institution of Civil Engineers of Ireland
    (ICEI)   35, 44, 46
Iqbal, Sir Muhammad (1877-1938)   73,
    167, 197
Ireland   8, 18-21
  Census of   44, 48
  Government of Ireland Act 1920   67
  Home Rule   19, 23
  Irish War of Independence   113
  Irish Unionist Alliance   23
  Land War   10
Irwin, Lord (1881-1959)   180, 181, 184
Islam   1, 31, 51-6, 68, 195, 196. *See also
    individual entries*
  in late-Victorian and Edwardian
    Britain   57-61
  practising   92-7
  Westernization of   3, 5, 85, 90, 163
Islamic Defence League (later, Islamic
    Information Bureau)   117
Islamic Review, The (aka *Muslim India and
    Islamic Review, Islamic Review
    and Muslim India*)   3, 64-5,
    67-9, 71, 72, 74, 77, 82, 86-90,
    94, 96-100, 104, 107, 108,
    128-31, 150, 154-6, 159, 161,
    162, 164, 170, 172, 189, 190,
    191, 198, 199, 212 n.60
Islamische Gemeinde zu Berlin e.V.
    (IGB)   151
Isma'ili Shi'a   117
Ismail, Khaja   97
'Is Our House in Order?' (Headley)   170,
    171
Ispahani, Mirza Hashim   102, 117
Ivy Lodge, St Margarets   67, 112, 115,
    141

jama'at   66, 154, 156, 158
James, Lawrence   185
Jammu and Kashmir   29-32, 41, 168,
    181
Jannat al-Baqi'   136, 229 n.80
Jannat al-Mu'alla   136
Jewish World   75-6

jheel   36
Jidda   132-4, 141, 229 n.69, 230 n.99
Johnson, Alice   13
Johnson, Anne   39
Johnson, Teresa St Josephine (first Lady
    Headley). *See* Allanson-Winn,
    Teresa (nee Johnson, 1871-1919)
Johnson, William Henry (1833-83)   38,
    39
Johnson-Winn, Cyril Norman (aka Cyril
    Allanson-Winn)   39, 41, 44,
    48, 50, 208 n.57
Journal of the Central Asian Society   162
Judaism   77

Ka'ba   137, 138, 140
Kamal-ud-Din, Khwaja (1870-1932)
    61-75, 77, 79, 86, 87, 90, 91,
    93-5, 97-9, 119, 122, 125,
    127-30, 142, 154-6, 163-5, 189,
    190, 195-7, 229 n.69
  death of   185
  Hajj   138
Karim, Prince Abdul   97
Kawkab al-Sharq   169, 170
Kemal, Mustafa (1881-1938; known as
    Atatürk)   121
Khan, Inayat (1882-1927)   149, 197
Khan, Maulana Zafar Ali (1873-
    1956)   64, 167
al-Khatib, Shaykh Fu'ad   125, 127, 134
Kheiri, Abdul Jabbar (1880-1958)   151
Khilafat delegation   118-19
Khilafat Movement (1919-24)   118-19,
    184, 198, 235 n.106, 238 n.36
Kidwai, Shaykh Mushir Hussain (1878-
    1937)   97, 102, 117
Kilbride, Denis (1848-1924)   23
kiswah   141, 144
Knight, E. F. (1852-1925)   31-3, 36, 37

Lahori Ahmadis   117, 150, 151, 152, 163,
    191, 215 n.47, 221 n.60
Lahori Ahmadiyyat   154, 198
Lamington, Lord (1860-1940)   147-8,
    163, 168, 238 n.51
Lawrence, T. E. (1888-1935)   133
Leitner, Gottlieb Wilhelm (1840-99)   60,
    61, 64

Liberal Unionist Party   19
Light, The   1, 3, 131, 154, 158, 164, 166, 167, 172, 199
Lindsay Hall ('London Muslim Prayer House')   93
Liverpool Muslim Institute (LMI)   2, 53, 58, 59, 64, 74, 107, 151
Lloyd, George Ambrose (1879–1941)   192
LMI. *See* Liverpool Muslim Institute
Lodge, Reverend Charles H.   148
Lofland, John   4
London   12–21, 23, 27, 29, 30, 32, 39, 41–6, 53, 59–64, 66, 67, 70–2, 75, 78, 79, 81, 86, 87, 90, 92–5, 97, 98, 104, 105, 109, 111–13, 118, 120, 123, 127–9, 131, 134, 138, 141–3, 145, 147–51, 153–6, 158
London Central Mosque Trust   193
London College of Physiology   149
London County Council   192–3
London Mosque Fund   64, 163, 168, 214 n.37
Louis of Battenberg, Prince (1854–1921)   103
Lovegrove, James William/Habeeb-Ullah (1867–1940)   158, 180, 192
Lovibond, Joseph Williams (1833–1918)   175

MacDonald, James Ramsay (1866–1937)   180
Mahmoud, Shaykh Abdel-Halim (1910–78)   198
Majid, Maulana Abdul (1896–1977)   98, 188
Mandate of the League of Nations   178
Maryon-Wilson, Sir Spencer Pocklington (1859–1944)   105
masjid   38
Maurice, F. D. (1805–72)   58
Mecca
  pilgrimage to (Hajj)   5, 60, 94, 97, 123–46, 152, 220 n.47, 230 nn.99, 114
  lure of   123–4
Medina   126
Mehmed V, Sultan (1844–1918)   85

'Method of Preaching Religion as Given in the Quran' (Kamal-ud-Din)   68
Mills, Martin   113–15
Mitra, Ashutosh   31, 32, 35–7
Moazzam Jah (1907–87), son of the Nizam of Hyderabad   186
mofussil   30
Mohye, Shaykh Abdul   127, 129, 132–5
monotheism   54
Morel, E. D. (1873–1924)   104
Mortimore, Frank Djaffar   64–5
Moslem Chronicle   172
Moslem World   81, 92
Moulavi, Vakkom (1873–1932)   92, 197
MSGB. *See* Muslim Society of Great Britain
muezzin   138
mufti   127
Muslim Society of Great Britain (MSGB). *See* British Muslim Society (BMS)

Near and Middle East Association   148
Nizamiah Mosque   168, 169, 171–3, 185–9, 192
Nizamiah Mosque Trust Fund   168, 172, 173, 175, 177, 186, 192, 193
Non-Cooperation Movement (1920–22)   118, 235 n.106
'Note to Self' (Headley)   52
Nur-ud-Din, Hakim (1841–1914)   65, 73, 87

Observer, The   79, 80, 82
Old Testament   52
Oliphant, Lancelot   127
'On Delivery from Human Peril' (Headley)   52
'On Recovery from Severe Mental and Physical Illness' (Headley)   107
Order of the Nahda (Renaissance) First Class   141, 143–5
Oriental Nobility Institute, Woking   60
Ottoman Empire   6, 152, 155
  end of   116–21
Ottoman–German alliance   5, 85, 121
Ottoman Society, The   102

Paigham Sulh 67, 72, 73
Pakistan Movement 167
Palestine 102, 125, 177–80
Palestine Arab Congress 178
Pan-Islamic Society/Islamic Society 61, 97
Pankhurst, Christabel (1880–1958) 105
Parkinson, John Yehya-en-Nasr (1874–1918) 64, 99, 100
Philby, Harry St John Bridger (1885–1960) 124, 125, 148
Phillipps-Wolley, Clive (1853–1918) 22
Pickard, Bashyr/William Burchell (1889–1973) 188, 191, 192
Pickthall, Muhammad Marmaduke (1875–1936) 2, 97, 101, 117, 120, 121, 124, 149, 167, 181, 186, 190, 197, 235 n.106, 238 n.51
'Pilgrimage to Mecca' (Headley) 124
Pitts, Joseph (*c.*1663–1739) 124
'Plan of Campaign' (1886–91) 19–20
Plumer, Lord (1857–1932) 178
Port Said 127–9
'Power of God's Love, The' (Headley) 12
Primrose League, The 19, 23, 24
Prophet Muhammad 5, 43, 51–6, 58, 60, 68, 80, 96, 137, 150

Qadiani Ahmadi movement 5, 147, 160
Qadiani Ahmadis 151, 195, 196, 215 n.47
Qadiani London Mosque (aka Fazl Mosque) 159, 163
Quilliam, William Henry Abdullah/Henri Léon (1856–1932) 1–2, 53, 58–61, 74, 98, 100–2, 107, 119, 121, 124, 149, 151, 154, 159, 176, 180, 185, 190, 195, 199
Qur'an 2, 63–5, 82, 96, 137, 157, 167, 182, 189

Ramakrishna Pillai, K. (1878–1916) 92
Rambo, Lewis R. 4
Rangila Rasul ('The Merry Sage') 164, 235 n.84
Rankin, Sir Omar Hubert (1899–1988) 148–9, 190, 192
Rawlinson, Sir Henry C., Major-General (1810–95) 39

'Religion of the Future, The' (Headley) 69, 154
religious conversion process 3–4
'Revelation of God's Protecting Care, The' (Headley) 52
Review of Religions, The 63, 64, 73
Richmond Asylum, Dublin 48, 50
Rida, Muhammad Rashid (1865–1935) 79, 130, 151, 197
Round Table Conferences (1930–32) 180, 181, 184–6
Royal Commission on Sea Coast Erosion 46
Royal Geographical Society, London 39
Royal Scottish Society of the Arts, Edinburgh 44
Russia 7, 30, 58, 117
Rutter, Eldon (1894–*c.*1956) 124, 135, 229 n.80

Sacred Mosque, Mecca 137, 138, 140
Sadiq, Mufti Muhammad (1872–1957) 151
Sadr-ud-Din, Maulana (1881–1981) 97–8, 221 n.60
sa'i 138, 139
Salafism 79
Salar Jung Indian Memorial House, Woking 64
salat al-jum'a 64, 65, 87, 167
Salisbury and Winchester Journal 16, 17
Sampson, Henry ('Pendragon') (1841–91) 203–4 n.30
Sa'ud, Ibn (1875–1953) 125, 136, 137, 146, 190
Sayal, Chaudhry Fateh Muhammad (aka Fateh Muhammad Sial 1887–1960) 65, 66, 74–5, 154
Schlagintweit, Adolphe (1829–57) 39
'Sea as a Constructive Agent, The' (Headley) 44
Second Boer War (1899–1902) 43
Second World War 192
Secret Intelligence Service, London 128
Self-Defence (Headley) 44, 92–3
Shafi, Sir Mian Muhammad (1869–1932) 166–7, 184, 197
shahada 55–6, 93, 212 n.71
Shah, Sirdar Ikbal Ali (1894–1969) 159, 176, 197

Shaw, Reverend W. H.   150
Shaykh al-Islam of the British Isles   59, 100, 149
Sheldrake, Bertram Khalid (1888–1947)   61, 98, 102, 149, 154, 155, 159, 171, 192, 239 n.60
Sikhism   31
'Simplicity in Religion' (Headley)   68–9
Singh, Maharaja Pratap (1848–1925)   30–1
Skonovd, Norman   4
Sladen, Douglas B. W. (1856–1947)   104
Smith, Reginald Bosworth (1839–1908)   58, 60
Société Internationale de Philologie, Sciences et Beaux-Arts   149
Society of Engineers, London   42, 111
South African Muslims   157
Spedding and Company   29, 32, 35
Spedding, Charles (1857–1925)   29, 32, 35
Spiritualism   149
Stanley, Henry, third Baron Stanley of Alderley (1827–1903)   59, 88, 124
Stanton, H. U. Weitbrecht (1851–1937)   66, 81, 92
Stephen, Nathan/Nur-ud-Din (1846–1928)   107, 149
'Strength of Islam, The' (Headley)   162–3
Suffragette, The   105
Suhrawardy, Abdullah Al-Mamoon (1870–1935)   61
Sunni Islam   31, 62, 100, 117, 151, 154, 155, 160, 166, 170, 171, 179, 196, 206 n.11, 218 n.131
sura   137

tawaf   138, 139
Taylor, Brian   3–4
Teachings of Islam, The (Ahmad)   67, 154
Thornton, D. Todd   21, 25
Thoughts for the Future (A[llanson]. W[inn])   43, 51–6, 68, 69, 77, 189, 212 n.60
Three Great Prophets of the World: Moses, Jesus and Muhammad, The (Headley)   122

tonga   30, 35, 36, 206 n.8
Toussoun (or Tusun), Prince Omar (1872–1944)   131, 142
Townshend, Lady   148
Treaty of Sèvres (1920)   119–21
Trust for the Encouragement and Circulation of Muslim Religious Literature   156–8
Turkey   5, 7, 88, 100–2, 109, 117–21, 123, 127, 128, 155
Turkish Nationalists   119, 121, 146
2LO London (BBC radio)   142

umma   7, 61, 99–102, 147, 155, 177–85, 197, 206 n.11, 240 n.3
Unitarianism   5, 53
United Family League, London   148

Vivienne, granddaughter of Lord Headley   126, 176, 186

Wahhabism   137, 155
Warley Lodge, Little Warley, Essex   10
Way of the Saiee   141
Western Awakening to Islam, A (Headley)   89–92, 152, 198
Western Europe   151, 197
Western Islamic Association (WIA)   159, 171, 192, 234 n.63
Westernization of Islam   3, 5, 85, 90, 163
Who's Who   13, 104
'Why Contention between Sister Religions?' (Headley)   56
'Why I became a Mohammedan' (Headley)   79
Whymant, Ameen Neville J. (c.1895–1970)   149
WIA. See Western Islamic Association
Wilhelm II, German Emperor and King of Prussia (1859–1941)   86
Wilhelm of Wied, Prince (1876–1945)   152
William Pitt the Younger (1759–1806)   8
Winn, George (1725–98)   8
WMM. See Woking Muslim Mission
Woking Mosque Trust   177

Woking Muslim Mission (WMM) 65,
      66, 74, 85, 86, 93, 95, 97–9, 102,
      122, 130, 144, 149, 151, 154,
      156, 158, 159, 163, 166, 168,
      177, 195–7
  Muslim Prayer House, Notting Hill
      Gate 118, 141
  'Tract Series' 90

World Islamic Congress (1931)
    180

Young Islam, The 191

Zam Zam Well 138, 141
Zogolli, Ahmet Muhtar (aka Zog I
    1895–1961) 153

www.ingramcontent.com/pod-product-compliance
Lightning Source LLC
Chambersburg PA
CBHW072130290426
44111CB00012B/1850